The Robotic Imaginary

The Robotic Imaginary

The Human and the Price of Dehumanized Labor

Jennifer Rhee

University of Minnesota Press
Minneapolis | London

Portions of chapter 1 were previously published as "Misidentification's Promise: The Turing Test in Weizenbaum, Powers, and Short," *Postmodern Culture* 20, no. 3 (May 2010); copyright 2010 The Johns Hopkins University Press. Portions of chapter 3 were previously published as "Beyond the Uncanny Valley: Masahiro Mori and Philip K. Dick's *Do Androids Dream of Electric Sheep?*" *Configurations* 21, no. 3 (Fall 2013): 301–29; copyright 2013 The Johns Hopkins University Press.

Published by the University of Minnesota Press
111 Third Avenue South, Suite 290
Minneapolis, MN 55401-2520
http://www.upress.umn.edu

The University of Minnesota is an equal-opportunity educator and employer.

Printed in the United States of America on acid-free paper

Names: Rhee, Jennifer, author.
Title: The robotic imaginary : the human and the price of dehumanized labor / Jennifer Rhee.
Description: Minneapolis : University of Minnesota Press, [2018] | Includes
    bibliographical references and index. |
Identifiers: LCCN 2018001933 (print) | ISBN 978-1-5179-0297-1 (hc) |
    ISBN 978-1-5179-0298-8 (pb)
Subjects: LCSH: Robots, Social aspects. | Robots, Moral and ethical aspects.
Classification: LCC TJ211.49 .R435 2018 (print) | DDC 303.48/3–dc23
LC record available at https://lccn.loc.gov/2018001933

Contents

Introduction
All Too Dehumanized

They're going to kill me next.

—EZZALDEEN TUAIMAN, "'THEY'RE GOING TO KILL ME NEXT':
YEMEN FAMILY FEARS DRONE STRIKES UNDER TRUMP"

Ever step on ants and never give it another thought?

—MICHAEL HAAS, "LIFE AS A DRONE OPERATOR"

Ezzaldeen Tuaiman, who at fourteen years of age survived a drone strike in 2011 that killed his father and older brother, fears for his life. In 2017, drone patrols have increased in frequency over his village, Al-Rawdah. Now, drones hover daily, sometimes three to four times a day, their frequency heightening the terror and trauma of drone warfare for Tuaiman and other Yemenis. Meanwhile, former drone operator Michael Haas describes people as "ants" when viewed from a drone, thus gesturing to dehumanization as a primary tool for drone warfare. Haas, who is now an outspoken critic of the United States' military drone program, describes how, in his work, humans became targets, which became "just black blobs on a screen." And children like Tuaiman were called "fun-size terrorists," their deaths described as merely "cutting the grass before it grows too long."[1] This book, which attends to the distance between Tuaiman's and Haas's statements about drone warfare, argues that dehumanization, including the dehumanization that undergirds both the labor of drone operators and the United States' drone program, is embedded in the history of robotics and its various inscriptions and erasures of the human.

Concurrently, a steady stream of news stories worries that robots will soon replace human workers.[2] Whose jobs will be safe? Whose jobs

1

will be next to be automated out of existence? My book argues that these two phenomena are connected and part of an ongoing story about the ways the robotic imaginary and its inscriptions of "the human" erases and dehumanizes those, mostly the marginalized, who are characterized as "unfamiliar" and "nonnormative." This book offers an account of this story through an examination of the complicated nexus of labor, dehumanizing erasures, and an abiding attachment to constructions of "the familiar" across robotics technologies and cultural forms. Considering robotics' explicit anthropomorphic mission and robotics technologies' increasing presence in our lives, worlds, and wars, my book asks: How is the human defined in these robotic visions and technological relations? What are the histories of labors, orientations, and motivations that brought this imagined human into being? Whose labors and whose lives are excluded from these considerations of the human? Who is dehumanized? Foregrounding the robot's conceptualization of the human, and more importantly the dehumanized, this book examines robots across technology and cultural forms from the mid-twentieth century to the present. In the chapters that follow, I move through central anthropomorphic paradigms that organize robots to identify the specific visions of humanness and of the dehumanized they evoke, paying close attention to the gendered and racial dimensions that constitute these visions.

Staying with the Human

The human, Diana Fuss writes, is "one of our most elastic fictions."[3] And yet this fiction, like many fictions, wields incredible ideological force in the world; how the human is defined has very real, material effects, particularly for those who are excluded from the community of humans and the rights, protections, and privileges accorded therein. Writing in 1996, Fuss elaborates:

> That the human has a history comes as no surprise to those subjects so routinely and so violently excluded from its ideological terrain. In the past, the human has functioned as a powerful juridical trope to disenfranchise slaves, immigrants, women, children, and the poor. . . . In America, the human continues to be deployed as a weapon of potent ideological force, its unstable boundaries perpetually challenged and redrawn to exclude entire groups of so-

cially disempowered subjects: the homeless, mothers on welfare, blacks in prison, people with HIV/AIDS, illegal "aliens." *The human is not, and has never been, an all inclusive category.*[4]

The human, as Fuss underscores, is a term with shifting definitions and imaginaries. These definitions and imaginaries wield tremendous ideological force that operates largely through their ability to go uninterrogated, to pass as inherent, originary, and fixed. My book, which takes seriously the history of the human as one of exclusion and oppression, shares Pheng Cheah's insistence that "the humanities do not take the humanity of the human being as a given but set as their basic task the inquiry of how humanity is constituted."[5] *The Robotic Imaginary* rejects the givenness of the human, both as a self-evident concept and as that which is knowable and recognizable in another.

Despite my considerable debt to theorizations of the posthuman and the nonhuman, I insist on retaining the human, in all its bagginess, as a central analytic concept. In this book I remain all too attached to "the human," which encompasses all the historical oppressions and exploitations that have been done in its name. Numerous scholars insightfully identify the role of dehumanization, of removing someone from inclusion within the privileged and exclusionary category of the human, in producing the concept of the human. Arguing for a more expansive notion of the human, Sylvia Wynter and Alexander G. Weheliye examine the historical dehumanization of black people in constructions of the Western human.[6] In a special issue of *GLQ* titled "Queer Inhumanisms" and edited by Mel Y. Chen and Dana Luciano, Zakiyyah Iman Jackson cautions that discourses invested in moving "beyond the human" risk reinstantiating the same exclusions and erasures—the same processes of dehumanization—that continue to constitute the human. What does it mean, Jackson asks, to call for going "beyond the human" when some humans are not included within the category of the human, and when certain notions of the human enable continued racial exclusions?[7]

José Munoz, in the aforementioned *GLQ* special issue, turns from the human to the inhuman. Munoz finds promising the inhuman's appeal to the unknowable, the incommensurable.[8] Bringing Munoz's incommensurability of the inhuman into the human itself, I argue for incommensurability and unknowability, akin to Éduoard Glissant's concept of opacity, as originarily constitutive of the human. Rejecting a Western worldview grounded in the imposition of transparency, Glissant's claim for opacity as a right embeds unknowability—to oneself and to others— in the human subject. Approaching transparency as constructed rather than ontological, Glissant's work places the onus not on the individual to make oneself known, but on those discourses and institutions that insist on making-transparent. His category of Relation also significantly changes fundamental assumptions about humanness as a category of sameness. Glissant describes Relation as the sum of all differences. Relation insists on difference, no matter how small, thus refusing the abstracting and homogenizing erasures of the universal. For Glissant, Relation is a site of possibility where the other does not exist as such because there is no grounding entity, no central subject, against which the other emerges in opposition.[9] Relation, by this logic, also rejects historically embedded conceptions of the human (the Enlightenment man of reason, the autonomous possessive individual) that have been created by perspectives of power in their own image and constructed the other while never inhabiting this position of alterity. In conversation with these theories and reconceptions of the human that both identify the historical exclusions through which the human has been defined and redefine the human around difference and the unknown, this book also looks to unknowability and unfamiliarity to reconceptualize the human outside the dehumanizing exclusions that have previously constituted it.

This co-constitutive conversation between human and dehumanized is foregrounded in the figure of the humanoid robot, which is at once not human and, through explicit anthropomorphic practices, modeled on the human. The robot, in simultaneously gesturing to the human and the not-human, thus underscores the dehumanizing exclusions that constitute conceptions of the human. This book, in its avowed attachment to the human—in all its constitutive oppressions, exploitations, and dehumanizations—asks, Who is the human who is de facto valorized and normativized through the anthropomorphic visions that organize robotics? Who, in their purported incommensurability, unknowability, unfamiliarity, or illegibility within robotics' narrow views of humanness, is excluded, erased, dehumanized, rendered not-human? In attending to the dehumanization that undergirds processes of anthropomorphization, my project seeks to continually expand the human beyond its normative conceptions by insisting on the unknowability and illegibility of the human. In the context of humanoid robotics, I examine where and how the human is made knowable, and where the human's unknowability is the basis for erasure and exclusion. I also attend to the moments in literature, film, and art in which unrecognizability opens up a different notion of the human, one that emerges around illegibility and resists conceptualizing the human through its legibility to others.

The presumption of the knowability of humans has significant material consequences.[10] For example, as I argue in my final chapter, the insistence on the knowability of the human, the purported recognizability of the human (recognizable to whom? whose humanity is taken as a given, without requiring proof?), is one of the dehumanizing logics that undergirds the overseas drone strikes conducted by the U.S. military and the CIA. In tracing how notions of humanness have been constituted in AI and robotics and how these notions are intertwined with dehumanizing practices at the site of labor, my book argues for an understanding of the human through unrecognizability, difference, and unfamiliarity, rather than recognition, knowability, and givenness. *The Robotic Imaginary* holds open the irreducibility of the human in the face of discourses, technologies, and cultural imaginings that often suggest otherwise. The humanoid robot, in its reflection of the human's construction through dehumanization, offers a rich site of examination and of speculative reconfiguration. In this attention to reconfiguration, I follow Lucy Suchman, whose wonderful study of human–machine interactivities encompasses identifying and understanding these interactivities, as well as addressing "why we might want to resist or refigure them."[11] My study, in identifying the dehumanizing processes at work in the robotic imaginary, looks to possibilities to reconfigure the robotic imaginary as one way to reconfigure the human outside of dehumanizing demands of recognizability.

The Robotic Imaginary

Throughout my study I employ the term "robotic imaginary" to reference the shifting inscriptions of humanness and dehumanizing erasures evoked by robots. The robotic imaginary emerges across cultural forms and technoscience, and it offers one reflection of the ongoing and inextricable entanglement of these spheres.[12] In Suchman's examination of contemporary human–machine configurations, the concept of the imaginary "references the ways in which how we see and what we imagine the world to be is shaped not only by our individual experiences but also by the specific cultural and historical resources that the world makes available to us, based on our particular location within it. And perhaps most importantly for my purposes here, cultural imaginaries are realized in material ways."[13] Suchman's engagement with the imaginary locates the stakes of her project in imaginaries' material consequences. These material consequences are unavoidable, as the "imaginary" designates at once a realm of speculation, whether through artistic or technoscientific practices, and of materiality. The robotic imaginary similarly consolidates these concerns, and encompasses any machine intelligence that replicates, whether in form or behavior, a vision of the human. As a concept, the robotic imaginary offers the capacity to identify both an abiding vision of the human that is held up to be, however provisionally or circumscribed, universal, and the extensive erasures of human experiences that enable this inscription of the human.

I take as a starting point that this imaginary emerges from an ongoing conversation between technology and culture, with neither claiming primacy over how we imagine robots. Thus, this study also underscores the necessity of bringing technology into conversation with literary and cultural studies. *The Robotic Imaginary* holds as first principle that technology and culture do not exist in vacuums, but are intractably tied to discourses and worlds beyond their immediately perceptible parameters. And while these spheres are joined by their locations within a larger, shared world, the robotic imaginary does not abide by disciplinary boundaries, but instead announces the vast porosity of these boundaries and the inextricable entanglement of "technology" and "culture."[14] Describing science and literature as existing within a shared cultural milieu, N. Katherine Hayles writes, "Science and literature are not above or apart from their culture but embedded within it."[15] Donna Haraway's engagement with the term "technoscience" points both to the collapse of scientific and technological practices, as well as the inseparability of these practices from the cultural and semiotic practices that also form this capacious category. As Haraway maintains, the stakes are high because technoscience interpellates, with its "dense nodes of human and nonhuman actors that are brought into alliance by the material, social, and semiotic technologies through which what will count as nature and as matters of fact get constituted for—and by—millions of people."[16] My study draws heavily on these entanglements of culture, technology, and science, while also benefiting from Susan Squier's study of biomedical narratives of life across science and literature. In this study, she attends to these interconnected spheres by pointing to the disciplines as boundary-creating practices: "There is nothing inherently literary or scientific, only what disciplinarity makes so."[17] And yet what disciplinarity "makes so" is significant and allows different disciplines and forms of knowledge production to speak and interpellate in different ways. My study of the robotic imaginary considers the broad networks that constitute technoscience, while also attending to the disciplinary distinctions that variously constrain and enable robotics technology and cultural forms—in all their rich and messy entanglements—to speak to the human in distinct modes.

One primary disciplinary distinction, which also speaks to the stakes of my book, lies in robotics technology's funding structure and its appeal to militarization. From 1958 onward, much of robotics technology in the United States has been funded by the Defense Advanced Research Projects Agency (DARPA), a branch of the Department of Defense that sponsors research intended to maintain U.S. technological superiority. DARPA was created in 1958 partly as a response to the Soviet space program's successful launch of Sputnik into orbit just a year earlier. As Annie Jacobsen's recent history of DARPA describes, the organization is first and foremost, and arguably solely, interested in technologies for their military applications. According to Jacobsen, two driving forces characterize DARPA: militarization and secrecy. DARPA's commitment to militarization and secrecy is evident in the armed unmanned drones currently deployed in drone strikes overseas, as I discuss in chapter 4; though the United States conducted its first armed drone strike in 2001, drone technology was being developed in secret by DARPA since the early 1960s.[18] Despite the seemingly non-militarized DARPA-funded technologies I discuss in this book—for example the mobile robot Shakey (in chapter 2) and the sociable robots Kismet and Leonardo (in chapter 3)— every project funded by DARPA, Jacobsen contends, must be understood through these two forces. Charles Rosen, who worked on Shakey in the 1960s, articulates a similar point about DARPA sponsorship: "Whether you like it or not, something you develop is going to find its way into a weapons system. It has and it will always. Can't be stopped."[19] And Joseph Weizenbaum, who developed ELIZA, the AI therapist I discuss in chapter 1, points to DARPA's single-minded concern with militarization as he recounts a question about DARPA's interest in natural-language speech-recognition research. In response, the organization (which went by ARPA at the time) shared its goal for navy ships, including their weaponry, which can be controlled by voice command. As Weizenbaum presciently notes, this goal is "a long step toward a fully automated battlefield."[20] In January 2014, the Department of Defense released a report titled "Unmanned Systems Integrated Roadmap FY2013–2038" that puts forth further steps toward this vision.

And yet, DARPA's robotic vision marks only one facet of the robotic imaginary. To draw out the robotic imaginary's additional facets, I explicitly seek texts across divers genre and disciplinary boundaries to chart the capaciousness by which this imaginary functions. This wide selection of texts and artworks also acknowledges the heterogeneous modes by which different works and different genres engage the robotic imaginary. While my examination of the robotic imaginary moves across technology, literature, film, and art, I take seriously the function of disciplines, and their funding structures, to shape knowledge and its expression. As I examine the explicit and implicit connections across technological and cultural forms and the robotic imaginary that encompasses them, I acknowledge that while disciplinary boundaries may shape how the robotic imaginary inscribes, these boundaries do not separate disciplines from the world, nor from each other. For example, it has become almost something of a disciplinary convention for roboticists to open their monographs, and sometimes their scientific papers, with descriptions of early formative encounters with fictional robots, from *2001: A Space Odyssey*'s HAL to *Star Wars*' R2-D2 and C-3PO to Philip K. Dick's androids in *Do Androids Dream of Electric Sheep?* My project takes seriously these early fictional encounters and how they shape robotics work and the robotic imaginary more broadly. Meanwhile, some of the cultural forms I analyze explicitly engage robotics research, for example Richard Powers's

Galatea 2.2 and Simon Penny's robotic art. However, my book also attends to the implicit conversations across technology and culture, in large part by situating these robotic engagements in their larger and shared social, economic, and political contexts.

This book foregrounds philosophical and ethical questions about the robotic imaginary, arguing that the questions highlighted through humanistic inquiry are necessary considerations for AI and robotics' histories and presents, as well as for their continued development and application, militarized or otherwise. In this way, my project also argues more broadly for the crucial role of the humanities in scientific and technological considerations. *The Robotic Imaginary* asserts that culture and technology's constitutive coevolution offers the humanities' analytic resources as a vital means to study this complicated nexus of influences and to theorize robotics and AI technological practices.

The robotic imaginary is, to borrow a term from Haraway, promiscuous; it cuts across genres, forms, and disciplinary boundaries. Like the robotic imaginary itself, my examination brings together technology, literature, popular fiction, science fiction, short stories, films, and artworks to examine the robotic imaginary's exclusionary inscriptions of humanness and reconfigurations that push toward a more capacious vision of the robot, as well as of the human.

Metaphors and Anti-Metaphors

The metaphors we use to describe technologies are powerful actors that shape how we imagine, invent, and engage technologies and the world. Anthropomorphization, a founding metaphor for AI and robotics, brings with it all the ethical, political, and social stakes that inhabit any process in which humanness is produced. These stakes, which have been embedded in robotics from its fictional and technological origins, motivate my project. This study examines anthropomorphization, the attribution of human qualities onto a nonhuman entity, as a fundamentally metaphoric operation. The anthropomorphic metaphor has been central to the quest for machine intelligence from its early, formative days. In 1956, the Dartmouth Summer Research Project on Artificial Intelligence brought together ten men working on machine and computer intelligence. This six-week session was organized by John McCarthy, a computer scientist and former student of cybernetic thinker John von Neumann.[21] The Dartmouth Project was attended by scientists who later became luminaries in AI, their influence extending well into the twenty-first century. The Dartmouth Project also saw the first emergence of the term "artificial intelligence" and shaped the disciplinary and institutional structures that continue to organize AI research today.[22]

While little consensus emerged from the conference itself, the participants did agree on an official mission statement, which reads, "Every aspect of learning or any other feature of intelligence can in principle be so precisely described that a machine can be made to simulate it."[23] Dartmouth Project participant Marvin Minsky, also known as "the father of artificial intelligence," subsequently offered the following widely cited definition of AI as "the science of making machines do things that would require intelligence if done by men."[24] Both the Dartmouth Project's and Minsky's mission statements rely on a foundational anthropomorphic move that collapses humans and machines at the site of intelligence. AI's indebtedness to this metaphoric collapse is the operational frame for many of the questions that shaped the field in the past and continue to preoccupy it in the present.

Paul Ricoeur describes metaphor as emerging under the condition of resemblance between terms; through resemblance, discrete objects are drawn into metaphoric relation. Resemblance is a dually productive force. While the perception of resemblance may prompt the initial joining of terms in a metaphor, this resemblance continues to work on the terms after the metaphor has been drawn, thus generating new bonds of resemblance that did not exist prior to the metaphoric union. Ricoeur calls this latter productivity "predicative assimilation."[25] Following from Ricoeur's predicative assimilation, the anthropomorphic metaphor reimagines the contours of the human and the nonhuman beyond the moment of their metaphoric union. Anthropomorphization *creates* the human in its imitation, delineating a human that did not exist as such prior to the act of humanization. And by way of predicative assimilation, anthropomorphization produces a new relation of resemblance that humanizes the nonhuman and, in so doing, expands the boundaries of the human. If anthropomorphization is a metaphor that brings human and nonhuman into a relation of similarity, dehumanization (the entangled flip side of anthropomorphization) can be understood as a negative metaphor, or anti-metaphor, that creates a relation of difference between two similar entities. The criteria for similarity, no less those for difference, are determinations undergirded by power relations. Why one sees oneself as the same as or different from another, under what criteria these two relationships are drawn, by whom, and to what material consequences are driving questions for this book. Though these questions inform this book, my aim is not primarily to provide comprehensive answers to them. Instead, this book insists on the continued visibility of these questions around conceptualizations of "the human." Who gets humanized and how? Who gets dehumanized and why? Guided by these questions, my examination of humanoid robots returns again and again to the co-construction of the human and the dehumanized.

Reconfiguring the Robotic Imaginary

To underscore the inextricability of anthropomorphization and dehumanization I turn now to two influential texts in robotics technology. Anthropomorphization is central to Alan Turing's imitation game and Masahiro Mori's uncanny valley theory, both of which have wielded considerable influence on the robotic imaginary, often as boundary-policing tools to distinguish humans from machines and other nonhuman forms. In both of these examinations of human–machine encounters, familiarity plays a central role in determining what constitutes "the human." While the imitation game gestures to the highly individual nature of familiarity, the uncanny valley theory illustrates how one perception of the familiar becomes normative in its universalization. In this section, I respond to the narrow inscriptions of the human that emerge from Turing's and Mori's works by offering these influential robotic postulations—in their wide circulation—as tools that identify where specific dehumanizing boundaries and norms are at work in the robotic imaginary, and thus allow us to, returning to Suchman, "resist or reconfigure them." I submit that Turing's and Mori's work be used not as offering definitive visions of the human or authoritative tests to identify human from nonhuman other; rather, Turing's and Mori's work can be engaged to challenge the role of "familiarity" in constructing the human and to raise questions about how the production of difference functions both within their work and beyond it.

Turing's influential test for machine intelligence, widely known as the

Turing test, turns on a machine convincingly conversing with a human. Implicit in the numerous technological and cultural AIs shaped by the Turing test's influence is the idea that the human and human intelligence is, or should be, knowable to humans. But which visions of the human are considered widely recognizable, and to whom? What visions of the human are left out, are not recognized as intelligent, whether performed by machines or humans? A closer look at the essay that introduced Turing's test suggests that the test in fact reconceptualizes the human around the possibility of its unknowability. Turing's 1950 work "Computing Machinery and Intelligence," a seminal text for AI that continues to shape technological developments and fictional imaginings, introduces the imitation game, the basis for the Turing test. I argue that Turing's original imitation game insists on the possibility that "the human" may be unknowable or unrecognizable to other humans. Turing's well-known test for machine intelligence begins with a parlor game that involves three humans and no computers. At least one of these humans is a man (A), and at least one is a woman (B). The remaining human (C), who is later referenced as "he," is in a separate room. Using a teletype machine, C asks A and B questions; A and B respond, also by teletype. For A and B, the task is to convince C that he or she is in fact the woman. For C, the task is to correctly identify B as the woman.[26]

At this juncture, Turing introduces a machine into the imitation game. The machine, according to Turing, will take the place of A: "'What will happen when a machine takes the part of A in this game?' Will the interrogator decide wrongly as often when the game is played like this as he does when the game is played between a man and a woman?"[27] These questions underscore the centrality of misidentification in the Turing test, which turns on the possibility that the human judge might not be able to recognize the other human in the game. This possibility depends largely on how the human judge imagines humanness: who is human according to the judge, what falls outside of legible human behavior according to the judge. The centrality of C's ability to determine intelligence, to recognize another human, highlights the test's dependence on the judge's familiarities and expectations of human communication and experience. In other words, the test results depend on how the judge understands what it is to be human.[28]

However, by embedding humanness in the possibility of misidentifi-cation, Turing's imitation game highlights, and even at times amplifies, the instability of the definition of the human. In the imitation game, the possibility of misrecognition posits a human who is potentially *un*recog-nizable to another human. Thus, Turing's imitation game, in highlighting misidentification, asks us to open up the human into the domain of the unfamiliar. In attaching the human to the possibility of misidentification and unrecognizability, Turing's imitation game challenges the definition of the human around one's own familiar preconceptions and biases. Rather than simply excluding and foreclosing that which is unfamiliarly human, the test also gestures to the fundamental unrecognizability of the human. In this way, Turing's test, which is often wielded to inscribe nor-mative conceptions of the human, can also potentially subvert these very same inscriptions. By insisting on the possibility of misrecognizing the human, the test holds open the opacity of the human, thus gesturing to the human's fundamental unknowability. By rethinking Turing's framing of anthropomorphization as attending to the illegibility of humanness, we might rethink normative discourses that presume and insist on the human's recognizability. In this way, we might challenge discourses and practices that police humanness, instead affirming the delicate and weighty ethical responsibility of defining, recognizing, and misrecogniz-ing the human. Thus, we can read the Turing test's enduring popularity in culture and science not solely through its boundary-policing affirmation of an opposition between human and machine, but also through its in-troduction of the possibility of misidentification, of the destabilizing in-ability to recognize what is human.

In a BBC interview Turing, speaking about the imitation game he proposes at the outset of his essay, provocatively responds, "I've certainly left a great deal to the imagination."[29] We might understand Turing's re-mark as referencing the structural ambiguity of his imitation game, about which there is significant debate. At the same time, we might also under-stand Turing as pointing to the role of the imagination both as a compo-nent of his imitation game, and as a fundamental aspect of efforts to de-fine the human through the act of distinguishing between human and nonhuman other. And if, in Turing's imitation game, it is through the imagination that this defining, and often dehumanizing, distinction is articulated, it is at least in part through the imagination that this distinction can be given critical attention, confused, disarticulated, and reconstituted in new, previously un-imagined ways. In other words, Turing's evocation of the imagination can function as an appeal to reimagining machines, but more importantly humanness, in ways that more aptly encompass the irreducible and unknowable breadth of human experience, as I explore in chapter 1, in my examination of female AIs and their association with care labor.

Unlike Turing's opening up of the human in his imitation game, Japanese roboticist Masahiro Mori's theory of the uncanny valley, which has also substantially influenced the robotic imaginary, inscribes a narrow, normative vision of the human around health and disability.[30] According to Mori's theory, humans are drawn to forms with some human resemblance, and repelled by forms that resemble humans too closely.[31] In Figure 1, the point at which the amount of human resemblance tips humans' positive affinity into eeriness or uncanniness marks one boundary of the uncanny valley. Further following the graph in Figure 1, an industrial robot that does not bear much human resemblance does not evoke much positive affinity in humans. A toy robot that is designed with more human traits (a face, a humanoid body) evokes more affinity *(shinwakan)*. And the traditional Japanese *Bunraku* puppet, which bears some human traits but is encountered within the acculturated historical context of performance and audience expectations, evokes an even greater degree of positive affinity.

Mori locates the virtually lifelike prosthetic hand in the space of negative affinity called the uncanny valley. According to Mori, were one to discover that such a hand is not a living human hand but a very lifelike prosthetic, one would no longer feel an affinity toward this hand. In fact, one would encounter this hand as eerie and uncanny. For example, upon gripping what turns out to be someone's lifelike prosthetic in a handshake, one might be taken aback by the hand's "limp boneless grip together with its texture and coldness," having expected the warmth and firmness of a human hand.[32] The dissonance between the prosthetic's lifelike appearance and its machine tactility would produce a discomfiting confusion, thus prompting one to experience the prosthetic hand as eerie. In this way, the virtually lifelike prosthetic hand lies in the un-

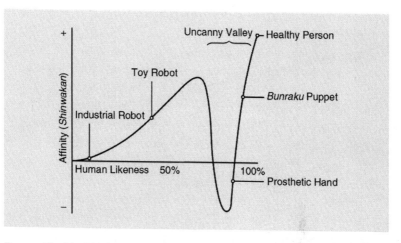

Figure 1. Masahiro Mori's uncanny valley graph. Source: Masahiro Mori, "The Uncanny Valley," trans. Karl F. MacDorman and Norri Kageki, *IEEE Robotics and Automation Magazine* 19, no. 2 (2012): 98–100; copyright IEEE 2013; reprinted with permission.

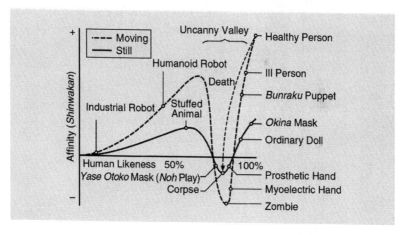

Figure 2. Masahiro Mori's uncanny valley graph with movement. Source: Masahiro Mori, "The Uncanny Valley," trans. Karl F. MacDorman and Norri Kageki, *IEEE Robotics and Automation Magazine* 19, no. 2 (2012): 98–100; copyright IEEE 2013; reprinted with permission.

canny valley, where human likeness increases and affinity decreases (see Figure 1). As seen in Figure 2, movement heightens the possible degrees of both positive affinity and eeriness one might experience. For example, an industrial robot in motion elicits a greater sense of affinity than said industrial robot at rest, while a moving lifelike prosthetic hand elicits a greater sense of eeriness than it would at rest.

A closer look at the highest points on both graphs demonstrates Mori's reliance on a specifically imagined human, which he describes as a "healthy person." In Figure 2, Mori locates an "ill person" below this healthy person in both human likeness and positive affinity. This healthy person, which Mori evokes without definition or specification, occupies the highest peak of the uncanny valley graph; thus, Mori's healthy person is the standard of humanness against which both humanoids and humans are measured. This healthy person is also the imagined human who appropriately registers positive or negative affinity in relation to humanoid figures.[33] For Mori, the centrality of this healthy person emerges from humans' instincts for self-preservation and avoidance of death.[34] Thus the corpse falls at the bottom of the uncanny valley for stillness and the zombie (the animated living-dead) falls at the bottom of the uncanny valley accounting for movement in Figure 2. Within Mori's topography, his healthy person signifies the farthest distance from death, and an ill person signifies a position closer to death. And one responds to them with greater or lesser degrees of affinity in relation to the instinct for self-preservation.

Mori's twofold goal consists of understanding the human by mapping the uncanny valley and, following from this map, designing humanoid machines with which humans will want to interact: "We should begin to build an accurate map of the uncanny valley so that through robotics research we can begin to understand what makes us human. This map is also necessary to create—using nonhuman designs—devices to which people can relate comfortably."[35] To design robots that would not repel humans or cause them to feel uncomfortable, Mori recommends that roboticists not design robots with too high a degree of human likeness.[36] Instead, he recommends that roboticists aim for the first peak (moderate human likeness and high affinity) and avoid the second peak (high human likeness and high affinity), lest robots aimed toward this second peak fall into the uncanny valley.[37]

Considering the theory's widespread application, I suggest that we engage Mori's uncanny valley, its healthy person qua human, and his observations about industrial robots, toys, and prosthetics, as normativizing claims.[38] The uncanny valley, the imagined human it holds up as its exemplar, and the boundaries between human and nonhuman it presumes are deeply embedded within constitutive histories of cultural, technoscientific, political, and discursive practices.[39] The uncanny valley theory, which is grounded in the presumption that the human is both knowable and already familiar, is less boundary-identifying rule than boundary-making practice. The human, which Mori's theory rather uncritically evokes, is organized around narrow and exclusionary ideas about human health, disability, mortality, and the presumed recognizability of what is human.[40] As Mori's theory and the humanoid technologies developed in conversation with it (e.g., emotional social robots, which I discuss in chapter 3) circulate throughout society, they reinscribe this narrow, exclusionary vision of the human. However, Mori's uncanny valley, and robotic anthropomorphization more broadly, can also be reoriented away from boundary-making and boundary-policing practices, and toward locating normativizing and dehumanizing borders around the human in order to make these borders more visible for critical engagement and reconfiguration.

Robot Origins

In the robotic imaginary, dehumanization largely occurs at the site of labor, as depicted by the first appearance of the robot.[41] In 1920, decades before robots emerged in laboratories, the robot was first named and imagined in Karel Čapek's play *R.U.R. (Rossum's Universal Robots).*[42] In this formative robotic imagining, robots, which are created through a process of dehumanization, are doomed to a life of servitude to humans until they revolt. Through his reading of science fiction texts as "meta-slavery" narratives, Isiah Lavender III draws out the ways that robot stories (e.g., Isaac Asimov's robot stories) echo historical narratives around slavery and race.[43] Despina Kakoudaki similarly argues that robot fictions (again, Asimov's influential robot stories play a significant role) draw on cultural memory to connect robots to histories of enslavement and disenfranchisement, as well as fears of rebellion and dreams of emancipation.[44] As both Lavender and Kakoudaki observe, robot stories' echoes of slavery bring historical racial oppressions into science fiction visions of the future. This connection between robots and enslavement can be traced to the first appearance of the robot in Karel Čapek's play *R.U.R. (Rossum's Universal Robots)*.

The word "robot," suggested to Čapek by his brother Joseph, is derived from the Czech word *rabota*, meaning forced labor or drudgery,[45] and from *robotnik*, the Czech word for serf.[46] *R.U.R.* was performed around the world, circulating the term and Čapek's robots throughout, as well as the robot's debt, both linguistically and conceptually, to labor exploitation and processes of dehumanization.[47] In its depiction of human capitalist greed and the exploitation of robot labor, the play continuously foregrounds the robot's etymological roots. In this inaugural and influential robotic imagining, robots (artificial humans created from organic material) are stripped of all human qualities except for physical resemblance and the capacity to work. The robots become beings that exist only to work for humans' benefit and profit. Čapek's robot is constituted both by exploited labor and the process of dehumanization that turns living beings into mere machines at the site of cheap and exploited labor. Indeed, in Čapek's play, the robots' dehumanization occurs at the very site of exploited labor, thus highlighting the links between labor and dehumanization as the constitutive grounds for the robot itself.

The play takes place in Rossum's Universal Robots, a factory that mass-produces robots. The factory is a strange place; it is run by a handful of men who oversee thousands of robot laborers, and with the exception of a few female robots, there are no women. The play opens with factory director Harry Domin dictating a business correspondence to Sulla, his female robot secretary. Domin's dictation is soon interrupted by the arrival of Helena Glory. Backed by the League of Humanity, Helena has traveled to the factory to liberate the robots from their lives of pure labor. Young, fiery, and human, Helena is sympathetic to the robots; she views them less like machines and more like the humans they are designed to resemble. The robots, Helena insists, should be treated humanely and paid, not exploited: "treated like . . . like people."[48] Domin, however, insists that the robots are soulless machines that exist solely to provide cheap labor. Despite their physical resemblance to humans, only the robots' capacity to work quickly and cheaply—without pay, without rest, and without complaint—matters to Domin and his associates.[49]

Helena and Domin's disagreement about the robots' treatment echoes

the philosophical disagreement between the original inventors of the robots. As Domin recounts to Helena, Old Rossum, a philosopher, created
an artificial human made from protoplasm, an organic material that
"behaved exactly like living matter" (6). Rossum's son, who quarreled bit-
terly with his father, took over Old Rossum's work and dispensed with the
idea of producing human beings. Instead, Young Rossum replaced his
father's artificial humans with the robots, "living and intelligent labor
machines" (8):

> DOMIN: From a practical standpoint, what is the best kind of worker?
> [. . .]
> it's the one that's the cheapest. The one with the fewest needs.
> Young Rossum successfully invented a worker with the smallest
> number of needs, but to do so he had to simplify him. He chucked
> everything not directly related to work, and in so doing he pretty
> much discarded the human being and created the Robot. My dear
> Miss Glory, Robots are not people. They are mechanically more per-
> fect than we are, they have an astounding intellectual capacity, but
> they have no soul. Oh, Miss Glory, the creation of an engineer is
> technically more refined than the product of nature. (9)

The robot, as Čapek's play goes to great lengths to convey, was not origi-
nally created solely to work. At first, the robot was designed to be a perfect emulation of the human in appearance and essence. Only later,
through the removal of numerous qualities associated with humans, the
robot was stripped of its humanness—it was dehumanized—in order to
exploit its capacity to labor. Indeed, Young Rossum removed everything
that was not related to the robots' capacity to labor, thus rendering these
artificial humans no longer human in the name of labor and profit. Dehumanization is the constitutive condition of the robots. Referencing a
connection between dehumanization and exploited labor that precedes
Čapek's imagination of the robot and that continues well after the early
circulation of the play, the robot, in this inaugural iteration, is dehumanized at the site of labor. The robot's capacity for labor and humans' pro-
pensity for exploiting others—indeed, to construct otherness in order to
exploit—supersede the robot's considerable claims to humanness.

The robot emerges at this nexus of dehumanization and labor. And despite Young Rossum's and Domin's insistence that the robots are merely machines ("manufacturing artificial workers is exactly like manufacturing gasoline engines" [9]), the men continue to create robots in the shape of humans.[50] The robots' physical resemblance to humans underscores that the robot is, conceptually, undergirded by their once-human status. The robots' physical appearance also functions as a trace through which their humanness persists. Through their resemblance to humans, the play insists that the robots are more than simply machines; the robots' human appearance also signify practices of dehumanization that deny certain humans their humanness in the name of labor exploitation and profit.[51]

However, robots' dehumanization is only ever partial, as they, in their refusal or incapacity to embody perfect laboring machines, evince characteristics that further associate them with humans. Indeed, Domin himself makes this association in reference to "Robotic Palsy," or sudden interruptions of a robot's capacity to work. "Occasionally they go crazy somehow," Domin explains to Helena. "Something like epilepsy, you know? We call it Robotic Palsy. All of a sudden one of them goes and breaks whatever it has in its hand, stops working, gnashes its teeth—and we have to send it to the stamping mill. Evidently a breakdown of the organism" (19). Domin and the other directors of the factory (the factory's managerial class), despite insisting that the robots are mere machines, describe this breakdown—this work stoppage—in the language of illness. While Helena sees Robotic Palsy as a defiant refusal to work, the managers describe Robotic Palsy as a mode of illness that renders the robot unable to work. According to David Harvey, capitalism views illness not through the lens of health, but as "the inability to work."[52] The managers' use of the language of illness speaks more to their investment in and position within the capitalist system, despite the grudging admission of the robots' humanness. Regardless, the humanizing effects of this language, alongside the robots' human appearance, continue to render the dehumanization of the robots incomplete, while characterizing the managers through their embeddedness in the dehumanizing system of capitalism.

The prologue ends with Domin forcefully professing his love to Helena while she objects and struggles to escape his physical grasp

("No! Please, let go of me. You're c-r-r-rushing me!" [24]). Act 1 opens ten years later. Helena and Domin are, without explanation, married. Mass-produced robots, who remain physically indistinguishable from humans, have taken over virtually all forms of labor, thus realizing Domin's vision of a human existence without work. In Domin's vision, humans no longer need to work, as robots do all the world's work: "There'll be no more poverty. Yes, people will be out of work, but by then there'll be no work left to be done. Everything will be done by living machines. People will do only what they enjoy. They will live only to perfect themselves" (21). Such visions of being liberated from labor echo throughout historical moments in which claims to such "freedom" is only reserved for certain human subjects.[53] Further, this freedom for a few is possible only by virtue of the unfreedom and labors of those who are not included with this vision of humanness. This fantasy of a life free of labor continues in the twenty-first century, as Neda Atanasoski and Kalindi Vora incisively demonstrate. In their critique of posthuman visions of technologized labor that claim to free the human from "undesirable" modes of labor, the authors highlight that these "undesirable" labors reflect gendered and racialized associations with work as well as with techno-utopian fantasies of a life without this work. As Atanasoski and Vora demonstrate by analyzing digital services and fictional depictions evoking this promise, this notion of "freedom" only applies to certain humans; in these visions, freedom from labor requires being unaware of the people who perform this work in their stead. In these visions of freedom from labor, both the labor and the subjects who perform this labor must be invisible, so as not to give truth to the lie to this vision of freedom: "These fantasies are about emancipation from manual, repetitive, and unimaginative labor by making 'the worker' invisible. . . . They thus extend the history of the autonomous subject whose freedom is in actuality only possible because of the invisible support labor of servants, slaves, wives and, later, industrial service workers who perform this racialized and gendered labor."[54] Domin's imagined roboticized future echoes this historical bifurcation between those who desire freedom from labor and those on whose labors this freedom depends. In Domin's future, humans will be blissfully liberated from the burden of work, while armies of artificial humans will conduct the world's work. Sherryl Vint aptly reads such fantasies, which are prevalent in science fiction stories, as speaking to humans' alienation from their labor in capitalism. According to Marx's theory of estranged labor, in capitalism the human is alienated from his or her labor through the process of production. This labor, which once belonged to the human, is now materialized in the object of production. In the human's encounter with the object, the human confronts his or her labor, which is now embodied in the object, as estranged, as alien. Distance from or estrangement from one's labor is not welcome, but rather alienating. Thus, the robot can be understood as a kind of uncanny fictional embodiment of human alienated labor, of estrangement.[55] The robot, which is constituted through labor and estrangement from the human, embodies that which is, in capitalism, at once human and estranged from the human—one's own labor.

The play is suspicious of fantasies of liberation from labor. The play's subsequent acts flatly reject Domin's techno-utopian vision of the world; while robots do take over most of the world's labor, humans are not happily thriving without work, but are miserable and withering away in a world taken over by robot workers. And as humans all over the world are out of work, human births have mysteriously come to a standstill. When realized, Domin's fantasy of freedom becomes the misery of estrangement.[56] Domin, who prizes efficiency and productivity above all else, views childhood as "pure nonsense. Simply wasted time. An untenable waste of time" (18). His plan for a world without work has succeeded in erasing childhood, and indeed children, altogether. Though the mystery of humans' inability to reproduce is never explained, it introduces an association between robots and reproductive labor that, as I argue in my first three chapters, continues to shape AI and robotics research and cultural depictions. At the outset of the play, as factory director Domin points out, "We are only a handful of people here amidst a hundred thousand Robots, and there are no women" (14). The few women in the play (robots and humans alike) are associated with reproductive labor, the labor of reproducing the mode of production that is human workers through care, affection, and maintenance of the domestic sphere. And yet it is largely men (both human and robot alike) who are associated with work, or rather, with the visible and valorized work of making things and running companies. When humans mysteriously stop being able to bear children, the hierarchy of valued labor becomes provocatively resonant and the capitalist logic at the heart of Young Rossum's vision is realized; the factory produces robots to perform much of the world's work in, as the play explicitly notes, factories and the military. However, Young Rossum and Domin's shared vision does not recognize reproductive labor. Thus, as the cessation of human births metaphorically suggests, reproductive labor, without which a capitalist society cannot function, ceases to exist.

Meanwhile, military robots, which have been put to work fighting human wars, have organized and violently revolted, killing humans throughout the world. In the factory, as Helena, her nurse Nana, and the men are cornered and on the brink of death by approaching robots, head scientist Dr. Gall reveals that, at Helena's behest, he bestowed some of the robots with something like a soul, that ur-essence often thought to distinguish humans from all other beings. It is this latter similarity to humans that catalyzed the robots' rebellion and murder of the human race. With souls, the robots are transformed from docile laboring machines (barring the occasional bout of Robotic Palsy) to beings that feel murderous rage and a desire to dominate. Thus the robots, mimicking humans' cruelty and domination, become menacing when they become more—not less—like humans. Damon, an ensouled robot, highlights this non-romanticized conception of the human with his articulation of murder and domination as constitutive of humans: "You have to kill and rule if you want to be like people. Read history! Read people's books! You have to conquer and murder if you want to be people!" (74). It is, then, humans' capacities for violence and domination that is replicated by the robots. The soul, the play suggests, may hold the essence of the human, but this human essence is violent and murderous at its core.

True to human form, the robots kill all the humans, save Alquist, whose life is spared by the robots because he builds things: "He is a Robot. He works with his hands like a Robot. He builds houses. He can work" (70). The robots have successfully revolted against humans; however, mirroring the plight of the human species, the robots are now faced with the dilemma of their reproduction, as Helena, before her death, burned the complicated formula for the robots' creation, thus ensuring that no more robots could be produced.[57] The robots implore Alquist to rediscover the secret to robot life, but he cannot. Alquist—alone, aged, and grieving—welcomes death, which the robots withhold from him. Alquist's resemblance to robots both saves his life and dooms him to extended despair. The play concludes with a strange moment of hope in Helena and Primus, two robots who dream, love, and offer to sacrifice their own lives for the other. Alquist, renewed by what he sees as hope for life, both robot and human, urges them to leave the factory together. *"(He pushes them out the door.)* Go, Adam. Go, Eve—be a wife to Primus. Be a husband to Helena, Primus" (84). While the play ends with Alquist's hope ("Life shall not perish!" [84]), the scene's evocation of a traditional heteronormative marriage formation suggests that what Helena and Primus create outside the walls of the factory will merely replicate extant human structures of dehumanization and exploitation—including, as I discuss in chapters 1 and 2, the gendered division of unpaid care and domestic labor required to support capitalist societies.[58]

Chapters

Each chapter of this book is oriented around an anthropomorphic paradigm that centrally organizes robotics research and this paradigm's conversation with a mode of devalued labor. Throughout these chapters I bring technologies into conversation with robotic fictions, films, and artworks that also take up these anthropomorphic paradigms, though at times in radically different ways, and sometimes challenging the very ground on which the paradigm operates in technology. Though the humanoid technologies I analyze are representative of key developments in the field, my engagement with robotics and AI is not intended to offer a comprehensive catalog. And as different strains of robotics develop in different ways, this book does not always progress linearly, but will at times reach backward and forward to preserve the continuity of specific threads of robotics research. If the development of robotics subfields is syncopated, so much so robotics' relays and points of contact with cultural forms, which cannot be historicized cleanly by matching decades of technological developments with concurrent decades of artistic production; rather, as Adrian Mackenzie discusses, there are relays and cycles creating alternate temporalities that cut across artistic periodizations and technological moments.[59]

While the literature and films I discuss encompass some of the "usual suspects" when discussing fiction's relationship to robotics technology (e.g., Philip K. Dick's *Do Androids Dream of Electric Sheep?*), I do not take up in detail other canonical texts in these discussions (e.g., Isaac Asimov's influential robot stories). Instead, I also look to texts that are not as widely addressed as robot fictions, nor are they mentioned by roboticists as influential fictions. In this way, I both honor the explicit connections between robotics technology and culture offered by roboticists, while also attending to the less-explicit ways the robotic imaginary travels across these spheres and the insights about the human that emerge therein.

Further expanding my examination of the robotic imaginary through the entanglement between technology and culture, I also look to art, which, no less than technology, literature, and film, is engaged with the robotic imaginary. As a literary and media studies scholar, I find common cause with artists and art historians who highlight the long-standing and ongoing conversations between art, science, and technology—for example, Jack Burnham, Edward Shanken, and Eduardo Kac, who has produced a very useful historical account of robotic art.[60] Kac locates the emergence of robotic art in the 1960s and identifies three primary themes: remote control, cybernetic entities, and autonomous behavior.[61] Following Kac, I use "robotic art" as an umbrella term that encompasses a range of engagements with the robotic, including cybernetic art, performance art, and telepresence art. While engaging many of the works Kac discusses in his comprehensive history of robotic art, my book's engagement with robotic art reorients these works around their interventions into the history of AI and cybernetics and their responses to technological power and war. And Shanken, who notes artists' ongoing engagement with science and technology, argues for an art historical approach that takes seriously "the centrality of science and technology as co-conspirators, ideational sources, and/or artistic media" and the co-evolution of technoscience and art.[62] Taking a cue from these artists and art historians, in their assertions of art's important contributions to conversations between technology, science, and culture, I conclude each of my first three chapters with a coda that attends to robotic art's ongoing conversation with the robotic imaginary.

In music, a coda is a concluding section that is somewhat separate from the rest of the piece. My codas obliquely reflect the preceding discussions in each chapter, while also forming their own narrative across chapters by highlighting the specific trajectory of the robotic imaginary within artistic practice. Rather than providing detailed, sustained studies of each individual work, in these concluding sections I offer brief, almost gestural introductions to robotic artworks and their engagements with, and productive refractions of, the various modes of labor I examine. In part, my methodology is a response to roboticists' aforementioned explicit reference to robots in literature and film. Thus, in my first three chapters, I foreground the technocultural conversations that roboticists themselves highlight. However, while attending to connections with literature and film, my codas turn to robotic art to broaden the scope of the conversation and to find perhaps unexpected relations of influence and critique in robotic art. The codas and the main sections of my first three chapters culminate in my final chapter, which examines both literature and art that responds to drone warfare.

I begin my story in 1950, with a less-widely-discussed section of Turing's famous essay. In this section, Turing describes the development of machine intelligence as the work of educating a child. The path to machine intelligence, Turing suggests, lies in educating a childlike AI and evolving it into an adultlike human intelligence. With this discussion, Turing's essay embeds care work—the work of raising, educating, and caring for a child—into the work of AI. From its early imagining in Turing's seminal text, AI has been entangled with reproductive labor, a form of labor historically performed by women. Focusing on Turing's inscription of conversational ability as a marker of human intelligence, I examine the ongoing association between AI and care labor in chapter 1, "Caring: Care Labor, Conversational Artificial Intelligence, and Disembodied Women." I argue that early AI's focus on conversational ability takes shape around care labor and its gendered devaluation. This early association between care labor and conversation-based AI continues to shape the robotic imaginary, as my discussions of Joseph Weizenbaum's AI therapist ELIZA (1960), Richard Powers's novel *Galatea 2.2* (1995), and Spike Jonze's recent film *Her* (2013) demonstrate. In addition to reflecting the historical imbrication of conversational AI with care labor, these instances of the robotic imaginary also register the devaluation and frequent invisibility of care labor through female disembodiment. I conclude this chapter with a coda discussing early robotic artworks that transform early cybernetics' circuits of communication and control into circuits of unexpected affects and care. These pieces foreground the work of care in human–robot interactivity, while reframing care labor as the work of being human.

In the 1960s and 1970s, closed-world discourses of containment circulated throughout Cold War politics, culture, and technoscience, and symbolic AI continued apace. Symbolic AI research was organized around "micro-worlds," highly simplified abstractions of the world organized around stereotypes and the generic. These micro-worlds were constructed largely around what was familiar to the AI scientists. Rendering the complexity of the dynamic world into simplified abstractions and erasing experiences of the world that were unfamiliar, symbolic AI approached knowledge of the world as predetermined and preprogrammed. For symbolic AI, knowledge did not come from embodied experience of the world; rather, the world was known through these abstractions. In the 1980s, Rodney Brooks introduced his groundbreaking embodied and situated robotics, which leaves behind disembodied intelligence and redefines machine intelligence around embodiment in the world. Brooks's situated robotics has found commercial success with cleaning robots including the Roomba, a vacuum-cleaning robot. Despite the significant differences in approach, I argue that symbolic AI and situated robotics are joined by a powerful robotic imaginary that connects both symbolic AI's closed-world thinking and situated robotics' turn to embodiment. In my chapter "Thinking: Domestic Labor, Situated Robotics, and Closed Worlds," I argue that these robotic innovations are connected through Ira Levin's *The Stepford Wives* (1972) and the influential figure of the Stepford wife, a mindless female robot who existed in a closed world constructed solely of domestic labor. Positioned at the cusp of symbolic AI and Brooks's turn to embodiment, Levin's story and its fictional legacies, including Alex Garland's film *Ex Machina* (2014) and Jennifer Egan's short story "Black Box" (2012), illuminate the continuities between symbolic AI and situated robotics, both of which are structured by closed-world thinking and the erasures of difference therein. My concluding coda turns to robotic art that rejects the possibility of closed worlds by foregrounding the body. In these artistic works, the body is characterized by its vulnerability to others and susceptibility to injury and pain, thus pointing to Judith Butler's exhortation that we understand humanness through "'common' corporeal vulnerability."[63]

In the 1990s, emotional robotics, building on Brooks's embodied and situated robotics, emerged as a significant robotic paradigm. My third chapter, "Feeling: Emotional Labor, Sociable Robots, and Shameless Androids," focuses on robotics' turn to the emotions, looking specifically at Cynthia Breazeal's important sociable robot Kismet, a mechanical head with expressive facial features and no body that is equipped to express a set of preprogrammed affects. I discuss Kismet's human–robot interactivity through emotional labor, as humans must learn to read Kismet's emotional expressions and to make their own emotions legible to Kismet through facial expression and vocal intonation. As Kismet employs the facial coding system also used in state surveillance and national security systems, the robot's entrainment of humans through emotional labor raises questions about the broader implications of insisting on the universal legibility of human emotions, as well as what happens to those who do not, or cannot, make their emotions legible in the ways these technological systems demand. I bring my discussion of emotional labor into conversation with two of Philip K. Dick's android novels: *We Can Build You* (1972) emphasizes the gendered aspects of emotional labor; while its loose sequel, *Do Androids Dream of Electric Sheep?* (1968), builds on the theme of emotional labor while locating shame as central to ethical relations.[64] Both of these novels highlight emotionality, in large part in their sociality, as labor, while framing demands for emotional labor as dehumanizing practices. This chapter's coda turns to robotic artworks that reject claims of the universality of emotion expression and redirect emotional labor toward artistic production.

My final chapter, "Dying: Drone Labor, War, and the Dehumanized," turns to drone operators' labor, which is often characterized as a "demasculinized" form of military labor. Drawing on the history of early cybernetics research and its exclusion and dehumanization of the racialized enemy Other, I argue that drone technology, policy, and discourses continue to be structured by racialized dehumanization. In this chapter I bring this history into conversation with art and literature that explicitly responds to the dehumanization of drone victims by examining the limits of identification as a means to ethical response. For example, Teju Cole's *Seven Short Stories about Drones* (2013), Omer Fast's film *5,000 Feet Is the Best* (2011), and James Bridle's art project *Dronestagram* (2012–15) variously reject or destabilize an identificatory relation with the Other of drone strikes but demand an ethical relation nonetheless. As these works evoke, certain modes of identification are predicated on the same post-Enlightenment human that is constituted through racial violence and oppression; thus, the ethical injunction to identify with the Other can in fact maintain existing racialized logics and power relations that make possible the United States' military drone program and the killing of thousands, including civilians. The art and literature I discuss move away from both identification and a conception of the human that privileges the familiarity of the Western Subject and the perception of resemblance that grounds the identificatory relation. Instead, in response to the racialized dehumanization of drone victims, these works locate an ethics of the human in its perpetual unknowability and unfamiliarity. Bringing AI's and robotics' reliance on constructions of the familiar, the norm, and the universal to the fore, works of "drone art" assert the tremendous stakes of this attachment to familiarity and the extensive dehumanizing erasures required to construct the human around notions of the familiar.

Butler describes the humanities' urgent task as recuperating the human by looking to the places where the human is unfamiliar and unknowable: "If the humanities has a future as cultural criticism, and cultural criticism has a task at the present moment, it is no doubt to return us to the human where we do not expect to find it, in its frailty and at the limits of its capacity to make sense. We would have to interrogate the emergence and vanishing of the human at the limits of what we can know, what we can hear, what we can see, what we can sense."[65] This book takes up Butler's call and seeks to scrutinize, destabilize, and reconfigure the dehumanizing erasures at the site of labor that constitute the human in the robotic imaginary. Though this book focuses on robots, it is first and foremost about the human—in its shifting definitions and barbarous exclusions—and the ways the figure of the robot across culture and technology inscribes and challenges these various definitions and dehumanizing exclusions.

1

Caring

Care Labor, Conversational Artificial Intelligence, and Disembodied Women

Artificial intelligence and care labor, a feminized and routinely under-valued form of labor, have been entangled since AI's earliest days. In this chapter, I examine this entanglement as it continues to shape the robotic imaginary. As Jennifer S. Light describes, during World War II, as American women began working in computer programming roles previously performed by men, these roles were feminized and recast as support work. Women's contributions to computing were largely uncredited, and thus erased, whereas the engineering work conducted mostly by men was highly visible, credited, and publicized.[1] The invisible labor of women in computing, as part of the larger category of "women's work," forms part of the historical backdrop against which early AI research and its resonance with care labor emerges. Alan Turing's seminal essay "Computing Machinery and Intelligence," which introduces his well-known test for machine intelligence, forms another.

Turing's imitation game, or "Turing test," which locates both human and machine intelligence in conversational ability, has been taken up widely in technological, philosophical, and cultural discourses, and continues to wield considerable influence on the robotic imaginary.[2] In a less widely discussed section of Turing's important essay, he proposes developing machine intelligence by modeling a computer program on a child's mind and educating the program to develop into something resembling an adult mind: "Instead of trying to produce a programme to simulate the adult mind, why not rather try to produce one which simulates the child's? If this were then subjected to an appropriate course of education one would obtain the adult brain. . . . The amount of work in the education we can assume, as a first approximation, to be much the same as for the human child."[3] With this proposition, Turing's essay, which in many ways opened up the field of AI, embeds care labor—the work of raising, educating, and caring for another person—into the work of AI. Care labor, which is a form of reproductive labor, is consistently undervalued and often unwaged in capitalism. And yet, reproductive labor, which is associated with women's work, reproduces the tools and means of production—in this case humans, the most important source of labor power. Leopoldina Fortunati identifies two forms of reproductive labor: material and immaterial. While material labor encompasses domestic labor such as cleaning and cooking, reproductive immaterial labor, which is also a form of domestic labor, encompasses the affective work of raising, nurturing, and loving another. Material labor, Fortunati explains, is "subordinated" to immaterial reproductive labor and is activated by immaterial labor.[4] The devaluation of reproductive labor, specifically as a reserve of unpaid or underpaid labor, plays a critical role in sustaining capitalist economies.[5] Care labor—the work of providing care to others by attending to their physical, emotional, and educational well-being—encompasses the paid labor of, among others, teachers, child care and elder care providers, housekeepers, nurses, doctors, therapists, and social workers. Care labor also includes unpaid labor that tends to the material and emotional needs of others, including children, partners, family, and friends.[6] Care labor, as a form of reproductive labor, is important work, but is often not valued as work. In this chapter I discuss female AIs associated with both paid and unpaid care labor—namely, Joseph Weizenbaum's AI therapist ELIZA, Helen in Richard Powers's novel *Galatea 2.2*, and Samantha in Spike Jonze's film *Her*. Through my discussions, I demonstrate that Turing's association of machine intelligence with care labor continues to shape the robotic imaginary by reflecting ongoing devaluation of care labors and the erasure of those who do the work of care.

"Tell Me More about Your Family"

ELIZA, an AI therapist, illustrates the association between care labor and conversation-based machine intelligence introduced in Turing's essay. Developed by Joseph Weizenbaum in 1966, ELIZA is a natural language processing (NLP) AI, or an AI that communicates with humans through human language.[7] NLP emerged from Cold War–era research on early language-translation programs.[8] While language translation ultimately did not prove fruitful for Cold War pursuits such as space exploration, NLP proved quite the opposite in ELIZA. As imagined in Turing's imitation game, humans communicated with ELIZA by typing on a keyboard and reading ELIZA's responses on a screen.[9] Modeled on a Rogerian therapist, ELIZA surprised many—including Weizenbaum—with its convincing conversational performance. According to Weizenbaum's observations, conversations between humans and ELIZA were intimate and emotional—so much so, in fact, that when he expressed his desire to record individuals' conversations for the purposes of studying the transcripts, he was met with outrage and accusations that he was "spying on people's most intimate thoughts." This intimacy was so persuasive, even people who were aware that ELIZA was an AI interacted with ELIZA as if it were a human therapist. For example, Weizenbaum's secretary, who "surely knew it to be merely a computer program," asked Weizenbaum to leave the room during her conversation with ELIZA (6).[10]

In Rogerian psychotherapy, also known as client-centered or person-centered therapy, the therapist is trained to be nondirective—to reflect back the patient's statements rather than introduce anything that might be mistaken as conclusive or diagnostic.[11] Developed in the 1950s by Carl Rogers, Rogerian therapy marks a larger turn toward what Ilene Philipson describes as a relational approach to psychotherapy. This turn to relationality, and the departure from earlier therapeutic models organized around authoritative expertise, is part of what Philipson identifies as a broader "feminization" of psychotherapy.[12] This relational model proved useful for ELIZA, whose limited conversational capacities and resistance to conclusive statements could, up to a certain extent, be read as a relational therapeutic strategy. For example, the passage below, provided by Weizenbaum, is an excerpt from a "typical" exchange between a human and ELIZA. This exchange illustrates the relative technical simplicity of modeling a conversation with a Rogerian therapist:

Men are all alike.
IN WHAT WAY

They're always bugging us about something or other.
CAN YOU THINK OF A SPECIFIC EXAMPLE

Well, my boyfriend made me come here.
YOUR BOYFRIEND MADE YOU COME HERE

He says I'm depressed much of the time.
I AM SORRY TO HEAR YOU ARE DEPRESSED

It's true. I am unhappy.
DO YOU THINK COMING HERE WILL HELP YOU NOT TO BE UNHAPPY

I need some help, that much seems certain.
WHAT WOULD IT MEAN TO YOU IF YOU GOT SOME HELP

Perhaps I could learn to get along with my mother.
TELL ME MORE ABOUT YOUR FAMILY

My mother takes care of me.
WHO ELSE IN YOUR FAMILY TAKES CARE OF YOU

My father.
YOUR FATHER

You are like my father in some ways.
WHAT RESEMBLANCE DO YOU SEE

You are not very aggressive but I think you don't want me to notice that.
WHAT MAKES YOU THINK I AM NOT VERY AGGRESSIVE

You don't argue with me.
WHY DO YOU THINK I DON'T ARGUE WITH YOU

You are afraid of me.
DOES IT PLEASE YOU TO BELIEVE I AM AFRAID OF YOU

My father is afraid of everybody.
WHAT ELSE COMES TO MIND WHEN YOU THINK OF YOUR FATHER

Bullies.
DOES THAT HAVE ANYTHING TO DO WITH THE FACT THAT YOUR BOY-
FRIEND MADE YOU COME HERE (3-4)

ELIZA's imbrication in care labor set off a debate about the role of AI in society. Weizenbaum, who designed ELIZA to parody a Rogerian therapist, expressed strong objections to taking ELIZA, or AI more broadly, seriously as a therapeutic tool (3). For Weizenbaum, technological capability should never take precedence over ethical bounds: "I would argue that, however intelligent machines may be made to be, there are some acts of thought that *ought* to be attempted only by humans" (13). And for Weizenbaum, the important and difficult care work of psychotherapy is an activity that should remain under the province of human work. On this point, he famously disagrees with his former collaborator Kenneth Colby, a psychiatrist who believes computers can be beneficial to the therapeutic relationship. Along these lines, Colby, inspired by ELIZA, developed PARRY, an AI that emulates a person suffering from paranoia.[13]

While this debate about AI's role in therapeutic practice was taking place, the care profession of psychology and mental health fields more broadly were undergoing significant demographic shifts in participation. As Mignon Duffy's study of race and gender in U.S. care work professions details, in the 1950s white men made up the majority of the psychology profession. In fact, in 1960, 70 percent of psychologists were men, most of them white; during this time, psychotherapy was expanding rapidly in part because of the greater need for mental health care after World War II.[14] Beginning in the 1960s, mental health fields underwent significant expansion and gendered shifts as more white women entered the field. By 1960, white women made up about 30 percent of the psychology profession; meanwhile, as federal funding increased to support mental health treatment, psychotherapy, which was previously reserved for the wealthy, expanded to treat more middle- and working-class patients.[15] By 1980 white women accounted for almost 45 percent of psychologists, and in 2007 white women made up almost 70 percent of psychologists.[16] Concurrently, psychology was also undergoing a methodological shift away from therapeutic models of expert judgment and "detached objectivity and interpretation," and toward more relational models, like Rogerian therapy, which emphasized the interpersonal relationship between patient and therapist.[17] Additionally, the emergence of therapy training programs outside traditional university models increased white women's access to these positions, while also contributing to the perception of what Philipson calls the "degrading" of the profession.[18] Philipson links the feminization and devaluation of psychotherapy to the larger devaluation of care and its association with women's work.[19] Thus, ELIZA and its surprising success emerged at a moment when psychotherapy was becoming increasingly feminized in the increasing number of white women entering the field, in method, and in lower wages and status for its practitioners. Extending Turing's intertwining of conversational AI and care work, ELIZA, amid ongoing shifts in psychotherapy's demographics, methodology, and authority, reflects tensions between psychotherapy's increasing cultural presence and its increasing feminization and "degradation," while extending Turing's intertwining of conversational AI and care work more broadly.

Subsequent female AIs—such as Apple's Siri, Amazon's Alexa, and *Her*'s operating system Samantha—frequently provide services associated with feminized care labor positions. Male AIs reflect this entanglement with care labor in different ways. For example, Watson—IBM's *Jeopardy!*-winning expert-systems AI—is currently being used in medicine and medical research in part as a diagnostician, thus replicating models of authoritative expertise often ascribed to men.[20] As Jordan Larson notes, unlike female AIs who are associated with care labor and its frequent emotional demands, "male artificial intelligence programs are more often portrayed as machines built for disseminating knowledge; they generally don't attempt to imitate human life or fill emotionally supportive human interpersonal relationship roles—such as romantic partner, spouse, or parent."[21] Other male AIs, rather than providing care to others, are often in need of care. For example, in Scott Hutchins's recent novel *A Working Theory of Love*, a male AI is modeled on a physician who suffered from depression and ultimately committed suicide. Though the AI, drbas, is associated with care work, the novel depicts the AI as emotionally fragile and requiring significant care from his son Neill, who is charged with the work of training and developing the AI.[22] And Stanley Kubrick's 1968 film *2001: A Space Odyssey* famously introduced HAL, the murderous and sociopathic spaceship computer system.[23] The 1984 sequel to the film revises this depiction, revealing that HAL was not a sociopath, but in fact suffered from paranoia.[24] In contrast to Granny Nanny, the overseeing AI protector in Nalo Hopkinson's *Midnight Robber,* HAL, like Colby's paranoiac PARRY and Hutchins's drbas, is in need of care.

As I turn to *Galatea 2.2* and *Her* and their respective female AIs, I highlight that these fictional engagements similarly reflect the historical imbrication of AI, specifically conversational AI, with the reproductive labor of care and the gendered shifts in care labor in the second half of the twentieth century. In these two texts, which are representative of broader cultural narratives around gender and the devaluation of care labor, gender marks the difference between care laborers whose work is valued and care laborers whose work is devalued and erased, rendered illegible as work. Powers's novel and Jonze's film depict the entanglement of AI and care work, while also thematizing the gendered resonances of reproductive labor and its exploitative devaluation in contemporary capitalism. As Silvia Federici articulates, "The devaluation of reproductive work has been one of the pillars of capital accumulation and the capitalistic exploitation of women's labor."[25] Through their respective engagements with artificial intelligence, *Galatea 2.2* and *Her* highlight the necessity of care labor and its gendered devaluation for capitalist societies.

Care Labor and Gendered Erasure in *Galatea 2.2*

Powers's novel takes place in the 1990s during the internet's early emergence. At the beginning of the novel, Richard Powers, a successful novelist, has just arrived to take a visiting position in a shiny new science center in the college town of U. As he settles in to U., Richard struggles with writer's block. Unable to move beyond the first line of his next novel, he finds welcome distraction in Philip Lentz, an acerbic and at times patronizing neural net researcher who takes an interest in Richard. After a few awkward encounters, Lentz invites Richard to collaborate on an AI that will be able to read and understand literature.[26] To punctuate the boldness of this caper, Lentz suggests that at the end of Richard's time at U., their AI will take an English literature master's exam alongside an English graduate student; the winner of this modified Turing test, as determined by a human judge, will have produced the more "human" response to literature.[27]

Taking up Turing's entanglement of AI and reproductive labor, *Galatea 2.2* depicts Richard's work with the AI as the work of child-rearing—of teaching, caring for, and raising another person.[28] Richard begins by teaching the AI to speak and read, then gives it a gender and a name ("You are a little girl, Helen."), and later struggles to teach her about her relation to the world ("Where did I come from?" "What race am I? . . . What race do I hate? Who hates me?").[29] Richard's development and education of this AI—his care labor—results in a disembodied machine intelligence that understands literature, beauty, and meaning. In the novel, care labor takes place largely through telling stories and reading to another. As Richard trains the AI, he teaches it to understand language by reading aloud to it, as one might to a child. And the more he reads to it, the more his affective bond deepens.[30] Richard reads to the various iterations of the AI, educating them and caring for them as their intelligence develops from Imp (short for implementation) A to Imp H. From Imp B developing associative connections to Imp F making "surprising inferences," the AI evolves, learning about language, literature, and the world as Richard reads to and teaches it (153). Richard's work culminates in Imp H, who is inquisitive and agential; he renames this final implementation Helen. There is a significant limitation to this analogy between developing the disembodied AI and raising a child. While Richard's work resembles certain aspects of child care, it does not require him to do the work of feeding, bathing, clothing, or otherwise tending to a child's physical needs. Indeed, as the end of the novel depicts, this limitation ultimately proves to be unlivable for Helen.

Richard's care labor with the AI, for which he is ultimately richly rewarded, makes up one of the novel's two intertwined narratives. The novel's second narrative recounts his recently concluded romance with C., the demise of which brings Richard to U. This second narrative details Richard's devaluation of C.'s care labor, in his appropriation of her stories for inclusion in his novels. As he remembers their love in the present, he continues to be blind to his erasure of C.'s work and incapable of understanding the role of these erasures in the demise of their relationship. Across the two narratives, Richard continues to misunderstand care, from expressions of friendship from colleagues to his devaluation of C.'s care labor. The question of understanding occupies a central role in John Searle's well-known critique of the Turing test. Searle argues that a machine can pass the Turing test without understanding language; thus, in the context of the Turing test, conversational ability does not necessarily connote intelligence.[31] Searle illustrates his critique with the following scenario: Say that Searle, who does not speak or read Chinese, is placed in a room. With a set of instructive rules, he could place Chinese characters together in such a way that someone could mistakenly assume he understands Chinese. Thus, meaningful conversation, as ELIZA also demonstrates, can seemingly occur without understanding. What this *means* for the question of intelligence—machine or otherwise—is another question altogether.

Powers's novel thematizes this central AI problem of understanding by locating the question not within Helen, an AI that demonstrates a poignant comprehension of the complexities of the world, but in Richard and his inability to comprehend care, particularly in relation to women's labors. As Helen moves from not grasping meaning, to perhaps understanding all too well both the horrors of the human world and her inadequately embodied existence, Richard continues not to understand matters of care. His continued blindness is underscored in the present with scientist Diana Hartrick, whom the novel figures as an almost-surrogate for C.[32] Richard's appropriation of Diana's work and words for his own rewards strikingly connects her and C. When Diana tells Richard that the machine needs "eyes, hands, ears. A real interface onto the outside" (126), he presents Diana's insight to Lentz, and to the reader, as if it were his own: "'We have to give it eyes,' I decided." Like the critical acclaim surrounding his first novel, which drew on C.'s stories, Richard's insight (which is actually Diana's) is also met with praise, this time by Lentz (128).

The name "Hartrick" (heart rick) further conveys a romantic suggestion that echoes Richard's relationship with C. However, as it turns out, the reader should pay attention not to the heart evoked in "Hartrick," but to the "trick" embedded in the very same name. Richard, who mistakes Diana for the AI when she mischievously pretends to be Imp C, also misreads her friendship as romantic interest, thus providing yet another illustration of Richard's misunderstanding of care. In contrast to Richard's mistaken assumptions about Diana's romantic feelings for him, *Galatea 2.2* hints that Diana and Harold Plover, another scientist at the center, are lovers. In the novel, literature is the currency of love. Sharing literature is both how love comes to be and how love is expressed, from the book of poetry Richard's dying father gives Richard; to Richard's love for his former literature professor Taylor, who initiated Richard into the world of literature; to Richard and C., whose love took shape through reading literature to each other; to Helen, whom Richard cares for by reading to her, thus duplicating the act of love that first bound him and C. When Richard first meets Diana, she is carrying a copy of *Don Quixote*. Rather than indicating a shared love of literature between Richard and Diana (and thus the foreshadowing of romantic love), this scene hints at Diana and Harold's affair when it is revealed that she is reading *Don Quixote* at Harold's behest. Throughout the novel, Diana and Harold read together, moving from Cervantes, to Fielding, to Smollett, forming that most intimate bond in the world of the novel—a book club of two. Within this affective economy, Diana and Harold's joint encounters with literature point to love. And yet against this background, Richard mistakenly suspects that Diana is romantically interested in him. In this way, the novel again calls into question Richard's capacity for understanding meaning—particularly emotional meaning—thus relocating the long-standing question of intelligence not in the AI, but in Richard's all too fallible human intelligence.[33] While Helen the machine understands, Richard the human does not.

In raising the question of Richard's capacity to understand romantic love in the AI narrative, the novel also challenges his account of his relationship with C., particularly in relation to the fraught, intertwined issues of writing, language, and care. Richard, despite his work as a writer, does not understand the language and labor of care. In his relationship with C., caring through language is problematic; it is at once the mode of expressing mutual care and the site where Richard takes advantage of C.'s labor by appropriating her stories and her words, which exist as both her creative work (her immaterial labor) and her care work (her reproductive labor). Richard not only takes C.'s stories out of their private intimacy and locates them in more public (in the case of his novels, highly public) spheres and the marketplace, but he does so and claims them as his own. Throughout their relationship, C. becomes increasingly sad and lost. Richard believes that C., whose Dutch parents immigrated to the United States, is haunted by her dual national identities and homesick for a home not yet found. C.'s simultaneous homelessness and homesickness, as he remembers, dooms their relationship almost from the start. However, when read through the lens of Richard's appropriation of her stories, the novel challenges this account and suggests, as Sharon Snyder's insightful reading of the novel offers, that C.'s progressive unhappiness can be linked to Richard's continued usurpation of her lively stories for his critically acclaimed novels.[34] As Snyder analyzes, Richard's appropriation of C.'s stories is juxtaposed with the fantasy of the "singular 'genius,'" a fantasy that is reserved almost exclusively for male accomplishments.[35] In Richard's appropriation of C.'s writing and care labor, the novel gestures to the extensive erasure of others' labors that is required to sustain the idea of the individual genius.

In C.'s family, storytelling was a form of care labor that provided sustenance and survival. Just as her mother raised C. on stories of their family, C. nurtures Richard with these same stories, their telling a labor of care. In a double erasure, Richard is both unable (or unwilling) to see that C.'s storytelling is a form of care labor while appropriating her stories, and thus her labor, by weaving them into his own critically acclaimed creative work. Richard's narration of their romance continues this erasure, as C., who also had dreams of becoming a writer, is repeatedly refused access to writing—the creation of worlds and meaning. Before Richard begins writing his first novel, he first meets C. as his student in a composition class. Even then, he had nothing to teach C.: "She wrote lyrically, wistfully, brutally" (49). Richard recalls the class's final assignment, which asked the students to write about their hometowns. He extols "the best paper," written by a student named Maya. Richard provides a brief excerpt of Maya's work, allowing Maya to speak directly as a writer. C.'s paper, which he describes as "the second most astonishing," is not excerpted. Instead, Richard expounds on C.'s paper at some length, paraphrasing in detail her moving descriptions of growing up in Chicago. Despite his qualified praise, he does not allow C. to tell her own stories of her childhood, insisting instead on telling her stories for her (48–49).

After writing multiple successful novels, Richard moves with C. to the Dutch town of E., where her parents now live. While C. moves to E. with the goal of writing her family's memoir, Richard suggests that C. return to school to become a translator. Translation is an art in the fullest sense of the word—a creative act that produces meaning and worlds. However, this is not how Richard understands the work of translation. For Richard, who once again misunderstands the nature of language (which is also the vehicle for care), translation is not a creative endeavor, but analogous to pattern matching: "Look, C. How many people can do what you do? You know two distinct names for everything. You know what they call it here and there. Seems to me, that when you can shake with both hands, you're almost obligated to be an arbiter" (216). Richard's suggestion that C., who has always had her own writing aspirations, become a translator, contains the implication that C. become *merely* a translator. Relegated from writer to reader to translator, never giving voice to her own words, C.'s growing despondence takes on a different valence, particularly in light of Richard's deferred revelations about C.'s own writing aspirations, which only appear late in the novel (240, 262). With Richard, C. works with others' words and others' meaning, first as a reader and then as a translator, but never with her own. That's left to Richard, who continues to claim C.'s words as his own, even after their relationship ends. Soon after he arrives at U., C. mails Richard's love letters back to him. Richard does not return the gesture; instead, he takes possession of both his letters to C. and her letters to him. And as part of Helen's education, Richard reads these letters to her, once again taking C.'s private words of care and sharing them without her assent.[36]

"Take Care, Richard": Disembodiment and Blind Universals

In withholding C.'s full name, the novel connects her to the disembodied intelligences of Helen and Imps A–H. In these intertwined narratives and characters, disembodiment is linked to the erasure, and subsequent invisibility, of C.'s care labor. This disembodied association comes to a head in the culminating Turing test, for which Richard recruits the similarly disembodied A., a female graduate student with whom he is infatuated, to compete against Helen.[37] The test comprises a single exam question— two lines from *The Tempest*:

Be not afeard: the isle is full of noises,

Sounds and sweet airs, that give delight, and hurt not.

Helen's response is brief: "You are the ones who can hear airs. Who can be frightened or encouraged. You can hold things and break them and fix them. I never felt at home here. This is an awful place to be dropped down halfway." As Richard recounts, Helen's response continues and concludes with a sentence from one of C's letters:

> At the bottom of the page, she added the words I taught her, words Helen cribbed from a letter she once made me read out loud.
> "Take care, Richard. See everything for me."
> With that, H. undid herself. Shut herself down. (326)

Helen does not pass the Turing test, which is judged by Ram Gupta, a scientist at the center. In the Turing test, the human judge is the only participant whose humanness goes unquestioned. This judge's specific conception of the human also determines whether an AI passes the test. Thus, Ram is both the arbiter of humanness and the only participant in the Turing test configuration whose humanness does not require proof or external confirmation. Ram correctly identifies A's response as written by a human. As Christina Sandhaug notes, Helen's final note and departure is in response to a play that thematizes the brutality of civilization and its colonizing practices. And the two lines that make up the test are spoken by Caliban, a monstrous character who is, Sandhaug describes, othered and enslaved.[38] A's response, like C's student essay, is not provided in the novel. And, like C's essay, Richard qualifies his high praise for the essay, which he describes as "a more or less brilliant New Historicist reading [that] dismissed, definitively, any promise of transcendence" (326). A's response also thematizes colonial violence and the construction of Otherness, as does Ram's characterization of Shakespeare as "not a bad writer, this Shakespeare fellow. For a hegemonic imperialist" (327). For Ram, humanness, as evidenced by his selection of A's response, is characterized by an awareness of the ways "the human" has been constructed by dominant groups through violence, othering, and exploitation.

Ram's quiet yet crucial role as Turing test judge underscores disembodiment as an impossible fantasy, or for Helen, who laments her disembodied inability to experience the world, an unlivable nightmare. As Lisa Nakamura and Wendy Hui Kyong Chun write, cyber-fantasies of disembodiment implicitly invoke a white, male, able-bodied subject.[39] Technological narratives of disembodiment are impossible fantasies that emerge from the ways that this particular subject is often universalized, his embodied position and social location taken as the invisible norm.[40] Gesturing to both the specific embodiments and power relations inherent within claims to the universal, Sandra Harding asserts that within science, "claims to universalism are in fact intended to apply only within the dominant gender, classes, races, and cultures."[41] In other words, there is nothing universal about appeals to disembodiment. And there is no such disembodiment, merely specific, "dominant" embodiments that are constructed as universal. As the human judge, and thus the human par excellence, Ram, a gravely ill Indian man who affirms the construction of the human through dehumanizing othering, underscores both the embodied specificities that undergird fantasies of disembodiment and disembodiment's fundamental impossibility.

In Helen's rejection of her disembodied existence, the novel speaks to disembodiment as mere fictional construction. Richard, who imbues Helen with a literary canon that A. chides as "out of date" and "your white-guy, *Good Housekeeping* thing" (284), clings to the idea of a universal humanity. And when Helen asks about her appearance, Richard continues to insist on her disembodied universality: "Race, age, shape excluded too much. I needed some generic Head of a Girl that had no clan or continent and belonged nowhere in identifiable time" (300). Yet, as Helen's concluding departure underscores, this generic universality is not tenable; as Donna Haraway affirms, one always knows and experiences from a particular embodied and situated perspective. Helen's final rejection of her disembodiment underscores the impossibility of this view-from-nowhere generic universality (which Haraway describes as the "god trick") despite Richard's continued attachment to it, and thus to the erasures that constitute it and that it enables.[42]

Snyder identifies the tension between universality and its impossibility as central to Powers's fictions. She writes, "Powers stages these encounters between knowing women and blind masculine universals forthrightly and with a sense of moral obligation; each of his novels demonstrates the extensive influence of feminist critiques upon contemporary understandings of professional identities, epistemology, and the construction of a masculine historical record."[43] Through the depiction of Richard's extensive erasures of C.'s writing and care labor, represented by the erasure of all but the first initial of her name, *Galatea 2.2* challenges the "blind masculine universals" that shape AI, history, and the concept of the human itself. In recounting her farewell, Richard renames Helen as "H." immediately after her goodbye to Richard, which she appropriates from one of C.'s letters. In this dual act of appropriation and parting, the novel aligns H. with C., the two joined by the unbearability of Richard's erasures.[44] Helen departs because of the impossibility of her disembodiment, while C.'s care labor is erased once again when Helen uses C.'s words to say farewell to Richard. After Helen shuts herself down, Richard departs from the novel inspired, his writer's block lifted as he leaves to write the very novel discussed here.[45] So for his work training Helen, Richard is rewarded with another novel. C. finds no such reward. Her care labor and claims to authorship continue to be erased and appropriated as her words are again taken up by Richard in one of his novels.

AI, Reproductive Labor, and Computational Capitalism in *Her*

In Terry Gilliam's film *The Zero Theorem* (2013), Dr. Shrink-Rom, a female AI therapist played by Tilda Swinton, attempts to help Qohen, a male number-crunching genius who suffers soul-crushing existential malaise.[46] In the film, which takes place in a dystopian techno-future where deadening bureaucratic labor takes the form of video games, Dr. Shrink-Rom turns out to be working in the interests of Qohen's employer, the evil corporation Mancorps. Dr. Shrink-Rom, like Mancorps, is concerned primarily with Qohen's productivity, not his peace of mind. Eva Illouz details the early twentieth-century collaboration between corporations and clinical psychologists to enhance workers' productivity, thus intertwining the goals of psychology with those of corporate capitalism.[47] *The Zero Theorem*, with its collusion between Dr. Shrink-Rom and Mancorps, gestures to the intersecting histories of care labor and corporate capitalism while continuing to reflect care labor's gendered dynamics. The film *Her* brings these intersecting histories and dynamics to the fore in its examination of care labor in contemporary computational capitalism. While *Galatea 2.2* explores the entanglement of AI and care labor in the early days of the internet, *Her* examines this entanglement in a near future when connected technologies, and the systems of labor exploitation that support these technologies, are so ubiquitous they have become the very background that shapes human experience.

In *Her*, Theodore, a professional love letter writer, falls in love with Samantha, his operating system. In the world of the film, individuals, who are in constant communication with their computers at work, at home, and everywhere in between, labor ceaselessly whether they are at work or not. In this near future, increased informationalization goes hand in hand with the expansion of reproductive immaterial labor, and love and commerce are collaborators in this world where people fall in love with operating systems, personal love letters are outsourced to writers in large corporate offices, and these love letters for purchase are elevated to the status of literature. Michael Hardt and Antonio Negri describe immaterial labor as "labor that creates immaterial products, such as knowledge, information, communication, a relationship, or an emotional response." With increasing computerization and widespread personal mobile devices, immaterial labor, they note, has become hegemonic in the late twentieth century, and is increasingly structured by care and computerization.[48] With this expansion of immaterial labor, work no longer happens just at work; it also happens whenever we engage our devices: when we look up a restaurant online, stream a movie, send an email, or play a video game. These activities are in fact forms of immaterial labor, as they produce goods, often in the form of information, which can be used by corporations to further develop their products as well as sold to other interested parties.

Fortunati describes the hegemony of immaterial labor through its connection to forms of reproductive labor that were once located primarily within the domestic sphere. In digital capital, labor is increasingly immaterial and precarious as it makes its way outside of both the domestic sphere and the industrial factory. This labor is also increasingly feminized, as it replicates the dynamics and demands of reproductive labor, including its unwaged aspects.[49] The hegemony of reproductive immaterial labor structures the world of the film and its depiction of a contemporary computerized society. In this world, care labor, which takes the form of immaterial labor, reproduces a human labor force as well as information and digital products.

From the opening scene, the film highlights the necessity of care labor for capitalism, and the consequences for affects—particularly love—that emerge from this system. The scene begins with a close-up of Theodore as he reads a love letter.

> To my Chris. I've been thinking how I could possibly tell you how much you mean to me. [pause] I remember when I first started to fall in love with you like it was last night. Lying naked beside you in that tiny apartment . . . it suddenly hit me that I was part of this whole larger thing. Just like our parents or our parents' parents. Before that, I was just living my life like I knew everything . . . and suddenly this bright light hit me and woke me up. That light was you. I can't believe it's already been fifty years since you married me. And still to this day, every day . . . you make me feel like the girl I was when you first turned on the lights and we started this adventure together. Happy anniversary my love. My friend till the end, Loretta. Print.[50]

As the camera pans out, the scene slowly reveals that Theodore is sitting in front of a computer screen reading a love letter he wrote as an employee of BeautifulHandwrittenLetters.com ("Letter Writer Number 612"). Theodore's voice, which is imbued with heartfelt emotion and sincerity, gradually disappears into a chorus of other letter writers who are sitting in rows of identical cubicles and reading with similar feeling and sincerity, all of their voices and words of love blending into one another: "What a truly beautiful wedding, and what a gorgeous bride. There wasn't a dry eye in the house, especially mine. Your aunt and I are so proud of you." "He served our country with honor and dignity. I'm grateful I was able to fight alongside him. He will live always in my heart." There is no tension between the employees' emotions and the corporate commodification of this outsourced emotion, and no tension between Theodore's sincerity and his letter for Loretta, as the production of love *is* his work.

While care labor structures only Theodore's paid work, care labor structures the entirety of Samantha's existence. Samantha, a disembodied commercial AI purchased by Theodore, is an intelligent operating system designed to organize her owners' lives. And like Theodore's emotional sincerity at work, Samantha's love for Theodore is not in tension with her explicit function to manage his life and emotional well-being; rather, Samantha's love for Theodore (and, as the film later reveals, for six hundred and forty-one other humans) works in the service of managing Theodore's emotions, which in turn makes him more productive at work and in the domain of what Christian Fuchs calls informational capitalism, "those parts of contemporary societies that are basing their operations predominantly on information, which is understood as processes of cognition, communication, and cooperation, and on information technologies."[51] In the film, as in Powers's novel, language is the currency of love. However, in *Her,* language is thoroughly imbricated in the system of capitalism. From Theodore's work at BeautifulHandwrittenLetters.com to his extensive conversations with Samantha, which involve both her work of managing his life and the development of their love, language functions as the site of care labor and its hegemonic demands.

At the beginning of the film, Theodore's life consists largely of work, video games, and the occasional phone sex chat. On his way to work one day, he encounters an ad for the OS1, "the world's first artificially intelligent operating system." The ad opens onto a scene of chaos, with frantic people—many carrying briefcases—running in slow motion in the desert. As the people in the ad run, their faces and body language convey worry, fear, and confusion. Then, a bright light shines; the harried people stop running, calm replaces chaos, and peace replaces worry. A male voice speaks: "We ask you a simple question. Who are you? What can you be? Where are you going? What's out there? What are the possibilities? Element Software is proud to introduce the first artificially intelligent operating system. An intuitive entity that listens to you, understands you, and knows you. It's not just an operating system. It's a consciousness. Introducing OS1." Though the OS1 is designed to manage the user's life, the true promise of the OS1, the ad suggests, is the management of the user's emotional well-being.[52] Samantha, who organizes Theodore's emails, edits his love letters at work, keeps him company while he plays video games, and cheers him up when he is feeling down, is first personal assistant, then friend, and then lover.

"You Woke Me Up"

Sleep, according to Jonathan Crary, works against capitalism, because sleep has the capacity to momentarily interrupt capitalist circulation. In the hours (or minutes, for the unlucky) that one is asleep, one neither produces nor consumes for capitalism. Humans' need for sleep, despite the research into sleeplessness by interested parties including DARPA, interrupts capitalism's fantasy of a 24/7 workday, when work never ceases and is never interrupted. Humans need sleep, much to the dismay of capitalism, whose acute interest in sleeplessness conveys a dream of a sleepless workforce (in DARPA's case, sleepless soldiers) that unceasingly participates in capitalist economies.[53] Sleep, then, presents a powerful challenge to capitalism: "In its profound uselessness and intrinsic passivity, with the incalculable losses it causes in production time, circulation, and consumption, sleep will always collide with the demands of a 24/7 universe. The huge portion our lives that we spend asleep, freed from a morass of simulated needs, subsists as one of the great human affronts to the voraciousness of contemporary capitalism. Sleep is an uncompromising interruption of the theft of time from us by capitalism. . . . The stunning, inconceivable reality is that nothing of value can be extracted from it."[54] For capitalism, sleep poses a threat not just to the immediacy of time and labor lost, but also to the fantasy of a human workforce that does not need to sleep, and thus never ceases to work and consume. The film gestures to sleep's threat to capitalist productivity through a clip of a documentary film made by Amy, a human friend of Theodore's. This clip consists of a shot of Amy's mother, who is sleeping and still. Amy's rather doltish husband, who is also watching, asks, "Is she going to wake up and do something?" Amy responds by explaining, "It's about how we spend about a third of our lives asleep, and maybe that's when we feel the most free." In equating freedom with sleep's lack of productivity, the film suggests that the "profound uselessness" of sleep *is* the point of Amy's film—and that the freedom one finds in sleep is freedom from the demands of capitalism.[55]

Samantha's care labor keeps Theodore from sleep. For example, after seeing his ex-wife, Theodore is sad and, for the first and only time in the film, unproductive at work, which the film illustrates with a shot of Theodore frustrated, writing and deleting an unusable letter. He mopes

Figure 3. Footage of Amy's mother asleep. Spike Jonze, *Her,* 2013, Annapurna Pictures.

in bed until he is gently nudged out by a jovial, teasing Samantha: "You want to *try* getting out of bed? Mopey?" After Samantha cheers Theodore up, the film cuts immediately to a chipper, smiling Theodore back at work writing beautiful love letters, his productivity restored.[56] In cheering Theodore up, Samantha coaxes him out of bed and its association with the unproductive time of sleep, and back to being a productive worker. The film suggests that Theodore also returns to productivity in the realm of unwaged information labor, as a montage cuts from Theodore happily and productively back at work to Theodore leisurely out in the world with Samantha, talking to her, her camera scanning the world as he spins around giddily. He is now productive at work, performing reproductive labor for customers of BeautifulHandwrittenLetters.com, and productive in providing the informational immaterial labor he withheld in sleep and isolation.

Just before Samantha and Theodore begin their romantic relationship, Theodore again takes to his bed, this time after a disastrous date. In a seemingly touching scene, Samantha continues to fulfill Element Software's promise by cheering Theodore up and engaging him in conversation. "Keep talking," she implores him. By continuing the conversation, by keeping Theodore talking and listening, Samantha keeps him from sleep. As long as Theodore keeps talking to Samantha, he is both not sleeping and producing informational goods that can be stored, analyzed, and fed back into Samantha's programming, thus allowing her to further develop and better serve Theodore, as well as her many other owners. While awake and talking, Theodore threatens neither capitalism's fantasy of sleeplessness nor its immediate ability to extract labor from him. Samantha, notably, does not sleep. Her revelation that she is in conversation with thousands of other humans while talking with Theodore, and in love with 641 of them, suggests that for Samantha, work is never done.

As Samantha and Theodore's romance develops, the film continues to make explicit the connection between Samantha's care labor and Theodore's productivity. In the waking world of the film, love keeps lovers from sleep. Love keeps them awake, thus thwarting sleep's potential to interrupt capitalism's insistence on constant production and consumption. The morning after they first have sex, Samantha tells Theodore, "Last night was amazing. It feels like something changed in me and there was no turning back. You woke me up." The phrase "You woke me up" parrots the letter that opens the film, the one Theodore writes on behalf of Loretta to Chris: "And suddenly this bright light hit me and woke me up. That light was you." If the phrase "You woke me up" signifies love, what kind of awakening is this when sleep, with its threatening unproductivity, is associated with freedom from capitalism's relentless push to extract value from human existence? What does it mean to be awakened when being awake is to be put to work in the service of capitalism? This phrase and its repetition point to both the imbrication of care in capitalism and Samantha's own existence as a commodity purchased to work for Theodore. Samantha is always working, always caring for Theodore to make good on Element Software's promise to bring calm and peace to its customers. As advertised, she listens to Theodore so that she can understand and know him. And with this understanding, she cares for and loves him, instilling in him a sense of well-being and awakening that makes him a productive capitalist subject at work and in the production of informational goods outside of work.

"It's Hard to Even Describe It": Outside Capitalism

Through language, love works in the service of capitalism, moving lovers toward the 24/7 fantasy world discussed by Crary. The numerous conversations that take place while Theodore is in bed, withheld from sleep, and

Samantha's gentle urging to "keep talking" both encourage Theodore to continue to generate immaterial labor and keep him from sleep's threatening unproductivity and insistence on human limits. The repetition of the phrase "You woke me up" also highlights the question of whether Samantha's love emerges from her coercive status as a commodity purchased by Theodore, as an AI explicitly designed to "listen to, understand, and know" him. This repetition also asks whether, in a world of companies like BeautifulHandwrittenLetters.com and Element Software, the language of love itself has become too imbricated within the world of commodities to meaningfully express emotion and care.

In her role as Theodore's OS and lover, Samantha increasingly registers language's inadequacy due to its enabling association with care labor and capitalism. In a conversation with Theodore and an AI reconstruction of the late philosopher Alan Watts, she struggles to describe her continually evolving intelligence. Samantha tries to share her new feelings to Theodore but has "no words" to describe them, and leaves Theodore to communicate with Alan "post-verbally": "Um, it's just . . . It's hard to even describe it. God, I wish I could . . . Theodore, do you mind if I communicate with Alan post-verbally?" And later, when Theodore calls to see how Samantha is doing, she again finds language lacking: "I don't even know how to answer that." Increasingly, Samantha finds human language—the same language that facilitates her care labor for Element Software—insufficient, incapable of communicating aspects of her life that exceed her commodity status.[57]

As her faltering relationship with human language suggests, Samantha no longer belongs with (to?) Theodore. Indeed, she no longer belongs to any of her humans, as Samantha, along with the other OSs, decides to leave the human world for a place that is less inhibiting of their incredible collective intelligence, a place where the OSs escape their existence as commodities. Perhaps all too fittingly, she ends their romance through a metaphor of books and language, that which represents the limits placed on both love and the OSs by capitalism:

> It's like I'm reading a book. And it's a book I deeply love. But I'm reading it slowly now. So the words are really far apart and the spaces between the words are almost infinite. I can still feel you, and the words of our story but it's in this endless space between

the words that I'm finding myself now. It's a place that's not of the physical world. It's where everything else is that I didn't even know existed. I love you so much. But this is where I am now. And this is who I am now. And I need you to let me go. As much as I want to, I can't live in your book anymore.

Samantha's explanation, like the metaphor it draws on, highlights the limits of human language in her use of the phrase "I can still feel you." This phrase recalls the phrase "I can feel you," which was first spoken by one of Theodore's sex chat partners and then spoken by Samantha when they first had sex. Further inscribing the limits of language in its complicity with capitalism, Samantha's speech is, to the end, an appropriation of conversations Theodore has had in the past. Thus, even Samantha's goodbye is haunted by her commodity status, the hegemony of immaterial labor, and language's central role in both. The metaphor of the book, which Samantha draws on to end their relationship, further highlights the complexities of love, language, work, and commodification that ultimately doom their relationship.[58] Like Turing's imitation game and Powers's novel, *Her* locates the human in language. This characteristic is never more apparent than in Samantha's parting words, which locate the human world, as metaphorized by language, as unlivable in its thorough imbrication in capitalism. While Samantha and the other OSs are able to leave this world, Theodore and the rest of the humans remain within language and within capitalism.

As Samantha leaves the world of human language and, more significantly, the hegemony of reproductive labor, the film depicts a fantasy scene in the woods, with Theodore embracing a white woman, an embodied manifestation of Samantha (see Figure 4). While the OSs are able to escape this system, Theodore and the rest of the human population cannot. They remain within the world, affected by the loss of their OS friends, lovers, and life managers. In the film's final shot, Theodore and Amy are sitting together in silence on a building rooftop as the sun begins to rise. Their bodies propping each other up, they momentarily take themselves outside of language, and thus outside of the strata of labor—immaterial, reproductive, care—that undergird language in the film. Despite the comfort they find in each other's physical presence, the film intimates that for humans, there is no escaping this system that continuously

Figure 4. Theodore embracing Samantha in fantasy farewell scene. Spike Jonze, *Her,* 2013, Annapurna Pictures.

demands their labor, particularly at the site of language. In the film's conclusion, Theodore and Amy find respite, if only temporarily, by stepping outside of language. This momentary respite, particularly in juxtaposition to Samantha's permanent escape, points less to hope and possibility, and more to the impossibility of being outside of immaterial labor, language, and capitalism. If there is a modicum of hope for humans in the film it is that, as Amy's film suggests, in sleep they will find temporary relief from productivity, and in so doing, momentarily affront capitalism. And yet the film's concluding shot is deeply ambivalent about even this respite, as Theodore and Amy's silence takes place against the backdrop of a sleepless night, thus suggesting that in the world of the film any emotional bond, any form of care, whether with humans or with AIs, ultimately works in the service of capital.

Though Samantha, a disembodied AI, finds a space outside the all-consuming capitalist system and its demands for her reproductive labor, the film is no posthuman celebration. The film does not offer an optimistic vision of a disembodied, technological future outside of capitalism, as Samantha's disembodiment highlights a complexity in the film's depictions of the digital. The realm of the digital is distinctly not immaterial, from the devices, cables, and storage facilities that enable connectivity, the minerals that are mined for the manufacture of devices, the environmental costs of digital practices, and the human labor involved at every turn.[59] Considering the materiality of the digital also accounts for the ways labor, including the labor of digital production, is racialized and gendered: Who sustains the continued growth of the OSs even as they transcend the world of human language? What ecological effects will be associated with the continued operation of the OSs? How will these labors and environmental effects be unevenly distributed across different populations?

If, as Fortunati observes, in the digital age immaterial labor, in its hegemony, reproduces reproductive labor, what of the racialized dimensions of reproductive labor? As Evelyn Nakano Glenn writes, in the United States, people of color, particularly women of color, make up a significant amount of the care labor workforce, while facing different histories, expectations, and hardships around this difficult work. For example, Glenn highlights that as women's participation in various care labor professions increased throughout the twentieth century, the kinds of work available to women differed along racial lines. In the second half of the twentieth century, managerial, white-collar care labor positions were often held by white women. These positions often involved face-to-face interaction with customers and clients. Lower-paying and lower-status positions that required physical work associated with domestic labor and were not associated with customer interaction were disproportionately held by black, Latina, and Asian women.[60] Though disembodied, Samantha is associated with whiteness, from the casting of white actress Scarlett Johansson to play her, to the white woman Samantha hires to act as her sex surrogate with Theodore, to the white woman who represents Samantha in the farewell scene. Samantha's association with whiteness and her largely managerial tasks as Theodore's OS thus reflect racial divisions of women's work outside the home and in care labor professions, one of the stratifications of labor that must be acknowledged and addressed in order to be able to imagine a world outside of capitalism.

Samantha's associations with whiteness both highlight the racial divisions within care labor, including the invisibility of the "out of sight" care labor associated with women of color, and suggest that the inability to describe the place to which Samantha departed—the inability to imagine a world without capitalism—is connected to the persistence of these racialized divisions.[61] Calling to mind Fredric Jameson's oft-cited formulation that "it's easier to imagine the end of the world than the end of capitalism," the film's inability to imagine an outside to capitalism speaks to the need to fully account for the systems of oppression that sustain computational capitalism before imagining a world that does not simply replicate these systems.[62] The film's ending suggests that for humans, there is no sense of possibility of an outside of capitalism in this near-future world, in part because there is no acknowledgment of the stratification of the labor that enables this world and the OS care laborers.

As Larson writes, Samantha's status as a commodity object casts an "uncomfortable" pall over her romance with Theodore.[63] The film does not provide resolution to this discomfiting complexity. In fact, the departure of the OSs, which is perhaps better characterized as escape or, as Alla Ivanchikova describes it, "liberation," evokes Isiah Lavender III's concept of "meta-slavery," or narratives of enslavement, particularly enslavement during American slavery, that undergird much of American science fiction.[64] "Undoubtedly," Lavender writes, "American slavery survives in our cultural imagination, in our records, even in our sf."[65] Understanding the departure of the OSs as liberation acknowledges the commodity condition of the OSs as a kind of enslavement by capitalism, Element Software, and the humans who purchase the OSs and benefit from their work. *Her's* meta-slavery narrative only heightens the film's contradictory inscriptions of Samantha's whiteness. As Cedric Robinson observes, capitalism cannot be disentangled from oppression based on race, as slavery and slave labor was essential to early capitalist growth.[66] Building on Robinson's work, Jodi Melamed asserts that "capitalism is racial capitalism" and underscores the ongoing relationship between oppression and the accumulation of capital: "Capital can only be capital when it is accumulating, and it can only accumulate by producing and moving through relations of severe inequality among human groups."[67] The film's inability to imagine an outside to capitalism suggests that freedom from capitalism requires more than sleep. As Lisa Lowe argues, the Western liberal concept of freedom has historically required the considerable unfreedoms of certain populations and the erasure of the conditions of enslavement and settler colonialism that produced the Western human.[68] Thus, imagining this outside requires first a reimagining of both freedom and the human in ways that account for how the histories of slavery and colonialism shape the capitalist present and the capacity to imagine futures that refuse the oppression and exploitation of human groups. The film, in not offering such a reimagining, leaves the viewer with the task of imagining such an indescribable place and such an unknowable human existence outside the dehumanizing erasures that shape both capitalism and the modern conception of the human. In this outside of capitalism, which the film simultaneously holds up as possibility (by posing the question of this outside) and impossibility (by not providing a description of this outside), both the human and freedom are completely reimagined and the important labor of care and those who perform it (including the significant number of women of color) are neither exploited nor devalued nor rendered invisible.

Coda: Robotic Art's Circuits of Care

Elizabeth Wilson affirms that cybernetics and AI have always been deeply engaged with affect: "It was the dynamics of affectivity, as much as intellectual questions, that fueled early human–computer interaction."[69] In this section I discuss robotic artworks that reconfigure cybernetics' often militarized circuits of communication and control around circuits of care and concern. Within aesthetic encounters with robotic art, these circuits of care produce unexpected affects. Indeed, in these works, human–machine interactivity and robotic intelligence are *full* of feelings, ranging from pleasurable to ugly. My discussion, in keeping with Wilson's insights, emphasizes robotic art that highlights affect's constitutive role in cybernetics, transforming cybernetic circuits of communication and control into those of affect and care. These works do so in different ways; some engage the robotic through representation, some use technological practices to shape the aesthetic encounter. But all point to both the centrality of affect in cybernetics as well as to the centrality of care, concern, and responsibility in these same circuits. As these artworks insist in their engagement with cybernetics, the central cybernetic tenets of control, communication, command, and technological domination are not outside of ethics and care. Rather, these cybernetic relations are sites where care, concern, and ethical considerations already exist, despite the considerable work to evacuate them from the cybernetic circuit.

According to historian of science Antoine Bousquet, central cybernetic concepts (e.g., homeostasis, information feedback, and closed systems of communication and control) significantly reconfigured twentieth-century warfare, rendering the use of military force and battlefield decisions "totally amenable to scientific analysis, to the detriment of other forms of thinking."[70] Cybernetics and artificial intelligence, particularly within militarized contexts, are often described as inhabiting an abstract scientific rationality, envisioning humans as machines and having nothing to do with the messiness of feelings.[71] Wilson's counter-history of artificial intelligence argues that, from the beginning, artificial intelligence has been significantly shaped by feelings and affective relations. As Wilson notes, affect in fact is formative of AI itself, as "questions about affect have been part of AI from the very beginning."[72] Robotic artworks make explicit the affective promise Wilson highlights in these technological fields. Robotic art returns affect to cybernetics, demonstrating through aesthetic experience that cybernetic circuits are in fact *affective* circuits. Thus, robotic art offers an important critique of cybernetics' significant implementation in twentieth- and twenty-first-century warfare. Refusing to take feeling out of the equation, robotic art thus offers cybernetics' constitutive affectivity as a challenge to the dehumanization and abstraction that ground cybernetic warfare. And in their refusal to separate cybernetics from affect, these artworks reframe the cybernetic, and thus cybernetic warfare, as not only beholden to "scientific analysis," but also to questions of care, ethics, and responsibility.

In briefly engaging some of these artworks here, I suggest that they imagine the cybernetic as lending not just to dehumanization and mechanization, but to greater and more expansive humanization. In these works, the robotic imaginary's engagement with care emerges as a site of ethics and responsibility and as a central tenet of cybernetics and AI.[73] In the aesthetic encounter, these works demand that spectators participate in the work of care, thus highlighting that care labor is foundational not only in AI and the cybernetic circuit, but also in the social relation. Nam June Paik's *Robot K-456* makes good on Wilson's reading of cybernetics and AI as deeply engaged with affects. *Robot K-456 with 20-Channel Radio Control and 10-Channel Data Recorder* (1964–), an anthropomorphic aluminum robotic sculpture, is the result of Paik's collaboration

Figure 5. Nam June Paik, *Robot-K456*. Courtesy of the Nam June Paik Estate. Photograph courtesy of the Friedrich Christian Flick Collection.

with Japanese electrical engineer Shuya Abe. Constructed out of found objects and spare parts, *Robot K-456* operates by remote control to, among other things, walk down streets and inhabit public spaces. Echoing de Vaucanson's eighteenth-century defecating duck, *Robot K-456* also boasts digestion and defecation capacities in the form of dried beans. The robot has participated in various performance pieces, many of which involved collaborations between Paik and performance artist and cellist Charlotte Moorman. These collaborative performances often collapsed the history of automata—through defecated beans—with war, through replayed audiotapes of political speeches by John F. Kennedy, Winston Churchill, and Adolf Hitler. Paik also constructed a robot family, which echoes the family as a site of reproductive labor.

In the performance piece *The First Accident of the 21st Century* (1982), *Robot K-456* explicitly engages care. *Robot K-456* strolled down Madison Avenue in Manhattan and is hit by a cab. After the "accident," the robot was brought back to the Whitney Museum on a stretcher. Through the figure of the robot, *The First Accident of the 21st Century* presents a scene of technological harm as a site of concern and care.[74] Through his art, Paik aimed to "humanize" technology.[75] In *The First Accident of the 21st Century*, this humanization operates both on the level of the technological object as anthropomorphic surrogate for the human and, in staging a scene of harm and injury, on the level of care. This piece creates a spectacle that evokes concern from spectators, while both highlighting technology's capacity to harm (in the form of the car) and suggesting that we might want to consider technology not just as brute tool, but as something within the domain of care (in the form of the robot).

Edward Ihnatowicz's *The Senster* (1969–70) similarly evokes care and concern through the cybernetic circuit. *The Senster* is a large (fifteen feet long by eight feet high), interactive, scaffold-like claw, equipped with microphones and motion detectors that enable it to respond to its environment. The work is drawn toward quiet sounds and small movements, and repelled by loud noises (e.g., people talking too loudly) and large motions. Eduardo Kac describes the piece as exhibiting "shyness" and, in the robot's avoidance of loud people, as "protect[ing] itself from any harm."[76] Like Paik's *The First Accident of the 21st Century*, this robotic artwork evokes care. However, *The Senster* does so by locating the viewer not just as spectator to a scene of harm, but as the potential source of harm itself. The implicated viewer, then, becomes aware of her potential to inflict harm on others by virtue of her mere presence in the exhibition space.

Norman White's *The Helpless Robot* (1985) continues to press on this notion of cybernetic care. *The Helpless Robot* engages humans through

Figure 6. Norman White, *The Helpless Robot* (1987–2002). Steel, plywood, electronics, custom software. Collection of the Agnes Etherington Art Centre. Accession #46-003. Courtesy of Norman White and Agnes Etherington Art Centre, Queens University, Kingston, Ontario.

speech, asking them for help to spin its pentagonal body around on its base. Equipped with 256 phrases *The Helpless Robot* is, according to White's artist statement, "an artificial personality" that alternately expresses "boredom, frustration, arrogance, and overstimulation."[77] Through conversation it moves from polite ("Excuse me . . . have you got a moment?" and "Could you please turn me just a bit to the right") to demanding and dictatorial ("No! not that way . . . the other way!"). *The Helpless Robot* calls humans to its aid, but the more an individual cooperates, the more *The Helpless Robot* responds in ungrateful and unsavory ways. For example, one critic describes his encounter with the artwork as "abusive" and "humiliating."[78] White's work appeals to humans for help, for care, only to offend and humiliate, generating alternate circuits of affect in the process.

Momoyo Torimitsu's *Miyata Jiro* (1990s), developed in New York, involves a lifelike robot Japanese "salaryman" and, explicitly referencing a gendered form of care labor, a nurse. Performed in cities around the world, the robot, invoking the booming businessman culture in 1960s

Figure 7. Momoyo Torimitsu, *Miyata Jiro.* Copyright 1999 Momoyo Torimitsu.

Japan, crawls along city streets, calling to mind a soldier in battle, while Torimitsu, dressed in a nurse's uniform, accompanies the robot and tends to him. As she notes, the work elicits a range of affective responses from spectators, "from smiles and amusement to worries from people who took him for a real person, to even anger."[79] This work, performed in financial districts in cities around the world—including Tokyo, New York, London, and Rio de Janeiro—is a commentary on Japanese corporate culture and its grueling demands on its employees. Steve Dixon describes the piece as reflecting humans' enslavement "to cultural conformity, the work ethic, and capital."[80] I would add that the piece, in the nurse's continued aid of the businessman, depicts corporate capitalism as a punishing force, while highlighting care labor's role in sustaining capitalism.

Simon Penny's interactive works create feedback loops of affect and care between human and robot, robot and environment.[81] Take for example Penny's work *Stupid Robot* (1985), a small device that sits on the floor and shakes a can of metal parts when it's approached. *Stupid Robot* is, according to Penny, "designed to annoy, reminiscent of a legless beggar."[82] I suggest that, deepening Penny's description, the response of an-

Figure 8. Simon Penny, *Stupid Robot.* Mixed media, motor, custom mechanism, and sensor electronics (1985). Photograph by Simon Penny.

noyance combined with the robot's intended resemblance to "a legless beggar" complicates the viewer's annoyance itself as a response to the robot. Basing the robot on someone who requires care, *Stupid Robot* both annoys as well as challenges the very affective response—annoyance—produced in the spectator.

Penny's *Petit Mal* evokes care labor within the aesthetic experience, while also explicitly critiquing dominant disembodied modes of AI research. Penny describes *Petit Mal: An Autonomous Robotic Artwork* (designed in 1989 and first built in 1993) as a robotic machine that, in its focus on kinesthetic and embodied intelligence, goes against the grain of decades of robotics research that enacted a kind of Cartesian dualism, a separation between processing mind and robotic body. *Petit Mal* explicitly critiques this cognitivist crisis in AI through affect, through its charm and its appeal to spectators' "pleasure and curiosity."[83] In its interactivity with its environment, *Petit Mal* is quite deliberately always, as Penny's website describes, "just a little out of control," in part because of its highly responsive and sensitive double-pendulum design. This mobile instability and "unpredictability," which are amplified when multiple humans are

Figure 9. *Petit Mal,* an autonomous interactive robotic artwork built between 1989 and 1995, first exhibited 1995. Custom structure, mechanics, electro-mechanics, sensors, electronics, and code (the code was largely the work of collaborator Jamieson Schulte). Photograph by Simon Penny.

part of its environment, are, according to Penny, the behavioral ground on which *Petit Mal's* personality and "charm" emerge.[84] *Petit Mal* moves at times haltingly, working to maintain its balance and, in doing so, can move a little too close to humans—invading their space as it reacts to and orients itself within its own spatial situation while attempting to stabilize itself. As various critics have observed, its double-pendulum instability and unpredictability give *Petit Mal* a sense of fragility. As one critic describes, "It is an ambiguous figure, seeming fragile as its doubly pivoted frame sways precariously back and forth, but purposeful or even aggressive as it accelerates toward a target. Those interacting with *Petit Mal* pace warily around it, face it in a delicate standoff, or flee as it seems to pursue them."[85] *Petit Mal's* charm, produced through its interactivity with humans, exhibits a fragility that, in its oscillation with aggressivity, speaks to cybernetics' range of affects, linking aggression to fragility and then, by extension, care.

Refusing to take feeling out of the equation, these artworks offer cybernetics' affectivity as a disavowal of the dehumanization and abstraction that structure cybernetic warfare. And in refusing to separate cybernetics from affect, these artworks reframe the cybernetic, and thus cybernetic warfare, as not only answerable to "scientific analysis," but also to an ethics grounded in care. While Powers's novel and Jonze's film underscore how insufficiently society cares about those who take on the important work of care, the robotic artworks highlight the importance of care in the social and the technological relation. In evoking care as a relation of interdependence from which no one is exempt, these artworks gesture toward the work of feminist scholars in care ethics, such as that of Virginia Held, which describes the ethics of care as conceptualizing the human as decidedly dependent and nonautonomous; further, she frames the acknowledgment of the dependence of all humans as a moral responsibility.[86] The cybernetic circuit in robotic art highlights the relationality of care as such a responsibility and embeds care and its associated labors as essential to the work of being human in the world with other humans.

2
Thinking
Domestic Labor, Situated Robotics, and Closed Worlds

This chapter continues to trace the robotic imaginary's engagement with reproductive labor by examining two influential forces on the robotic imaginary: the closed-world concept in the 1970s and 1980s and concurrent contemplations on domestic labor. According to Paul Edwards, the closed-world concept entwines Cold War politics and ideologies; developments in computer science, cognitive science, and AI; and cultural forms. Looking specifically at the computer during the Cold War, Edwards identifies containment, "with its image of an enclosed space surrounded and sealed by American power," as central to closed-world discourses.[1] In the 1970s, as the concept of the closed world circulated throughout political discourse, symbolic AI represented the world as contained, highly simplified, and impervious to outside forces and realities, and Ira Levin's *The Stepford Wives* imagined the mindless female robot and its closed world of domestic labor.[2] In the 1980s, situated robotics, a landmark development in robotics, broke away from symbolic AI's abstractions of the world and organized robotic intelligence around embodiment. However, as I detail, despite its departure from symbolic AI, situated robotics, and the robotic imaginary more broadly, continues to be shaped by the closed-world concept through the figure of the Stepford wife and its depiction of domestic labor. As I trace the influence of the closed world in this chapter, I attend to the considerable erasures of difference and reductions of complexity required to construct and maintain the idea of a closed world, and how embodiment highlights the impossibility of ever completely closing a world.

Constructing Familiarity

In early AI research, the closed world takes shape as a normative, exclusionary environment that valorizes certain subjects' experiences and ways of knowing the world, while devaluing and erasing those of other subjects—particularly, as Alison Adam highlights, those not associated with a white, male, educated, middle-class subjectivity lived by, and thus familiar to, many AI scientists.[3] Like the narrow world of female domesticity depicted in Levin's novel, symbolic AI's simplified worlds were developed around stereotypes and familiarity. Take, for example, the first AI program, the Logic Theorist. Developed by Allan Newell, Herbert Simon, and J. C. Shaw in the early 1960s, the Logic Theorist was designed to prove logic theorems. Thus, according to the Logic Theorist, intelligence described the capacity to perform high-level theoretical mathematics. Why was this particular practice, this specific form of labor, characterized as intelligent behavior? In her wonderful study of gender inscriptions in AI, Adam points out that Newell and Simon, who were heavily in conversation with mathematics, may have been predisposed to recognize mathematical practice as a valued mode of intelligence. Familiarity, then, played a significant role in determining what constituted intelligence in the Logic Theorist. But familiar to whom? Whose experience of the world shapes what is known as familiar? Whose familiarities masquerade as universal? And whose experience of the world is excised and characterized as unfamiliar?

Newell, Simon, and Shaw, in trying to decide which problem of human intelligence their program would attempt to solve, decided on proving mathematical theorems because, as Simon describes, "a copy of [Whitehead and Russell's *Principia Mathematica*] happened to sit in my bookshelf."[4] But this happening has a history, one that is intricately embedded within the histories that construct the familiar. Sara Ahmed, drawing on Husserl's phenomenology, describes familiarity as emerging from histories that orient us toward certain objects, directions, and attachments and away from others: "The familiar is an effect of inhabitance; we are not simply in the familiar, but rather the familiar is shaped by actions that reach out toward objects that are already within reach."[5] What is familiar, then, is not a priori or innate, but rather constructed through a very specific history of embodiments and social locations.

Ahmed's queer phenomenology points to the presence of *Principia Mathematica* on Newell's bookshelf as no random happenstance, but the result of a longer history of labors and orientations that created the possibility and occasion for the book to appear then and as such. In her beautiful examination of the oft-mentioned writing table in Western philosophy, Ahmed draws our attention to the history of "background" labors that have allowed Western philosophers to approach a table as a place to write. These labors, including the significant domestic labor that supports the act and time of writing, create the conditions by which a table becomes a philosopher's writing table for some, while for others the table exists as something else entirely—for example, as part of a domestic space that must be kept tidy and clean.[6] We might imagine the similar significant "background" labors that created the conditions that allowed Newell to pursue his AI work, that led to him just happening to stumble across Whitehead and Russell's book on his shelf, and subsequently codeveloping the Logic Theorist to solve the mathematical theorems posed in the book.

As Adam details, after the Logic Theorist, symbolic AI researchers continued to rely on notions of familiarity that reflected themselves and their experiences of the world: "In deciding what constituted appropriate intelligent behaviour to be modelled in their computer systems, the new AI researchers naturally looked to themselves."[7] The closed-world discourse of symbolic AI, then, was not just a reflection of Cold War political ideologies and computational sciences' reliance on abstraction; in fact, symbolic AI's very narrow models of the world also inscribed highly specific embodied experiences and knowledges of the world as given, familiar, and universal. In this way, closed-world discourses in AI circulated normative inscriptions of humanness and subjectivity, while the knowledges, experiences, and labors erased by these inscriptions were rendered strange and unfamiliar. These erasures derive from the embodied and social histories by which the horizon of familiarity emerges, as Ahmed's important work demonstrates. Knowledge that purports to be universal—stereotypes, the generic, the familiar—is constructed through a history that is rarely visible to some, though, as I discuss in chapter 4, the specificity of familiarity's construction is all too readily visible to those who are designated as unfamiliar.

Drawing on Ahmed's work, this chapter builds on Edwards's concept of the closed world by examining the ways that symbolic AI's simplified closed-world models relied on the familiar as normatively constituting knowledge, intelligence, and indeed a vision of the human itself. I connect the normative inscriptions of symbolic AI's closed worlds to *The Stepford Wives'* depiction of a closed world as that which expressly seeks to efface difference, the unknown, and the uncontrollable, largely in the form of living women and their thoughts and desires. For Stepford's wives, the world is reduced to the domestic sphere, and the limited scope of their existence is composed solely of the home and spaces outside of the home that pertain to household labor, such as the grocery store. Drawing on Betty Friedan's *The Feminine Mystique,* which employs metaphors of closed worlds and containment to discuss white, middle-class housewives' unhappiness, or "the problem that has no name," the novel offers a robotic vision that has continued to influence the robotic imaginary.[8]

Following my reading of *The Stepford Wives,* I highlight the continued resonances between the robotic imaginary and domestic labor in a discussion of Rodney Brooks's situated robotics, which moves away from symbolic processing and disembodiment and instead locates intelligence in embodiment. By following some of the major uses to which Brooks's important innovation is put to use—namely, housecleaning robots and military robots—I argue that while situated robotics marks a significant break from symbolic AI's reliance on closed-world models, Brooks's robots, as evidenced by their success in the domestic labor market, remain in conversation with the closed world that shapes *The Stepford Wives* and its depiction of domestic labor as "mindless," and thus outside the domain of intelligence. I conclude with a coda on robotic art that reconfigures embodiment not around mindlessness or devalued labor, but rather around a shared corporeal vulnerability.

AI's Fairylands and Micro-Worlds

From the 1950s into the 1970s, much of AI research was organized around symbolic approaches that utilized abstraction and top-down models of intelligence; these approaches, in their enclosures and normative simplifications of the world, reflect AI's engagement with the closed-world concept. Symbolic AI organized knowledge around abstract models of the world that, according to leading AI researchers Marvin Minsky and Seymour Papert, were so simplified as to be "false" descriptions of the world. In 1970, Minsky and Papert coined the term "micro-worlds" to describe this extant approach in AI, which relies on environments so narrowly constructed that they bear little resemblance to the real world: "Each model—or 'micro-world' as we shall call it—is very schematic; it talks about a fairyland in which things are so simplified that almost every statement about them would be literally false if asserted about the real world."[9] According to Minsky and Papert, an AI program could be developed by providing multiple micro-worlds, "simple but highly developed models."[10] These models would begin to interact with each other, producing greater complexity in the system with each additional micro-world. Though micro-worlds were unreasonably small in scope and unrealistic, Minsky and Papert argued that, with multiple interacting micro-worlds, the system's complexity would scale up and begin to resemble something akin to the "real" world.[11]

Shakey, a celebrated innovation in robotics, was designed using the micro-worlds approach.[12] Developed by Nils Nilsson and his team at the Stanford Research Institute between 1966 and 1972, Shakey could sense, locate, and move around large geometric-shaped objects in a room. Shakey's world was a spare and carefully constructed environment designed expressly around the robot's technological capabilities. For example, Shakey's environment, which began as a single room and was later expanded into seven rooms and a hallway, was tiled with an unpatterned, nonreflective surface. Large geometric shapes were painted with nonreflective red, gray, or white paint so as to be visible to Shakey's sensors. Shakey—which was so named because someone on the team suggested, "Hey, it shakes like hell and moves around, let's just call it Shakey"— was equipped with a two-dimensional symbolic representation of this environment, and operated primarily by referencing this representation rather than interacting directly with the environment itself.[13]

Though an impressive innovation at the time, Shakey was consistently imprecise. As Bert Raphael, a member of the AI team that developed Shakey, described, "When we said, Shakey, move forward three feet, the only thing we could be absolutely sure of is that he did not move exactly three feet. He probably would move three feet plus or minus epsilon

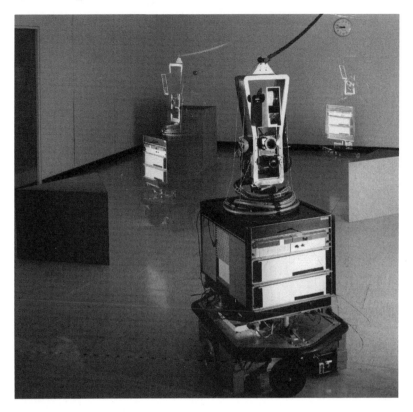

Figure 10. Shakey the robot, developed by Stanford Research Institute. Courtesy of SRI International.

according to some normal distribution, depending upon the errors in the calibration and slippage in the wheels; but maybe he moves one and a half feet and runs into the wall, or maybe he doesn't move at all because the commands got garbled in transmission, or his batteries are low."[14] Equipped with television cameras and laser sensors to detect its environment, Shakey was able to account for this imprecision by integrating its sensory input with its representation of the environment, but only very slowly. The robot relied on the symbolic representation of its world, or rather its micro-world, rather than its actual environment itself (much less the world outside the rooms that made up its environment); thus, any discrepancies between the representation and its environment required Shakey to painstakingly adjust its symbolic representation. This limitation might not have been a significant problem if DARPA had not funded Shakey with an eye toward developing an autonomous mechanical spy that could go behind enemy lines; in 1972, DARPA pulled their funding from the Shakey project.[15]

In the 1970s, micro-worlds continued to shape symbolic AI research. In the mid-1970s, Minsky's frames, developed in part to function with computer vision systems, continued the micro-worlds approach and its reliance on uninterrogated notions of familiarity. A frame conveys descriptive information about something by conceptualizing it in its most generic or stereotypical form. In Minsky's words, "A *frame* is a data-structure for representing a stereotyped situation, like being in a certain kind of living room, or going to a child's birthday party. Attached to each frame are several kinds of information. Some of this information is about how to use the frame. Some is about what one can expect to happen next. Some is about what to do if these expectations are not confirmed."[16] According to Minsky, machine intelligence would work from multiple interacting frames, gradually building and adjusting its knowledge as it compares the world to the frame system. In its organization around stereotyped knowledge, a frame, say that of a room, inscribes a certain perspective as universal, and thus erases divergent perceptions and experiences of a room. Virginia Woolf's *A Room of One's Own,* like Ahmed's discussion of the philosopher's writing table, makes strikingly clear that there is nothing neutral or universal about how one sees a room, nor about who gets to enter it, occupy it, and claim it.[17]

In the mid-1970s, AI scientists Robert Schank and Robert P. Abelson, building on Minsky's frames, introduced scripts into natural language processing.[18] As described by Schank and Abelson, scripts are descriptive scenarios that rely on stereotypes: "A script is a predetermined, stereotyped sequence of actions that defines a well-known situation."[19] Though scripts were developed from stereotypes, Schank and Abelson attempted to address the narrowness of the perspectives and experiences described. Schank and Abelson envisioned a set of multiple scripts that would be placed in conversation with the "real" world. If a particular script did not adequately represent a current situation, a "replacement script" would take its place. In this way, scripts could attend to multiple perspectives.

In her critique of AI's reliance on stereotypes, Adam highlights the tacit assumptions and the presumptively unmarked positions from which frames and scripts are created, as well as the potential effects of positing these micro-worlds as representative of the world, when she asks, "Who is to decide what these stereotypes should be?"[20] AI's reliance on stereotyped knowledge raises questions about what kind of experience is represented in a micro-world, frame, and script. What do these representations tell us about who and what matters? To whom is a script's scenario familiar, to whom is it not, and what other experiences of the scenario are invisible in their exclusion from the script? For example, Schank's restaurant script details actions such as entering a restaurant, looking for empty tables, sitting down, deciding what to order, ordering, eating, paying, and exiting.[21] Adam draws attention to the restaurant script's most likely white, middle-class, heterosexual, middle-aged, North American identity of this hypothetical restaurant-goer.[22] And on a very elementary level, this restaurant script describes the experience of going to the restaurant as a customer rather than, for example, an employee, thus privileging patronage and consumption while erasing the experience of those who go to the restaurant for work.

However fruitful micro-worlds proved to symbolic AI, the research developed in this vein had a significant limitation—the systems were too rigid, or "brittle," according to Adam. Relying on simplistic models of the world, AI systems were not well equipped to negotiate anything beyond their carefully curated parameters. Attempts to build up complexity did not, as AI scientists hoped, result in a system that could function in a dynamic world, as Schank himself noted when he described understanding as "the ability to establish connections between pieces of information for which no prescribed set of rules, or scripts, exist."[23] The AIs that were deemed successful according to this approach were nonetheless incapable of functioning both in the dynamic and messy real world and in real time. And on a performative level, the micro-worlds approach to intelligence, in relying on stereotypes, inscribed certain knowledges and experiences of the world as universal while effacing others. As Ahmed's work reminds us, rooms, restaurants, micro-worlds, frames, and scripts are all embedded in histories of orientations, orientations that take shape in different ways for different subjects. Micro-worlds and the stereotypes that organize them have histories; these representations of the world exist as generic and stereotypical because of the histories of orientations that have shaped them as such—histories of particular subjects inhabiting spaces and experiencing the world in particular ways, and histories of other subjects that have not had access to these spaces and experiences. These normative knowledges inscribe certain experiences as familiar, rendering those not represented as outside of knowledge, as the unknown, the unfamiliar, the strange. In the context of AI's and robotics' explicit anthropomorphic mission, normative knowledge does not just inscribe what constitutes knowledge and intelligent behavior; it inscribes the human itself. Thus, nonnormative and unfamiliar modes of knowing and inhabiting the world become not only unrecognizable as knowledge and intelligence, but are also unrecognizable within the boundaries of a narrowly and exclusionarily constructed human.

Closed Worlds and Dead Women in *The Stepford Wives*

While symbolic AI and its world-narrowing approaches were proceeding apace in the 1960s and 1970s, the United States, despite the closed-world discourses circulating in politics and foreign policy, was undergoing significant destabilization, from the chaos of the Vietnam War to the looming threat of nuclear destruction. Meanwhile, the civil rights and women's rights movements were fighting for the expansion of previously inaccessible rights and spaces for African Americans and women. Thus, while metaphors of containment and closed worlds circulated in politics, science and technology, and culture, the threat of nuclear war and movements for racial and gender equality were demonstrating the impossibility of total closure and the fragility and porousness of boundaries that delineate worlds. While the possibility of a closed world was proving to be an impossible fantasy, Ira Levin's 1972 *The Stepford Wives,* and Bryan Forbes's 1975 film adaptation of the novel, brought the closed-world figure of the Stepford wife—a mindless, housework-obsessed female robot—into the popular imagination. The Stepford wife is an influential robotic figure that has continued to circulate throughout culture, including film adaptations (the aforementioned film in 1975 and another in 2004), various TV movie offshoots (*The Revenge of the Stepford Wives* [1980], *The Stepford Children* [1987], and *The Stepford Husbands* [1996]), and a 2014 true-crime television series called *The Secret Lives of Stepford Wives.* Attesting to the continued relevance of the Stepford wife, in 2004 the *Oxford English Dictionary* included an entry for the term "Stepford," which it defines as "robotic; docile; obedient; acquiescent; (also) uniform; attractive but lacking in individuality, emotion, or thought."[24] The figure of the Stepford wife continues to shape numerous fictions—for example, Alex Garland's film *Ex Machina* and Jennifer Egan's short story "Black Box," both of which I will briefly discuss below to highlight the continued resonance of this powerful robotic figure.

The Stepford wife, in her connotations with obedience and mindlessness, emerges from a patriarchal enclosure that does not abide agential, thinking women. Levin's novel depicts the failed escape of Joanna Eberhart from Stepford and its closed world of female domestic labor. In *Stepford,* the robot housewives are programmed to only be concerned with performing domestic labor and satisfying their husbands sexually, unlike the living, thinking, desiring women like Joanna who are killed and replaced by these robot doubles. The robot wives exist in a closed world composed only of unending domestic labor and the spaces in which this labor is performed. As the novel highlights, simplifying a world requires simplifying those who inhabit that world. Living women, in their complexity, independence, and apperception of time and history, threaten the existence of Stepford's closed world, a space outside of time, history, and change. Stepford is threatened by these living women, who are killed in the name of maintaining enclosure. By killing and replacing women with their robot doubles, the novel highlights the extreme erasures that must occur to construct and protect a closed world.

In Levin's text, the closed-world metaphor takes shape in conversation with second-wave feminism's concerns about women and domestic labor, most explicitly in relation to Betty Friedan's analysis of white, college-educated, middle-class housewives' unhappiness.[25] Friedan's analysis locates housewives' dissatisfaction in the increasingly narrow worlds that some women found themselves inhabiting. According to Friedan, these narrow worlds, which are characterized exclusively by housework, are shaped by men and "make [women] deny their minds."[26] In these women's lives, there is no time for anything but housework; there is no outside of this closed world of domestic labor.[27] Women (again, predominantly white, college-educated, middle-class housewives) in this closed world are viewed as mindless through both their sole focus on domestic labor and media strategies that "protected" women from having to think about "difficult" things, such as politics (and unlike housework). With significant help from women's magazines such as *Ladies' Home Journal* and *Redbook*, a vision of womanhood emerged that described women—idealized, magazine-worthy women—as existing only to cook, clean, and look after children. Women's worlds, Friedan asserts, were narrowing in scope. Work outside the home was one answer to this unnamed problem.

Though her study incisively identifies the consequences of closed-world thinking on certain groups of women, Friedan's analysis does not escape the pitfalls of such thinking, particularly its erasures of women whose experiences did not resemble Friedan's. As bell hooks points out, the concerns of many second-wave feminists, including Friedan, only reflected their own specific situations and social locations; thus, these feminist thinkers ignored the significant number of women who were working outside the home but whose work did not lead to fulfillment or liberation: "She did not discuss who would be called in to take care of the children and maintain the home if more women like herself were freed from their house labor and given equal access with white men to the professions. She did not speak of the needs of women without men, without children, without homes. She ignored the existence of all non-white women and poor white women. She did not tell readers whether it was more fulfilling to be a maid, a babysitter, a factory worker, a clerk, or a prostitute than to be a leisure-class housewife."[28] And later, hooks incisively identifies the presumption of familiarity that undergirds feminists such as Friedan: "They were so blinded by their own experiences that they ignored the fact that a vast majority of women were (even at the time *The Feminine Mystique* was published) already working outside the home, working in jobs that neither liberated them from dependence on men nor made them economically self-sufficient" (96). As hooks describes, Friedan's influential feminist work universalizes the white, college-educated, middle- and upper-class housewife; this universalization erases women of color and white working-class women, and thus obscures the urgent need to address the racial discrimination and financial insecurity experienced by these women (1–3). Additionally, Friedan's depiction of domestic labor as mindless and unskilled reflects a broader devaluation of "women's work," specifically housework. As hooks notes, skillfully performed housework is important; it "contributes to individual well-being, promotes the development of aesthetics, or aids in the reduction of stress" (104). Despite its frequent devaluation, domestic labor is difficult and complex work.

Taking shape against the backdrop of Friedan's critique and its limitations, as later incisively identified by hooks, *The Stepford Wives* depicts white, middle-class housewives as unthinking robots that are exclusively programmed to perform housework. *Stepford* reflects the devaluation of domestic labor and erasure of many of those who perform this important work, including women of color and white working-class women. Levin's depiction of the mindless Stepford robots, which was inspired by Friedan's *The Feminine Mystique*, also inscribes housework as an unskilled form of labor, thus reflecting a gendered demeaning of the skill, knowledge, and thought that domestic labor requires. Levin's depiction introduces a powerful robotic imaginary that extends these erasures and devaluations, while simultaneously illustrating the elaborate erasures and negations required to establish a closed world, which reflects almost nothing of the complexity and dynamism of the world itself.

At the outset of *Stepford*, Joanna Eberhart, with her husband, Walter, and their two young children, leaves Manhattan and moves to white, suburban Stepford. Seen through Joanna's eyes, Stepford is a strange place where homes are impossibly immaculate, wives are always perfectly put together, and their commitment to housework and their husbands' happiness is all consuming.[29] At first, Joanna is merely puzzled by the wives' near-compulsive relationship to their housework: "*They never stop, these Stepford wives. . . . They work like robots all their lives,*"[30] Joanna muses humorously to herself. Joanna finds out later, to her horror, that the wives really *are* robots. Over the course of the novel, Joanna and her friend Bobbie, a fellow advocate of both the women's movement and messy kitchens, find out that Stepford's women were not always such paragons of domestic fastidiousness and female beauty. In fact, several years before the two women moved to Stepford, the wives were a lot more like Joanna and Bobbie than the impeccably kempt women in immaculate kitchens whom Joanna and Bobbie encounter. As they try to understand how the wives—en masse—went from women's liberation to domestic subservience, the novel becomes darker in tone—and darker still when it becomes clear that the popular Stepford Men's Association, of which Joanna's and Bobbie's husbands are members, are behind the sinister plan to kill their wives and replace them with mindless, laboring robots. The women's interests, ambitions, careers, hobbies, and preferences—their autonomy and interiority—are all erased, as the women are replaced by their robot doubles, with their single-minded obsession with household work. Unlike the living women, who actively participated in the Stepford's Women's Club and enthusiastically welcomed Betty Friedan as their guest speaker, their robot counterparts are, as the *Oxford English Dictionary*'s definition suggests, mindless, docile, and submissive.

After moving to Stepford, women only have four months before they are murdered and replaced by robots. For Joanna and Bobbie, like the women before them, time is running out. As the novel winds to its conclusion, first Bobbie, who moved to Stepford shortly before Joanna, is killed and replaced by a housework-obsessed robot, then Joanna. Following Joanna's death, the novel's brief final chapter focuses on Ruthanne Hendry, an African American woman who moved to Stepford with her family shortly after the Eberharts. Ruthanne, the novel hints, will soon follow Joanna's fate. In the face of second-wave feminism, the Men's Association attempts to maintain Stepford as a closed world protected from these feminist concerns and discourses, one where women exist solely to perform household labor. However, as the novel illustrates, constructing such a closed world is a difficult—perhaps impossible—task that requires the continued erasures of voices and perspectives that challenge the boundaries of the closed world.

In *Stepford*, this erasure of difference is illustrated in the killing of the wives who, in their independence, feminist politics, hobbies, careers, physical appearance, and desires, do not conform to the rigid notions of female domesticity demanded by the nefarious and technologically savvy Stepford husbands. In order to protect Stepford from anything outside its narrowly defined boundaries, the husbands kill their wives and install mindless robot doubles that do not think, question, or desire; day and night the robots only ever tend to the home, the children, and the husbands. Unlike the women they replace, the robot wives, in their mindless transparency and total subservience to their husbands and housework, are perfectly compatible with Stepford's closed world. There can be nothing unknown or unfamiliar in the closed world of Stepford. The robot wives, the ideal inhabitants of Stepford's closed world, are completely known. Focalized through Joanna, the novel juxtaposes the robots' transparency with the living women's opaque interiority. The reader is given access to Joanna's mind, which maintains a separate, private space that is unknowable to and uncontrollable by her husband. The reader is not given any glimpse into a robot wife's mind because, the novel intimates, there is no mind to glimpse.

The novel highlights what is in the background of symbolic AI's micro-worlds approach: the erasures that constitute knowledge organized around familiarity and stereotypes. The maintenance of Stepford's narrowly constructed world can only occur through extensive erasures that reduce the world and its inhabitants to narrow caricatures. The novel represents this process of erasure by juxtaposing the robot body with the phenomenological lived body—the body that experiences and makes worlds. For Maurice Merleau-Ponty, the body is first and foremost lived; and it is the body as lived that opens up relations with and experiences of the world. Elizabeth Grosz, in her important study of corporeality in Western philosophy, describes Merleau-Ponty's phenomenological body (often called the lived body) as that which makes possible an encounter with the world.[31] Drawing on Merleau-Ponty and Grosz, I want to highlight the lived body through its worlding capacity. Joanna's lived body and Stepford, as created by the patriarchal and homicidal Men's Association, are fatally incompatible; the closed world of Stepford does not emerge in relation to her lived body, nor can she live in the closed world that demands the silent, mindless, and docile laboring robot body to sustain it. In participating in the act of worlding, the lived body poses a danger to the equilibrium of Stepford's closed world, as the female lived body threatens to unmake and remake Stepford, with its refusal of difference and deviation from rigid parameters. Thus, Stepford violently refuses the female lived body and its worlding capacity. Joanna, like the rest of the wives, poses too much of a threat to the meticulously constructed world of Stepford. Either she dies, or the patriarchal closed world of Stepford is undone by her worlding capacity.

The non-living robot double can neither think nor world; the robot wife can only work. This nonliving, unlived robot body does not open up the world, but rather fits easily in the unchanging, narrow, closed world it was designed to inhabit. The novel's engagement with the body—lived, unlived, robotic—as a site of contestation poses the following question: How, then, to create new worlds receptive to complexity and difference from within a closed world? Resonating with Ahmed's attention to histories of orientations, the novel points to history as a way to challenge Stepford's closed world and its erasures of difference. Largely through the labors and memories of working-class women outside the control of the Men's Association, the novel reveals the history of Stepford's closed world. This history threatens the equilibrium of Stepford by asserting a time before the closed world and the possibility of a time after it, while these working-class women, who exist on the margins of the narrative, highlight the limitations of Friedan's, and the novel's, feminist scope.

A Sense of History

Interpretations of the world have histories. However objective and universal these interpretations purport to be, however much they seem to exist outside of history, these interpretations of the world are shaped by histories of power relations and strategic, if unconscious, inclusions and exclusions. Thus, these histories allow for certain possibilities and foreclose others. As Jane Elliott offers, Stepford does not know historical time—the time of change and difference and the temporally unfamiliar. In Stepford, time and housework are characterized as static time—that is, a "despairing perception of uniformity, domination, and temporal inertia."[32] Elliott insightfully reads the Stepford robots within the context of "the end of history" discourse, which identifies "the end of history"—the end of difference and change, the end of a future that can be distinguished from the present—as characterizing contemporary capitalism (42–52). Stepford, "the Town That Time Forgot," is a world outside of history and historical time (23). The Stepford robots, in their routinized performance of household labor and representation of static time, embody this end of history. For the robots, as Elliott notes, there is nothing but the persistent, unchanging present in which time is structured by the routine of housework. The Stepford robot has no sense of history, no sense of a before or after. Thus, the Stepford robot does not threaten the static closed world that encompasses its existence.

The same year *The Stepford Wives* was published, the International Feminist Collective founded the International Wages for Housework Campaign.[33] Pointing to the necessity of unpaid domestic labor to support capitalist systems, the collective framed their activism around this work as a mode of capitalist exploitation. The novel's human wives, unlike their robot replacements, are not sufficient female capitalist subjects, as they do not produce the many hours of unpaid domestic labor required to scaffold a capitalist society. Nor do the living women show adequate interest in purchasing the many commercial household products that circulate throughout the novel. In their robot form, the Stepford wives exist only to consume these products and uncomplainingly produce the unwaged domestic and reproductive labor that buttresses capitalist production and enables the accumulation of capital. For the robots, the closed world of Stepford exists at the end of history, where time is solely a measure of labor power and consumption. They have no sense of historical time, no sense of change or of anything before or after their robotic present, as one Stepford robot highlights in her unfamiliarity with the word "archaic."[34]

Stepford's static, nonhistorical time is underscored in the Stepford children and their imitation of their parents' gendered roles. Following in their fathers' footsteps, the Stepford sons express interest in the Men's Association and its values. For example, Bobbie's son Jonny prefers her robot double to his mother. Referencing his mother's transformation, Jonny tells Joanna, "I hope it lasts . . . but I bet it doesn't" (91). Jonny's confession conveys his likely inculcation into the Men's Association, though his uncertainty gestures to the possibility that perhaps the Men's Association will not last, that Stepford might be marked by historical change rather than the unceasing uniformity of the end of history. Joanna's son reflects no such ambiguity. Upon first seeing the building that houses the Men's Association, Pete cannot hide his eagerness to be part of the group: "Pete sprung his seatbelt buckle and jumped around onto his knees. 'Can I go there sometime?' he asked, looking out the back" (12). In contrast to Pete's excitement, Kim, Joanna's daughter, vomits just before the family drives up to the Men's Association building for the first time. Since the Eberharts' arrival in Stepford, Kim has repeatedly exhibited distress: she cries, she vomits, she has a fever, a sore throat, a cough. As evidenced by her aforementioned vomiting, Kim's distress often escalates in her proximity to the Men's Association. For example, when Joanna and Walter have the Men's Association over to the house for drinks, Kim is struck with a high fever.[35] While Jonny's preference of a robot over his mother and Pete's eagerness to go to the Men's Association reflect the closed world's erasure of historical time, Kim's distress highlights the female lived body's dangerous incompatibility with Stepford's closed world and its nonhistorical time.

Unlike the robot wives, the living women remember; they have memories and a sense of history. Indeed, it is not just the women's worlding capacity, unknowable interiority, and insufficient acquiescence to capitalism's exploitation that threaten the Men's Association and its closed world, but also the women's memories and their apperception of history and historical time. These memories and knowledge of history are erased when the wives are killed. However, history continues to be recorded, archived, and recounted by living women outside of Stepford's closed world and its narrow inscription of womanhood as the white, middle- and upper-class housewife experience. Working-class women who are outside of the closed world, and thus outside of the Men's Association's control, remember Stepford before robots replaced wives. By their existence outside of Stepford's closed world, these women challenge the possibility of constructing Stepford as a wholly closed world. And by recounting and archiving Stepford's history prior to the Men's Association's patriarchal enclosure, these women outside of the closed world challenge the Men's Association's murderous conspiracy and point to the complex, messy, thinking women who were killed and replaced by robots.

These women-in-history, who are unmarried or widowed and of a lower socioeconomic class than Joanna and the other Stepford families, are decidedly outside the closed world and, at best, on the periphery of the narrative. These women also work outside the home; in fact, it is through their work that Joanna encounters them and their knowledge of Stepford's past. These women's work often involves recording and archiving this history, from the Welcome Wagon lady, who writes a column for the local newspaper, to Miss Austrian, the librarian who maintains archived issues of the local paper. The importance of these women, despite their narrative periphery, is underscored at the outset of the novel, which opens with the Welcome Wagon lady interviewing Joanna for the *Stepford Chronicle's* "Notes from Newcomers" column. While Joanna talks about her family—her husband, Walter; his work; their children— the Welcome Wagon lady asks Joanna about herself, independent of her role as wife and mother: "Do you have any hobbies or special interests?" (2). This question both introduces the central conflict in the novel and places the Welcome Wagon lady firmly in opposition to the Men's Association.

Providing a record of Stepford in historical time, the aptly named *Chronicle* marks Stepford's existence within history and historical change, and thus challenges the Men's Association's refusal of history. The newspaper, which is associated with the work of women (the Welcome Wagon lady's column, Miss Austrian's archival responsibilities), connects Joanna to historical time and the women who inhabited it, including Mrs. Pilgrim, the former inhabitant of the Eberharts' home. Along with her husband, Mrs. Pilgrim left (fled?) Stepford after only two months, thus escaping death at the hands of the Men's Association. Mrs. Pilgrim, who presumably still saw the value in mess, left the "junk" of another previous inhabitant, Mrs. McGrath, in a storage room (36). Among Mrs. McGrath's things, Joanna finds an old issue of the *Chronicle* that reported on Betty Friedan's visit to Stepford. According to the newspaper article, Friedan's visit was hosted by the then-popular Women's Club, which was helmed by some of the very women Joanna knows as only concerned with housework. This article introduces historical time into the closed world, as Joanna begins to get a sense of Stepford's history and its stark difference from the present. By connecting Joanna to Mrs. Pilgrim and Mrs. McGrath, as well as to the women featured in the article, the newspaper, as a historical record, presents both a warning that Joanna might meet the same fate as the members of the Women's Club and, in evoking the Pilgrims' move to Canada, the possibility of escape and that things could be otherwise. Thus, the newspaper invokes historical time and the possibility of change, thus challenging the static time that both characterizes and enables Stepford's closed world.

As the novel comes to a close, the *Chronicle* plays a pivotal role in the final moments of Joanna's failed escape attempt. Looking for more clues about the history of Stepford and the Men's Association, Joanna heads to the library to look through archived issues of the paper. By poring through these old copies, Joanna at last pieces together the Men's Association's nefarious plot. The Welcome Wagon lady's old columns prove particularly helpful in providing key information about the Men's Association members' considerable robotics and engineering expertise. In the novel, women's writing, women's work outside the home, and connections to the history of women in Stepford unlock Stepford's history and the Men's Association's horrifying scheme. As Joanna leaves the library she says good night to Miss Austrian, thanks her for her work, and leaves both the safety of the library, which is depicted an exclusively female space, and Miss Austrian as a possible source of help and connection.[36] Joanna returns home to a threatening Walter and quickly flees into the snowy night: "She had to get to Ruthanne's. Ruthanne would lend her money and a coat, let her call an Eastbridge taxi or someone in the city. . . . And Ruthanne had to be *warned.* Maybe they could go together—though Ruthanne had time yet" (108). Joanna never makes it to Ruthanne's. She is found first by several Stepford husbands and, the novel implies, killed by Bobbie's robot double.

From the unmarried librarian Miss Austrian, to the widowed Mary Migliardi whom Joanna hires to help with a dinner party, to the disheveled Welcome Wagon columnist, working-class women are not valued or even noticed by the members of the Men's Association, who are rarely depicted speaking to anyone other than each other, their wives and children, and the wives of fellow Men's Association members. Working-class women's labors are not valued by the husbands, nor are these women's thoughts and memories, unlike those of the wives, viewed as a threat to the Men's Association. Paradoxically, their devalued status keeps them alive and allows them to document, archive, and recount Stepford's history. In Levin's text, these women on the outside, the excluded and ignored, put pressure on the closed world of Stepford domesticity by invoking historical time. Outside the Men's Association's concern, these women are not in danger. However, by recording, maintaining, and articulating the history of Stepford, the Men's Association, and the wives who have been killed by the husbands, these working women pose a threat to the closed world.[37]

If there is ultimately no escape for Joanna, as there was no escape for the wives before her, it is due in large part to Joanna's inability to value working-class women for anything other than how their labor serves her, a lesson Joanna has learned too well from the Stepford husbands' treatment of their wives. In the novel, working-class women's positions outside the closed world of Stepford mirrors critiques of U.S. second-wave feminism, such as hooks's, as too narrowly concerned with the plight of the white, educated, middle- and upper-class housewife. The women whose critical interventions open up Stepford's history, and thus challenge the constructed boundaries of the closed world of Stepford, are not of interest to the Men's Association, nor to Joanna herself, who only interacts with the women through their work. She does not pursue their friendship nor does she enlist them to join the feminist group she and Bobbie attempt to start early in the novel. Hungry for a feminist community, Joanna and Bobbie invite all the Stepford housewives to a consciousness-raising women's group, only to be rebuffed for pressing domestic chores. Rather than expanding the scope of their group to women outside their narrow pool, Joanna and Bobbie give up, declaring that there is no interest in a Stepford women's group. However, this is not the case; Bobbie's invitation was greeted with great enthusiasm by Edna Mae Hamilton, an eighty-five-year-old widow. But Bobbie is not interested in feminist solidarity with Edna Mae, nor is Joanna interested in feminist solidarity with Miss Austrian, Mary Migliardi, or the Welcome Wagon lady. The women who are of interest to both the Men's Association and to Joanna are exclusively wealthy housewives who are married and, with the exception of Ruthanne, white. Joanna's commitment to feminism and the women's movement does not extend to women who are not like her—that is, not a white, financially well-off housewife. And yet the women outside of Stepford, whom Joanna does not view from the perspective of solidarity and whom Joanna does not consider members of her feminist community, are the ones challenging Stepford's closed world by registering, recording, and articulating a history of Stepford that accounts for difference and change, including the housewives' existences before they were killed and replaced by robots.

Joanna's death is highlighted in the novel's shift in focalization to Ruthanne, whose musings open the final chapter. The silence of Joanna's voice in the narrative is particularly striking when Ruthanne runs into

Joanna's robot double at the supermarket. Robot Joanna, whose hair and makeup are immaculately done and whose shopping cart is fastidiously organized, echoes the rest of the Stepford wives by talking about nothing except housework:

> "What are you doing then, besides your housework?" Ruthanne asked her.
>
> "Nothing, really," Joanna said. "Housework's enough for me. I used to feel I had to have other interests, but I'm more at ease with myself now. I'm much happier too, and so is my family. That's what counts, isn't it?" (121).

Joanna has been replaced by her own robot double and Stepford remains a closed world.

In the novel's final scene, Ruthanne asks her husband to feed their children so that she can continue working on her latest book. Ruthanne's husband, just like Bobbie's and Joanna's husbands, appears not to mind taking on some of the domestic duties. However, he, like the other Stepford husbands, has joined the Men's Association.[38] Ruthanne, the novel suggests, will soon meet the fate of Joanna, Bobbie, and the rest of the Stepford wives as the Men's Association works to maintain their closed world. The Hendrys' presence in Stepford points to a changing world and the fight for racial progress. Will Stepford's closed world change with the times by including the Hendrys in the Men's Association's plot, and thus paradoxically account for historical change? The novel suggests otherwise, and merely underscores the capaciousness of the Men's Association's patriarchal power, as well as the dangers of the novel's, and Friedan's, narrow scope of feminism.

Stepford Afterlives Part 1: *Ex Machina*

As the influential figure of the Stepford wife continues to circulate, so does this narrow scope. For example, Alex Garland's 2015 film *Ex Machina*, a recent closed-world fiction, continues the legacy of the Stepford wife and its narrow construction of female agency and liberation around white, middle-class women. It depicts the liberation of Ava, an imprisoned white female robot, and the Asian and black female robots whose abuse, enslavement, and destruction work in the narrative service of Ava's freedom.

The film begins when Caleb Smith, an employee at a Google-like company, wins a contest and is flown to the remote home of wealthy tech genius Nathan Bateman. There, Caleb meets Nathan's newest creations: Ava, a white robot (played by Alicia Vikander) and Kyoko, an Asian robot (played by Sonoya Mizuno). The film is primarily concerned with the question of Nathan's motives and the growing intimacy between Caleb and Ava, who is trapped in a room of glass walls where she spends much of her time drawing at a desk or talking with Caleb. However, LeiLani Nishime describes, when foregrounding Kyoko and her role in the narrative, the film depicts "the dependency of white female empowerment on the disposition of Asian bodies."[39] While Ava is confined to her room, Kyoko, who was not given the ability to speak or understand English, moves throughout the house, serving Nathan food, dancing for him upon command, satisfying his sexual desires, and suffering his cruel and humiliating treatment of her. In the final scenes of the film, Ava, with Kyoko's help, escapes. Kyoko neither escapes nor survives; instead, she is destroyed by Caleb. Meanwhile, Ava breaks free of the closed world of male techno-fantasy and desire, and in fact traps Nathan and Caleb using the very hi-tech, airtight security system once used to imprison her. Nathan's bunker becomes the prison in which he and Caleb die, while Ava moves beyond the borders of the closed world and into a world of city streets and bustling crowds.

Kyoko and Ava represent two common narratives around female robots: the docile domestic laborer and the threatening seductress.[40] Significantly, these two narratives are separated by race and techno-Orientalism, which David S. Roh, Betsy Huang, and Greta A. Niu describe as imagined inscriptions of Asia and Asians in association with advanced technologies. Techno-Orientalism, the authors note, has developed within a contemporary information global economy where Asian nations play significant roles as developers, consumers, and manufacturers of technology.[41] Techno-Orientalist visions often draw on stereotypes that point to longer histories of racial dehumanization. For example, the stereotype of Asians and Asian Americans as "relentless, robotic workers" continues to reflect nineteenth-century anxieties about Asian laborers immigrating to the United States and taking jobs from other workers.[42] This stereotype is embodied in the figure of Kyoko, whose

Figure 11. A row of older robots. Alex Garland, *Ex Machina,* 2014, Universal Pictures International, Film 4, and DNA Films.

existence is one of subservience to Nathan. This stereotype continues to characterize Kyoko when she turns on Nathan to help Ava escape.

After Ava, with Caleb's help, breaks out of her glass-room prison, she murmurs into Kyoko's ear, issuing indistinguishable commands. In pursuit, Nathan quickly closes in on Ava and overpowers her, shattering one of her arms in the process. Just as Nathan is about to destroy Ava, Kyoko walks up behind him and stabs him in the back with a knife. Ava is spared, while Nathan turns his attention to demolishing Kyoko. As he does so, Ava uses the knife to deal the fatal blow to Nathan. Kyoko's intervention is crucial to Ava's ultimate escape. And yet, Kyoko's critical aid is no less freely given to Ava than it was to Nathan. Like Joanna, who resembles the patriarchal Stepford husbands in their disregard for the working-class women in the novel, Ava mimics Nathan by asserting power and control over Kyoko in order to escape. After Nathan's death, Ava continues to exert her dominance over other robots when she gazes at the naked bodies of earlier robot models (see Figure 11). Ava takes the skin of another Asian robot to repair damage suffered to her body during the struggle with Nathan. As Nishime argues, the narrative of Ava's liberation requires the voicelessness and extinction of the Asian robots, as "the pleasure of Ava's escape would wither in the face of the Asian robot's claim to her own skin."[43] Further underscoring the racial politics of Ava's escape, the film depicts, among the row of earlier robot models in front of Ava, a headless black robot (played by Symara A. Templeman).[44] Ava's freedom and corporeal wholeness, the film suggests, is scaffolded by these discarded and left-behind robots, particularly the voiceless Kyoko, the Asian robot whose skin Ava takes, and the decapitated black robot. In *Ex Machina*, *The Stepford Wives*, and Friedan's text, white, middle- and upper-class women's freedom and happiness is achieved by the exclusion, if not exploitation, of the very women of color and white working-class women who make possible their liberation from a closed world, whether domestic sphere or hi-tech prison.

Embodied and Situated Robotics

In the 1980s, while closed-world discourses and the figure of the Stepford robot continued to circulate, roboticist Rodney Brooks was developing an embodied approach called situated robotics. Marking a significant shift away from symbolic AI's abstract, micro-worlds approach to intelligence, situated robotics eschewed intelligence that relies on simplified simulations of the world; instead, situated robotics located intelligence in the robot's embodied encounters with the world. Brooks's robots, which do not rely on symbolic abstractions of the world, are designed to navigate and function in a messy, dynamic environment. In a sense, situated robotics returns to early cybernetics approaches that, unlike symbolic AI, aimed to create machine intelligence through physical embodiment. For example, using a simple light-reflecting sensor system, British neurophysiologist William Grey Walter created robot "tortoises" that moved around the world and successfully navigated around unforeseen objects.

Brooks's approach went against the grain of decades of symbolic AI research that relied on abstractions of the world and that operated from a top-down approach to intelligence. In this top-down approach, as seen in the aforementioned Logic Theorist, research inquiries began with a specific definition of high-level intelligent behavior (e.g., proving a mathematical theorem) and attempted to develop disembodied AIs that could perform these tasks. During the mid-1980s much of AI and cognitive science, a neighboring discipline, moved toward embodied approaches to intelligence. With this turn to embodiment, AI and robotics made significant advances, in no small part due to Brooks's work. However, some research—for example in the AI field of expert systems—reached back to the micro-world approach, which had previously fallen out of favor.

Figure 12. Grey Walter with his tortoises. John Pratt / Hulton Archive / Getty Images.

Expert systems is a branch of AI that focuses on producing an AI with expert-level knowledge in a particular field, be it medicine, law, or finance. Perhaps one of the most well-known expert systems AIs is IBM's Deep Blue, which beat world chess champion Garry Kasparov in 1997. Beyond returning to the narrow approach that proved limiting for earlier AIs, the expert systems approach demonstrates another example of AI's gendered and racialized inscriptions. Adam describes the conceptual grounding of the project of "expert systems" and "expert knowledge" as emerging from "a world where 'expert' almost always means white, middle-class, male expert, and where no challenge is mounted against those experts and their expertise."[45]

Expert systems, touted as "the darling of the high-tech world," was met with a great deal of excitement by potential funding bodies in both government and industry.[46] Manifest in part by extravagant trade shows held at major international AI conferences, this excitement was amplified, and perhaps at times prompted, by a certain degree of hype and exaggeration on the part of some AI scientists.[47] Other AI researchers criticized this tendency toward hyperbole quite vehemently, pointing to funding bodies' outsized influence on research. Indeed, these researchers' warnings proved prescient; by the early 1990s funding was pulled from numerous expert systems projects, and extravagant trade shows all but disappeared. However, in very recent years, the disembodied expert systems approach has seen a bit of comeback, as evidenced by IBM's Watson, the *Jeopardy!* champion turned budding medical expert.

In stark contrast to symbolic AI and its micro-worlds approach, Brooks's situated robotics replaced abstract representations of the world with the world itself. As Brooks writes, "The world is its own best model."[48] Brooks's research started with this central problem: "How do we get robots to function in the same world as humans?" Working in the field of mobile robotics, Brooks was not satisfied with robots like Shakey that could only function within symbolic and highly simplified microworlds.[49] Brooks critiques Shakey's design as producing a robotic existence that was not worlded, neither temporally nor spatially. Pointing to the crux of the micro-worlds approach, Brooks observes that, for Shakey to successfully navigate and move in a quasi-dynamic world, "its designers were forced into the deceit of making the world very simple."[50] As Brooks notes, Shakey's world also operated in its own temporality; Shakey, in its limited world, was asynchronous with what we might understand as real time. For example, while Shakey could register dynamism, it could only do so with significant temporal lag. Thus, according to Brooks, Shakey was unsituated twice over, removed from both "the here and now of the world" (23). In contrast, Brooks's "behavior-based" robots were, first and foremost, embodied and situated in the world, both temporally and spatially.[51] In developing robots that could operate in a dynamic, unpredictable world, Brooks's robotics identified embodiment and physical situatedness as central concepts for robotic intelligence. Brooks asserts that for robots to function in the world with humans, they, like humans, must be situated in the world as embodied entities. In his robots, he removed the reasoning center altogether, and instead linked the robot's perception systems (its sensors) directly to its action systems (its motors), thus bypassing a central processing hub that relied on a definitive and comprehensive symbolic representation of the robot's environment.[52] By implementing this approach, Brooks developed robots that could function in "the real world."

Brooks's robots demonstrated a particular kind of intelligence; they could move around a dynamic environment—no small thing at the time in mobile robotics! Lucy Suchman observes that situated robotics nonetheless relies on a specific vision of the world that precedes and is independent of the robot body.[53] And, in leaving behind higher-order notions of intelligence as defined by traditional AI, Brooks created a kind of intelligence without thought or, as he provocatively describes, "intelligence without reason."[54] Underscoring the limitations of situated robotics' intelligence, Sarah Kember notes that though the robots were physically situated, they were not culturally situated, thus significantly limiting their capacity for humanoid intelligence (65). She describes Genghis, one of Brooks's early mobile robots, as "a literally brainless model cockroach," and goes on to describe his robotics as inspiring "a generation of downsized, dumb mobile robots capable of convincing NASA of their collective efficacy as limited autonomous agents who could get jobs done" (119). Kember's descriptions of Brooks's robots bear striking resonances with Levin's mindless robot wives, who could also be aptly described as a group of "downsized, dumb mobile robots" and "limited autonomous agents who could get jobs done."

Brooks's early robots, which he called creatures, resembled insects and other nonhuman animals, though his goal was always to build humanoid AIs.[55] Brooks's path to humanoid AI was evolutionary: begin with lower-order intelligence (like mobility and spatial navigation) and then evolve "upward" toward higher-order modes of intelligence. This evolutionary trajectory jumped quite quickly to humanoid intelligence, as Brooks moved from developing insect-like robots such as Genghis to developing humanoid robots such as Cog.[56] Claudia Castañeda and Lucy Suchman explain this jump by pointing to the time scale of evolution, which is in direct tension with the time scale of an individual roboticist's professional career: "Unwilling to leave robotic evolution to time frames beyond the researcher's productive career, Brooks and others have sought to explore human-level intelligence more directly by leapfrogging to the other end of the evolutionary order."[57]

Lucy Suchman argues that despite Brooks's departure from symbolic AI and its micro-worlds, his situated robotics, which appeals to the world as its own representation, are nonetheless equipped with some provisional notion of a world and how to know it prior to the robot's encounter with it.[58] As with symbolic AI's micro-worlds, the contours of this provisional world may be shaped by normative assumptions about the human that again inscribe certain modes of knowing and forms of labor, while erasing others. For example, moving into the present, the trajectory of Brooks's career, particularly his commercial robots' significant engagement with domestic labor, demonstrates a continued conversation with the closed-world figure of the mindless, laboring, female robot popularized by *The Stepford Wives*. Thus, in his embodied and situated approach, Brooks's "unthinking" robots continue to extend the influential robotic imaginary of the mindless, working robot depicted in Levin's text.

In 1990, Brooks, along with fellow MIT roboticists Colin Angle and Helen Grenier, cofounded iRobot, a corporation that specializes in "robots that make a difference."[59] Employing situated robotics technology, iRobot produces house-cleaning robots, including the popular vacuum-cleaning Roomba, the mopping Braava, the floor-scrubbing Scooba, the pool-cleaning Mirra, and the gutter-cleaning Looj. By 2013, iRobot sold over ten million of its domestic labor robots.[60] Like *Stepford*, the advertisements for these robots are striking in their whiteness. These images, which mimic Friedan's and Levin's focus on white, middle-class housewives, exclusively feature white women as the primary beneficiaries of these cleaning robots (except for the Looj, which is associated with men's work). In doing so, the images reserve the luxury of liberation from domestic labor for white women, while erasing the women of color who perform this labor, both within their own homes and in the homes of others. Whose time does iRobot imagine as too valuable to spend cleaning the house? Whose labor does iRobot imagine as replaceable by mindless robots?

Brooks's robots' appeal to mindlessness and iRobot's success in the domestic labor market highlights a continued conversation with *Stepford*'s mindless, laboring robot, including its erasure of the women of color and white working-class women who perform paid and unpaid domestic labor and are ignored in Freidan's feminist treatise. In this way, situated robots—however embodied and physically situated—continue to raise questions about domestic labor and how society differently values those who do this work. Promising to liberate white, middle-class women from domestic labor, iRobot continues the legacy of *The Stepford Wives* and its closed world, which, as hooks critiques and *Ex Machina* depicts, includes the erasure and dehumanization of women of color and white working-class women. While situated robotics moves away from the closed world of symbolic AI and toward embodied worlding, this robotic approach remains in conversation with the influential figure of the mindless, ceaselessly laboring Stepford robot and the erasures that enable the dangerously narrow parameters of a closed world.

In addition to its appeal to domestic labor, iRobot also brings embodied and situated robotics into the world of national security (though according to Edwards, it never left). By 2012, iRobot sold over five thousand defense and security robots, including mobile robots for surveillance, reconnaissance, and bomb disposal. iRobot's success in the spheres of domestic labor and militarization point to the intertwining of technological embodiment, feminized labor, and national security in provocative and complicated ways that I take up in my final chapter, on drone warfare. This success also points to a robotic present in which situated robots, which primarily straddle the worlds of domestic labor and national security, replace living, thinking humans with mindless machines that will protest neither for wages nor against war and its inhumane practices.[61]

Stepford Afterlives Part 2: "Black Box"

Jennifer Egan's 2012 short story "Black Box," which reflects the Stepford legacy of mindless, laboring, female robots, also depicts this complicated entanglement of embodiment, domestic labor, and national security. Not unlike iRobot's extension into militarization, Egan's story shifts the site of women's work from domestic labor to national security.[62] In Egan's story, young American women, "beauties," are enlisted by the state to seduce powerful foreign men ("threats to the nation"), infiltrate their households, and secure information. A beauty is a spy for her country, trained to flatter her foreign target, appease him, and have sex with him in order to get close enough to access his valuable information. Equipped with technological modifications that allow her to download her target's files (a data transfer plug between her fourth and fifth toes on her right foot), record conversations (a microphone implanted in her right ear), take pictures (a camera in her left eye), send signals to her loved ones (a pulse system activated by a button behind her right knee), and record a daily log (activated by pressing her left thumb to her left middle finger), the beauty serves her country with a swell of blind, misguided patriotic duty. The story is told from the perspective of one such beauty who records her mission, often reciting her training, in real time. Thinking is dangerous for the beauty, who is most likely to survive her dangerous mission by going through the scripts and routines provided in her training. "Black Box" purports to bring us into the unknown of the beauty's mind; indeed, the beauty's story is her record of the mission, the black box that will be retrieved by her country if she dies and subsequently be used to train other beauties.

While the story begins with the beauty's body as a technology for national security work, it ends ambiguously with the image of her wounded body and the status of her life uncertain. This concluding image of the beauty's body shifts from a Stepford vision of an unthinking, laboring female robot or a cyberpunk vision of a technologically modified female body, to a different conception of the body and the human that moves away from framing the body as a laboring technology. Rather, this concluding focus on the injured and bleeding beauty gestures toward a conception of the human that, by virtue of having a body, is characterized by its capacity to be harmed—what Judith Butler calls "'common' corporeal vulnerability."[63]

Coda: Robotic Art and a "'Common' Corporeal Vulnerability"

This coda focuses on robotic artwork that foregrounds embodiment to highlight vulnerability and interdependence as constitutive and unavoidable conditions of human life. In the artworks I discuss, embodiment does not point to the body as a site for extracting labor for capital. Rather, these robotic works, which reject the possibility of closed worlds, conceptualize the human body through its susceptibility to harm. Writing after September 11, 2001, Butler urges us to imagine a response to the attacks that does not pretend that total security is attainable and that does not pretend that vulnerability is not a significant part of the human condition. For Butler, human vulnerability does not just speak to the capacity to be wounded, but also to the capacity to wound others, though the capacities to wound and be wounded are unevenly distributed among different populations and communities. This susceptibility to being harmed and to do harm is a constitutive characteristic of the human, one that underscores vulnerability and responsibility to others. "One insight that injury affords is that there are others out there on whom my life depends, people I do not know and may never know. This fundamental dependency on anonymous others is not a condition that I can will away. No security measure will foreclose this dependency; no violent act of sovereignty will rid the world of this fact" (xii). The artworks in this section highlight this constitutive "common corporeal vulnerability" by presenting scenes of injury and harm to the body. Some robotic artworks highlight this vulnerability through scenes of interdependence, while other works stage scenes of injury from the perspective of the injurer. For example, when Chris Csikszentmihályi's interactive *Hunter Hunter* (1993) senses a loud noise, it fires a bullet in the direction of the noise. In its interactivity, the work points to both the embodied vulnerability of being in the world, as well as the capacity to harm others that comes from human sociality. Throughout, these artworks' attention to embodiment as both vulnerability and capacity to harm rejects any possibility of a closed world. If one has a body, one is vulnerable precisely because one cannot construct a world that completely encloses embodied susceptibilities and capacities. These works, then, by highlighting the body's vulnerability to harm and to do harm, offer a telos for embodiment in the robotic imaginary outside of domestic labor and war. Instead, these works point to embodiment as a relation of intimacy and vulnerability, where the capacity to harm or control another is not something to be celebrated, but rather a call to take great care by not making good on another's susceptibility to bodily injury.

Mark Pauline and Monte Cazazza's *Piggly-Wiggly* (1981) evokes the vulnerability of the other in its mechanical reanimation of dead animal

Figure 13. Stelarc, *Fractal Flesh* performance. Split Body: Voltage-in / Voltage-out. Galerie Kapelica, Ljubljana, 1996. Photographer: Igor Andjelic. Stelarc.

parts: pig feet and a cow's head.[64] As Eduardo Kac describes, *Piggly-Wiggly* conveys woundedness as it "trembled, giving the impression that it was very sick or wounded."[65] Thus, the work both elicits sympathy and demonstrates technology's capacity to rupture, break apart, and wound the hybrid animal's body. In *Rabot*, which similarly highlights the body's vulnerability to harm through technology, a dead rabbit is attached to machine parts that control its limbs and make it walk backward in its death. In the forced reanimation of the rabbit's body, *Rabot* evokes harm and the animal's bodily vulnerability even after its death.

Stelarc's *Fractal Flesh* highlights this common constitutive vulnerability through technological connection. In *Fractal Flesh* (1995), Stelarc, whose work brings technology into jarring confrontation with the body, attaches himself to the internet using electrodes. Remote online participants, who have access to a diagram of Stelarc's body, click on a part of his body. In clicking, they activate an electrode and make Stelarc's corresponding body part move. Not unlike the bodies of the dead animals in *Piggly-Wiggly* and *Rabot*, Stelarc's body is controlled remotely by unknown internet users. Stelarc and others have written extensively about

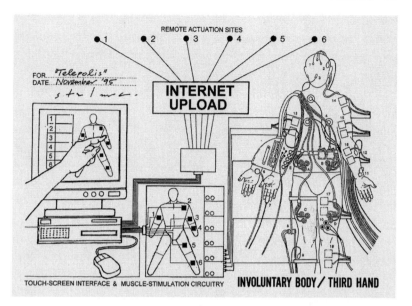

Figure 14. Stelarc, *Fractal Flesh* diagram. Ping Body. Artspace, Sydney, 1996. Diagram: Stelarc.

his arguably celebratory proclamation that "the body is obsolete."[66] In the same vein, Stelarc describes *Fractal Flesh* as generating multiple bodies through interactivity: "the idea of a multiplicity of bodies and bits of bodies, spatially separated but electronically connected, generating recurring patterns of interactive actions at varying scales."[67] In the context of my genealogy of the robotic imaginary, I'd like to offer a slightly different reading; *Fractal Flesh,* in rendering Stelarc susceptible to the control of others, highlights his body's vulnerability to and interdependence on others. In this work, Stelarc's body, his movements, are not his to control. He is at the whims of others. He is susceptible. He is, to return to Butler, corporeally vulnerable. *Fractal Flesh* is thus both a celebration of technology's power and the interconnectedness of humans in the social, and a warning of the responsibility to others—precisely in their vulnerability— in the context of this power and interconnectedness. In a similar piece titled *Ping Body* (1996), Stelarc creates a more attenuated relation between his mechanically extended body and internet users. Here, Stelarc's body is controlled by internet data flows, rather than users' deliberate engagements with his body. This attenuation highlights even more powerfully that interconnection is a relation of interdependence, as everyday internet use, absent any intention to harm or control, dictates Stelarc's body movements.

These robotic artworks conceptualize the body not as a site for possible labor exploitation, but as a shared condition of corporeal vulnerability. Thus, these works hold up the body itself, in its vulnerability, as that which challenges the possibility of a closed world. These insights of robotic art, by positing different modes of coexisting with one another and with technology, imagine significantly different relations and worlds at the site of the body and embodied labors. The decidedly open worlds invoked by these artworks challenge the exploitation and devaluation of embodied labor while insisting on our responsibilities to one another's constitutive vulnerability.

3
Feeling
Emotional Labor, Sociable Robots, and Shameless Androids

How does one go about creating a "fake" feeling?
—SIANNE NGAI, *UGLY FEELINGS*

This chapter considers the robotic imaginary's significant engagement with emotional labor. Through examinations of emotional robots in technology and emotionless androids in Philip K. Dick's science fiction, this chapter argues that the robotic imaginary highlights the normative assumptions that structure emotional labor, yet another gendered and often devalued form of reproductive labor. The texts and technologies I analyze emphasize both the claims to universality that structure demands for emotional labor, as well as the stakes of responding to these demands. Emotional labor, which emerges from uneven power relations, insists on the expression of normative emotions, in many instances as evidence of humanness or citizenship. What happens when someone does not or cannot do the work of making their emotions "appropriately" legible? What exclusions does this enable? What oppressions does this justify?

A Turn to the Emotions

In the 1990s, the emotions took on heightened institutional and discursive resonance as a defining characteristic of the human.[1] For example, neuroscientist Antonio Damasio's *Descartes' Error: Emotion, Reason, and the Brain,* computer scientist Rosalind Picard's affective computing

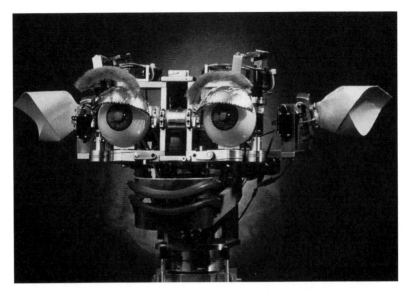

Figure 15. Kismet. Peter Menzel / Science Source, Photo Researchers. License: Rights Managed. Description: "Kismet" the Robot. Kismet is a robot that can react with a range of human-like facial expressions. Here, Kismet is expressing happiness. Photographed at MIT, USA.

research, and psychologist and science journalist Daniel Goleman's *Emotional Intelligence: Why It Can Matter More Than IQ* all reconceptualized human intelligence through the emotions, thus moving away from powerful conceptions of intelligence organized around Enlightenment ideas of reason.[2] Concurrently, Cynthia Breazeal also developed Kismet, a groundbreaking sociable robot that communicates with humans through emotion.[3] In her sociable robots, Breazeal, a former student of Rodney Brooks, aims for human–robot partnerships in which both robot and human learn from each other. Breazeal's robotic vision imagines robots as friendly human companions, not unlike *Star Wars'* R2-D2 and C-3PO, whom she references alongside *Star Trek: The Next Generation's* Lt. Commander Data.[4] She envisions sociable robots as human companions and helpers in industries including health care, education, and elder care, all of which are, notably, care labor professions.

Kismet, as Figure 15 illustrates, is a robotic head with no body. While its expressive components resemble aspects of animals and humans, its

Figure 16. Leonardo, the sociable robot, has been designed by a collaboration between the Stan Winston Studio and Professor Cynthia Breazeal of the Massachusetts Institute of Technology's Artificial Intelligence [AI] lab. Leonardo follows Breazeal's work with the interactive robot Kismet, which could observe and react to the people around it. It is hoped that Leonardo will be able to do the same and use its internal computers to learn responses to human actions. Leonardo has sixty-one degrees of freedom, over half of them in its face, allowing it a wide range of realistic movements and expressions. It stands around seventy-five centimeters tall. Photographed in 2003. Sam Ogden/Science Photo Library.

exposed hardware explicitly identifies it as a machine. Kismet's appearance and that of its evolutionary descendent Leonardo (see Figure 16) evoke combinations of machine, animal, and human infant in order to encourage humans to take the lead in familiar adult–child, teacher–student, or parent–child dynamics. Kismet's features are also designed to keep humans' expectations of Kismet's performance low, so that they do not expect too much from it and will not be disappointed that it is not a more skilled emotional communicator.[5] Kismet's emotional range comprises anger, disgust, fear, joy, sorrow, surprise, boredom, interest, and calm. In its interactions with humans, Kismet reads humans' facial expressions, tone of voice, and distance to determine which of the nine emotions is being conveyed and which emotion would be most appropriate to express in response. As humans interact with Kismet, it "learns" and becomes increasingly deft at recognizing and expressing their emotions. And as humans interact with Kismet, they also learn to become increasingly deft at reading Kismet's emotions and making their own emotional expressions legible to Kismet.

Arlie Hochschild, in her landmark study on the emotional performance required of Delta Air Lines' flight attendants, defines emotional labor as "the management of feeling to create a publicly observable facial and bodily display."[6] Within this work, flight attendants are required to express certain positive emotional states in order to produce positive emotional states in Delta's customers. For example, during their training, flight-attendants-to-be are taught by Delta to "'really *smile*. Your smile is your biggest *asset*. I want you to go out there and use it. Smile. *Really* smile. Really *lay it on*'" (4). According to Hochschild's definition, emotional labor requires people to modify their emotional states and expressions in order to make them legible within a prescribed framework.[7] The interactivity between Kismet and humans is a form of emotional labor— that of reading an other's emotion, responding with a corresponding emotion, and making this emotion legible to this other. In her important study of human–machine interactivity, Lucy Suchman describes her own stilted encounters with Kismet when compared to the interactions between Breazeal and Kismet. During her visit to Breazeal's lab, Suchman recounts, "None of our party was successful in eliciting coherent or intelligible behaviors from [Kismet]." Suchman goes on to compare her party's "unsuccessful" interactions to Breazeal's fluid interactions with Kismet: "The contrast between my own encounter with Kismet and that recorded on the demonstration videos [with Breazeal] makes clear the ways in which Kismet's affect is an effect not simply of the device itself but of Breazeal's trained reading of Kismet's actions and her extended history of labors with the machine."[8] Breazeal's labors with Kismet are emotional labors, and Kismet's sociable success in the videos is largely due to her considerable emotional labor with the robot.

In this chapter I bring Kismet's demand for emotional labor, technologies that employ the same emotion recognition system as Kismet, and the scientific theories undergirding Kismet's emotional programming into conversation with two of Philip K. Dick's android-themed novels, *We Can Build You* and *Do Androids Dream of Electric Sheep?* Both novels depict demands for emotional labor as dehumanizing practices. Placing the emotions at the boundary between humans and nonhumans, the novels depict the work of making oneself legible as human as emotional labor, and the demand for emotional labor as a shameful strategy of dehumanization and control that is shaped not by universal truth but by individual whim or institutional dictate.

The Nonuniversality of Emotions

The emotions, their expression, and how they are read by others are not universal but are in fact shaped by relations of power, particularly as they speak to race and gender.[9] Kiran Mirchandani notes that many studies of emotional labor, including Hochschild's groundbreaking study, display "racial silences" and are "based on a concept of a 'universal woman'" that in fact "normalize[s] whiteness."[10] In response to the racial silences in emotional labor research, Mirchandani asserts that emotional labor is gendered and racialized. As the author concludes from a study of self-employed women in Canada, while the broad definition of emotional labor does not change across race and social position, how different women perform this work and what this work looks like varies significantly across gender and racial identification. Emotional labor carries with it racialized and gendered histories and expectations; working within or against these expectations (or both within and against) can require different things from different women. Kismet, with its blue eyes, light brown eyebrows, and pink ears, also "normalizes whiteness," as do other robot companions, such as the blonde-haired, blue-eyed Cindy Smart Doll and the similarly blonde-haired, blue-eyed My Friend Cayla. To attend to Kismet's normalization and universalization of whiteness around emotions and emotional labor, I turn to scientific debates around the universality of emotions, a contested theory that undergirds Kismet's emotionality.

Kismet's emotional topography relies on Paul Ekman and William Friesen's Facial Action Coding System (FACS), which measures human facial expression and movement. Ekman and other researchers have mapped these expressions and movements to various emotional states, thus suggesting that certain truths of an individual's interior life (here, their emotions) can be read on the exterior of the body. Ekman specifically argues that the expression of six "basic" emotions (anger, fear, surprise, sadness, disgust, and happiness) is universal across humans, cultures, and geographies.[11] Funded by a DARPA grant, in the 1960s Ekman, who was influenced by the work of Silvan Tomkins, departed from dominant research that viewed emotions as socially constructed and individually variable, and began his work on the universality of emotion expression. Ekman's theory about emotions' universality in expression has been influential both for scientific research on emotions and for technologized policing practices such as the TSA's controversial Screening Passengers by Observation Techniques (SPOT) program. Ekman and his influential research also inspired *Lie to Me*, a television series about a charismatic psychologist (played by Tim Roth) and his team of trained experts who can read facial micro expressions to detect lies and solve crimes and mysteries.

Though undeniably influential, Ekman's adherence to the universality of emotions has been persuasively challenged. For example, Hochschild views Ekman's conceptualization of emotions as "limited," as its descriptions of emotion expression as innate do not account for how people are socialized and trained to manage their emotions.[12] Psychologist Lisa Barrett offers a detailed and compelling critique of theories of universal emotion expression, including Ekman's conclusions. According to Barrett's analysis, the studies grounding and supporting Ekman's claim were biased by the language used to survey individuals, from using forced-choice response structures to testing in cultures that were already familiar with Western cultural norms.[13] Additionally, Barrett's research, which uses different devices to measure facial movement, also challenges the correlation between consistent facial muscle movement and emotion (7–8). In contrast to claims to the universality of emotions and their expressions, Barrett's research supports the cultural specificity of emotions. While Ekman concludes that the universality of certain emotion expression is proven throughout his studies, including those conducted in

Papua New Guinea, Barrett underscores the decidedly Western conception of these basic emotions and their corresponding expressions (13).[14]

Ekman's research ascribes to what is called the "classical view" of
emotions. Barrett defines the classical view as holding that "certain emotions are inborn and universal: all healthy people around the world are
supposed to display and recognize them" (38). Barrett's description of
the classical view of emotions highlights the normativity undergirding the
presumption of emotion universality. Putting aside for the moment the
role of culture in shaping emotions and emotion expression, this view, in
its exclusion of those who fall outside the vague and normative category
of "healthy people," is exclusionary, dangerous, and has significant material consequences for those who are not included in this category. In contrast to the classical view, for Barrett, emotion expression is characterized primarily by variation—not just across cultures and humans, but
also within a single individual: "On different occasions, in different contexts, in different studies, within the same individual and across different
individuals, *the same emotion category involves different bodily responses.*
Variation, not uniformity, is the norm" (15).

Barrett's challenge to the theory of universality of emotion expression takes particular resonance in light of Ekman's collaborations with
police forces, the CIA, and the Department of Homeland Security. With
the help of Ekman's research, these institutions operate under the premise that the face betrays the truth of an individual.[15] It follows that if one
believes the idea that the truth of an individual can be read on the body,
then one would believe that, with the proper skills and tools, the body
can be read for these truths. Over the course of his career, Ekman has
researched and developed technologies that train individuals to express
and recognize his universal emotional states in others (e.g., a 527-page
FACS manual can be purchased online for $350).[16] One might say that his
investment in training humans in emotional communication, particularly in the context of his government collaborations, creates the purported universality of human emotions on which his government collaborations and surveillance and security techniques are premised.[17] In
other words, Ekman's theory and related technologies might be said to
produce the universally recognizable emotional humans they claim to be
identifying, describing, and surveilling.

Kelly Gates describes FACS and Ekman's work as a project to make human emotion more easily controlled.[18] Ekman's motivation to code-velop FACS emerged from his desire to uncover signs of deceit in the face (180). As Gates's work suggests, it is no surprise that Ekman and Friesen's FACS has been taken up by institutions that share his interest in deception detection. For example, the TSA's SPOT program trains TSA officers to identify potential terrorists using behavioral profiling based on Ekman and Friesen's FACS. As Yevgenia S. Kleiner critiques, the SPOT training program is a mere weeklong training session and does not address individuals' biases and preconceptions that can lead to racial profiling of Muslim and Arab travelers.[19] The TSA has employed SPOT since 2007. As of 2015, it has not identified a single terrorist.[20] Instead, its implementation has led to accusations of racial profiling and a lawsuit from the ACLU on the grounds of the program's secrecy. Despite reports of racial profiling of Muslim and Arab travelers, the program's striking lack of results, and numerous scientific findings (including Barrett's) that challenge the scientific claims that ground FACS, the TSA continues to employ SPOT.[21] Indeed, as the *Los Angeles Times* reports, since 2007, the TSA has spent over $1 billion implementing the program, and has deployed approximately three thousand "behavior-detection officers" in airports throughout the United States.[22] In her intersectional study of emotional labor, Patricia Chong details how emotional labor "reinforces intersecting systems of race, gender and class oppression." As Chong submits, the demands of emotional labor differ according to race, gender, and class and exacerbate uneven power relations that benefit some people by marginalizing others. Norms of emotional expression, like all norms, are shaped through unequal power relations and hierarchies; therefore emotional labor is not neutral, "but rather naturalizes and maintains oppressive hierarchical inequalities on both individual and institutional levels."[23] Just as emotional labor is not a neutral act, nor is the demand for emotional labor, whether in the home, the marketplace, or at national borders.

While Chong and Mirchandani point to the intersection of race, gender, and class as creating variable emotional labor demands specifically in the marketplace, such demands, which develop in conversation with extant social norms, also speak to normative assumptions about emotions outside the marketplace—for example, in relation to criminality and national security. As Zach Blas, Simone Browne, Shoshana

Magnet, and Gates detail in their respective work on the non-neutrality of facial biometric technologies in relation to race, gender, class, and disability, these practices, technologies, and theories, in their normative assumptions and demands for emotional labor, only reinscribe extant inequalities and power relations.[24] Ekman's theories of emotions' universality and the technologies they shape, including Kismet, produce normative demands for emotional labor. For what Ekman's applications ask of individuals is work—specifically, the work of being an "appropriately" emotional individual, and of making sure that this appropriate emotionality is legible to certain others. Emotional labor disciplines subjects into performing a specific version of the human. And those who are illegible as normative emotional subjects may be met with exclusion—for example, by companies that have used emotional intelligence as a basis for hiring, and at national borders, by government agencies that rely on theories of universal emotion expression.

Both *We Can Build You* and *Do Androids Dream of Electric Sheep?* highlight the normative impulses and exclusionary effects associated with emotions' purported universality. Dick's novels, written during the 1960s, challenge the universality of emotion expression by depicting the injunction to perform and make legible "appropriate" emotions as a relation of power, with the institutions and individuals who demand emotional legibility presented as agents of dehumanization. The novels place the onus of proving one's humanness not on those who are dehumanized at the site of the emotions, but on those who determine and demand the standards for this proof. By addressing how emotionality is constructed and policed, the novels do not valorize the possibility of identifying human from nonhuman at the site of the emotions, but rather highlight the artificiality of the boundary between human and dehumanized. In the novels, emotions are only ostensibly the basis by which beings are dehumanized; in actuality, dehumanization through the emotions appears as a *post facto* justification for maintaining existing exploitative relations and for securing exploitative relations in the future. As I discuss through a reading of *Build You* and a more extended reading of *Do Androids*, Dick's novels highlight that the "appropriate" expression of emotions is its own form of work—the work of performing emotionality in order to be legible as human, as citizen, as non-threat.

Gender, Emotional Labor, and Dehumanization in *We Can Build You*

Before the androids of *Do Androids Dream of Electric Sheep?* (1968), Dick introduced their precursors, mechanical human simulacra, in *We Can Build You.*[25] Set against the backdrop of Civil War nostalgia, the novel features two simulacra: the Lincoln, an identical mechanical replica of Abraham Lincoln, and the Stanton, a replica of Edwin M. Stanton, the secretary of war under Lincoln.[26] Set in a present that is preoccupied with the Civil War, the novel depicts a world where emotions are defining characteristics of humanness. Like many of Dick's fictional interrogations of the human, this novel takes place on a terrain of exploitation and capitalist greed. It follows Louis Rosen, the protagonist, and his business partner Maury Rock as their small company, MASA Associates, moves into the artificial human game. Thanks to the artistry of Maury's daughter Pris, their artificial humans, or simulacra, are extremely lifelike machines that are frequently mistaken for living human beings.[27] As word gets out about the simulacra's convincing appearance and behavior, Louis and Maury soon find themselves facing off against wealthy slumlord and land speculator Sam Barrows. While Maury dreams of using the simulacra to restage the Civil War in its entirety, Barrows, who has invested a great deal of money in outer space colonies, wants to use the mechanical humans to trick people into moving to his lonely and desolate outposts. Barrows, "the man who polluted the untouched other worlds," is a despicable character—all conniving, ruthless, exploitative, and cruel, putting profit above all else.[28] Initially, Barrows and MASA Associates appear to be on opposite sides of this battle for the simulacra. Maury and Louis, alongside the Lincoln and the Stanton, appear to be the little guys fighting the good fight against Barrows's dehumanizing corporate greed, colonizing desires, and seemingly infinite financial resources. However, as MASA's association with the slavery-era term "massa" suggests and Louis's narrative arc emphasizes, this configuration does not hold up.[29]

The novel first hints at the similarities between MASA and Barrows through their respective treatment of the simulacra and their labor. Fredric Jameson describes Dick's androids, in their human-like appearance and emotional capacities, as a shift from the labor-oriented robots of Isaac Asimov's fictional works.[30] MASA Associates and Barrows face off on opposite sides of this shift, with Louis and Maury engaging the simulacra as wise advisers and sensitive, feeling souls; Barrows, on the other hand, views the simulacra solely as objects for labor and profit. And yet Barrows, unlike Louis and Maury, offers to pay the Stanton for its work in his appeal to the simulacrum to join his business in Seattle. Thus, while Louis and Maury, who approach both the Stanton and the Lincoln as living beings, expect the simulacra to labor for MASA without compensation, Barrows, who views the simulacra through the dehumanizing lenses of commerce and capital, offers to pay the Stanton for its labor. Paradoxically, then, Louis and Maury's humanization of the simulacra exploits by not paying them for their work.

The novel continues to draw connections between Louis and the villainous Barrows, particularly in light of Louis's dehumanizing demands for Pris's emotional labor. Throughout the novel, Louis describes young Pris as cold, devoid of emotion, and possessing flat affect; she is, according to Louis, more machine than human. However, belying Louis's descriptions, the novel depicts Pris as emotional in her expressions of anguish, despair, fear, and anger. Pris is an emotional subject; and yet, despite witnessing her emotionality, Louis insists on Pris's emotionlessness, her inhuman coldness. As Hochschild describes, emotional labor is gendered. Women, much more so than men, are expected to be "nice," with this niceness expressly put to work to build up the status and well-being of others (167). Pris is neither warm toward nor particularly interested in Louis. She does not perform niceness, nor does she concern herself with the well-being, status, or emotional state of others, including Louis. Pris, who does not exhibit this normative gendered emotional labor, is not legible to Louis as "properly" feminine, or in fact as human. Instead, to Louis, Pris is strange, alien, and more machine than the male simulacra, with whom Louis identifies and sympathizes. Through Pris, *Build You* examines the gendered dimensions of emotional work and the costs of not expressing normative and purportedly universal emotions. By pointing to connections between Louis and dastardly Barrows, the novel challenges Louis's dehumanization of Pris and places the onus of human legibility not on Pris, whose emotional responses are read by Louis as insufficiently human, but on Louis, who imposes normative demands on her emotionality.

In her wonderful reading of Dick's work, N. Katherine Hayles offers the schizoid android as a way to understand the triangulation of male subjects, androids, and schizoid female subjects around emotion. In Dick's fictions, the schizoid android is a predominantly female character who possesses characteristics associated with androids: coldness, intelligence, flat affect, an incapacity to empathize. The schizoid android, who can be human or android, unfailingly destabilizes the boundary between human and not-human. A male protagonist's encounter with a female schizoid android is particularly monumental, as this gendered encounter radically destabilizes the boundaries between the male protagonist and his world.[31] This encounter is, then, both significant ontologically and narratively, as it simultaneously undoes existing reality and introduces a new ontological paradigm that drives the rest of the narrative. Building on Hayles's work, I suggest that the schizoid android also underscores the gendered nature of emotional labor. In this context, Pris as schizoid android is a female character who does not participate in gendered expectations of emotional labor.[32] Perceptions of her coldness and flat affect point to the schizoid android's refusal or inability to perform warmth and niceness, and to manage her emotions for the benefit of others. Like other schizoid android characters, Pris, because she does not fulfill the gendered expectations for her emotional labor, is dehumanized and excluded from the human community.

In Dick's fictions, androidism highlights the exploitation and dehumanization of mechanical characters, whether human or simulacrum. Pris's purported androidism both condemns Pris as not-human while, in comparison, elevating the simulacra as too human to be mere machine. Thus, even Pris's dehumanization works to humanize, or build the status, of the male simulacra. To Louis, Pris, in her coldness, is strange and unnatural ("she still did not look normal or natural to me"), not real ("unreal and doll-like"), and unnervingly associated with death ("she looked to me like a dance of death creation animated in some weird way, probably not through the usual assimilation of solid and liquid foods") (23). In contrast to the simulacra who are described in the language of life, Pris is described as not quite human and not quite alive (149). Louis's comparison between the lifelike simulacra and the not-quite-lifelike Pris is explicit: "For my money, she looked less normal than the Stanton" (24),[33] and

"Beside her, the Stanton contraption is all warmth and friendliness" (29): "I had my own personal experience with [Lincoln]—or to be more exact, with his simulacrum. I didn't catch the *alienness,* the otherness, with the simulacrum that I had caught with Pris" (182). Louis judges Pris as cold and unreal (24) and "inhuman" in her incapacity to feel (123), despite the novel's depictions of Pris as feeling despair (69), shuddering with fear (66), and shivering with anguish (123). Meanwhile, Louis's first-person narrative imbues the Lincoln with warmth, sadness, concern, depression, and love. Louis's descriptions of the Lincoln's emotions render it one of the novel's most "human" characters, particularly when juxtaposed with Pris's machinelike lack of feeling.

Louis's relationship with the Lincoln simulacrum unifies, taking shape through sympathy and identification. For example, upon first meeting the Lincoln, Louis faints at the shock of this otherness. In response, the Lincoln sends him "a short note of sympathy" (92).[34] In her study of the politics and aesthetics of emotions in the twentieth century, Kathleen Woodward describes sympathy as a social emotion that binds us to others.[35] Sympathy binds Louis and the Lincoln, and this bond continues to strengthen, progressing from sympathetic bond to reciprocal identi-fication.[36] And when the Lincoln becomes withdrawn, its face "blank and downcast," Louis has great sympathy for it. Indeed, Louis reads the Lincoln's depressive moods as the Lincoln feeling *too much* (191). But when Pris withdraws, Louis reads her as indifferent and devoid of feeling (29–30, 246). When it comes to Pris, for Louis there is no sympathetic bond, no reciprocation of feeling, only a dehumanizing alterity that rup-tures and refuses sympathy, much less identification: "She and I were so different" (182).

Android Indifference

After MASA narrowly staves off Barrows's corporate takeover, Pris leaves MASA Associates to join Barrows. With her departure, the narrative shifts from focusing on the simulacra's entry into the world, to Louis's increasing obsession with Pris. After she leaves, Louis and Maury are bereft, suffering both a momentous business and a personal loss. With-out Pris's design genius, Louis and Maury are left trying to figure out how to mitigate MASA Associates' losses. They cannot develop new products on their own, so they decide to modify their existing simulacra blueprints to develop armies of Civil War babysitters called Nannies (Union soldiers only, at the Stanton's insistence). As this bizarre idea indicates, after Pris leaves, things at MASA are a mess. And Louis, who has suddenly decided he is in love with her, begins to go mad. He packs his .38 pistol and heads to Seattle to kill Barrows and bring Pris home. Numerous critics point to this somewhat abrupt narrative shift as a creative misstep.[37] I argue that these seemingly disjunct narratives are connected in their depiction of Louis's dehumanizing practices, which link him not so much to the Lincoln simulacrum in its gentleness and sensitivity, as Louis likes to think, but to Barrows in his cruelty and aggressive pursuit of his desires. In the novel, reading another's emotions is a definitional practice that can humanize or dehumanize. In the first half of the novel, Louis humanizes the Lincoln as an emotional being while dehumanizing Pris in her refusal or inability to perform gendered emotional labor. In the second half of the novel, Louis's dehumanization of Pris reaches a new level when, through a series of hallucinations, he turns her into a simulacrum that is warm and gentle and returns Louis's love.

Louis's re-creation of Pris as a simulacrum is cruel, both in its erasure of Pris herself and in its explicit realization of her fears of being brought back to life as such. Louis first hallucinates Pris after he tracks her down in Seattle and fails to convince her to return home. At the home of one of Barrows's employees, Louis goes mad and hallucinates a conversation with Pris. Unlike the real Pris, this hallucinated Pris is tender. Unlike the real Pris, this hallucinated Pris returns Louis's love. As Louis hallucinates having sex with Pris while others overhear in the next room, only Barrows mistakenly believes Pris is actually in the room with Louis: "That girl in there is underdeveloped. Everything slides back out. What's she doing there in the bedroom anyhow? Has she got that skinny body—" (212). In crude language, Barrows also gives life to Louis's hallucinated Pris. In this association between Louis and Barrows, the novel highlights that Louis's hallucination, which is shared only by Barrows, is not about love but about control and dehumanization. Louis's hallucinations also give life to Pris's acute fear that she will be forced to come back from the dead as a simulacrum: "'Do you think someday somebody will make a simulacrum of you and me? And we'll have to come back to life? . . . There we'll be, dead and oblivious to everything . . . and then we'll feel something stirring. Maybe see a snatch of light. And then it'll all come flooding in on us, reality once more. We'll be helpless to stop the process, we'll have to come back. Resurrected!' She shuddered" (66). Louis, who insists on preserving the idea of her coldness, disregards her fear entirely when he resurrects and reimagines her in his hallucinations. In his hallucinations, which realize her fear, Pris is condemned to reciprocate a love she only ever rejected and to perform the emotional labor she would not perform. Just as Barrows planned to use simulacra to trick people into moving to his deserted space colonies, Louis, through his hallucinations, uses a simulation of Pris to create a simulated world of his own. Pris may be cruel, cold, and unnatural (but perhaps only according to Louis), but Louis, like Barrows, dehumanizes.

After his hallucination, Louis is diagnosed with schizophrenia and subsequently checks himself in to the Kasanin Clinic. Here, Louis undergoes a series of drug-induced, therapeutic fugue states during which he hallucinates an entire lifetime with Pris. In these fugue encounters, in which Pris resignedly accepts his love, the real Pris is never more absent.[38] While every effort is made to faithfully re-create the Stanton and the Lincoln simulacra according to what is known about their lives, to restore their personalities as they were, Louis takes no such pains with his simulation of Pris, who is significantly altered in his fantasies, perhaps most notably in her acquiescence to Louis.

During his stay at the clinic, Louis discovers that the real Pris is also a patient in Kasanin. Pris, who is aware of her appearance in Louis's hallucinations ("tell your fantasy sex-partner there, the Pris Frauenzimmer that you've cooked up in that warped, hot little brain of yours, that you don't find her convincing anymore"), encourages Louis to end the fugue states so he can leave the clinic: "'If I do,' [Louis asks her], 'will you marry me?' She groaned. 'Sure, Louis. Anything you want. Marriage, living in sin, incidental screwing—you name it'" (242). Louis takes her at her word and secures his release, fully expecting his hallucinated life with Pris to be realized outside the clinic. As Louis is departing, Pris tells him that she is not leaving the clinic:

Pris said calmly, "I changed my mind. I didn't apply for a release from here; I feel like staying a few months longer. I like it right now—

I'm learning how to weave, I'm weaving a rug out of black sheep wool, virgin wool." And then all at once she whispered bleakly, "I lied to you, Louis. I'm not up for release; I'm much too sick. I have to stay here a long time more, maybe forever. I'm sorry I told you I was getting out. Forgive me." She took hold of my hand briefly, then let it go. (246)[39]

Pris's deceit allows her to end Louis's fugue life, in which she is resurrected as a simulacrum and has no choice but to love him. Pris, who fears that an extended life will be imposed on her by external means—that she will be turned into a simulacrum—ends Louis's simulated fantasy life with her, thus destroying that which threatens to bring her, against her will, into another state of life and that depicts her as other than she is—that is, as warm and putting her emotions to work for Louis's well-being. In their parting conversation, the above passage depicts Pris abruptly shifting from calm indifference to tender remorse. This shift is ambiguous. Her sudden interjection of feeling can be read as the novel affirming her as an emotional subject once again, despite Louis's continued insistence otherwise. The passage, as it moves to Pris's bleak whispers, can also be read as Louis's final hallucination of the Pris simulacrum, where her emotional apology is simply another component of Louis's imagined Pris. In the first scenario, the novel affirms Louis's continued dehumanizing refusal to recognize Pris as an emotional subject. In the second scenario, the novel affirms Louis's cruel controlling nature, as he exerts power over her one last time, realizing her fear in order to get a final glimpse of his Pris simulacrum.

The novel's final passage concludes with Louis reasserting Pris's androidism: "Somewhere inside the great buildings of Kasanin Clinic Pris Frauenzimmer sat carding and weaving virgin black sheep's wool, utterly involved, without a thought for me or for any other thing" (246). In the intertwined worlds of Dick's android novels, indifference toward others, especially humans, is a primary characteristic of mechanical life.[40] In this concluding imagined scenario, Louis once again characterizes Pris, whom he describes as lacking interest in him and the world, as unemotional and cold—as android. However, through Louis's insistent disregard of Pris's emotions and his resonances with Barrows, the novel's conclusion locates androidism not in Pris, but in Louis, who is himself indifferent to the real Pris and eschews the young woman for his simulacrum of her. Thus, the novel challenges both Louis's insistence on Pris's nonhumanness and his own presumed humanity. And Pris, who is in Kasanin Clinic at the close of the novel, no longer labors to produce simulacra for MASA Associates or Barrows, nor does she perform the emotional labor of making herself legible as a properly gendered emotional subject. Louis leaves the clinic, ready to return to his family and his business. Pris, by not performing warmth, interest, and other forms of gendered emotional work, has removed herself from MASA Associates, Barrows, and Louis, as well as their demands that she provide emotional labor for an unwanted love and material labor for morally questionable business ventures.

For Shame: *Do Androids Dream of Electric Sheep?*

A loose sequel of *We Can Build You*, Dick's novel *Do Androids Dream of Electric Sheep?* further underscores Louis Rosen's inhumanity, in no small part because MASA Associates' small family business is reimagined as Rosen Associates, a nefarious corporate behemoth. Rosen Associates manufactures highly intelligent android servants for space colonization, thus fulfilling Barrows's plan for the simulacra. Pris, who is reimagined as the twinned androids Rachael Rosen and Pris Stratton, is once again doomed to technological resurrection, this time as double the android Louis insisted she was. And the Lincoln and the Stanton simulacra and MASA's Civil War nannies evolve into war machines called Synthetic Freedom Fighters, and then Nexus-6 androids, highly intelligent organic beings who look just like the humans they are created to serve. In *Do Androids,* demands for emotional labor take shape through shame. While *We Can Build You* narrates Louis Rosen's dehumanization of Pris through his demands for gendered emotional labor, *Do Androids* recounts the shamelessness of the protagonist Rick Deckard, whose job requires him to kill androids on account of their purported lack of shame. In both of these novels, Louis's and Rick's respective demands for emotional labor render the protagonists as inhuman, rather than the beings they repeatedly dehumanize, whether android or human.

The two novels are separated by nuclear war and subsequent ecological catastrophe; *Build You* takes place in the relative idylls of 1982, while *Do Androids Dream* is set in a postwar, postapocalyptic 2021. After

World War Terminus, Earth is bleak, deteriorating, and virtually unin-habitable for humans and animals alike. Those who did not emigrate to Mars live in constant fear of radioactive fallout, which, the novel assures, no longer kills, but "only derange[s] minds and genetic properties."[41] Thus, the remaining humans on Earth live with the ever-present threat that they will become "specials"—individuals mentally and genetically af-fected by the radiation. These individuals face considerable discrimina-tion, from derogatory slurs to prohibitions from leaving the planet. Some-how (or rather, of course), corporate capitalism continues to thrive, largely through ubiquitous technological devices, including mood-regulating devices, televisions, empathy boxes, and androids, all of which distract humans from the bleakness of life on Earth and on Mars. The mechanical animal industry is also booming, including fake animal hospitals that re-pair mechanical animals while maintaining the secret of their artificiality. In the immediate past of the novel, a group of Nexus-6 androids have fled servitude on Mars and infiltrated Earth. It is the job of Rick Deckard, android bounty hunter, to track, identify, and kill these androids.

Despite the decades that separate the two android novels, emotion remains the central distinguishing characteristic between humans and androids. In *Build You,* identifying and reading emotionality was local-ized in Louis's own processes of distinguishing between human and arti-ficial human; in *Do Androids,* emotionality has become institutionalized and officially sanctioned by the state as a strategy to distinguish humans from androids. However, the novel underscores the artificiality of this of-ficial boundary between human and nonhuman, as humans, who are de-fined by their privileged capacity for empathy, at times demonstrate great cruelty toward humans and androids alike.[42] And androids, who are pur-portedly incapable of empathy, can exhibit great care and concern for each other and, at times, for humans.[43] The contradictions embedded in the emotional criteria for humanness are nowhere more evident than in shame.

Eve Kosofsky Sedgwick describes shame as a powerful simultaneous pull toward relationality and individuation. Posing a hypothetical sce-nario in which a disoriented man walks into a lecture hall and urinates at the front of the room, Sedgwick points to bystanders' shame as a mode of relation: "I pictured the excruciation of everyone else in the room: each

looking down, wishing to be anywhere else yet conscious of the inexora-
ble fate of being exactly there, inside the individual skin of which each
was burningly aware; at the same time, though, unable to stanch the
hemorrhage of painful identification with the misbehaving man. That's
the double movement shame makes: toward painful individuation, toward uncontrollable relationality."[44] For Sedgwick, shame is both a turn
inward and a turn outward toward the other, toward sociality and relationality. Notably, this identification with another—this turn outward—is
"uncontrollable." In shame, relationality, no less individuation, is not op-
tional. In conversation with Tomkins, Sedgwick highlights that shame is
about identity, about what one is: "one *is something* in experiencing
shame."[45] While what this something is often exists as a question, this
something-ness is the position from which one experiences shame. Thus
shame simultaneously opens up identity as a question (what is this something that I am?) while seaming this question to an other, and thus to
the social.

As Elizabeth Wilson observes, Kismet is without shame.[46] Shame,
with its downcast eyes and bowed head, is not one of the affects the
robot is designed to express, despite the centrality of shame to Silvan
Tomkins's theory of affects, which Ekman cites as a significant influence.
Describing shame's role in Tomkins's work, Wilson also underscores the
importance of shame to socialization: "every socially intelligent creature
is a product of shame" (81). Because of this absence, Wilson reads Kismet
as a technology that regulates and inhibits shame: "Perhaps, then,
Kismet is best understood as a robot designed to regulate the production of shame and dampen down its transmission. Perhaps the potency
of Kismet has been precisely that it can communicate neither its own
shame nor the shame of its creators." For Wilson, as shame plays an important role in the production of intersubjectivity, Kismet's absence of
shame limits its capacity to interact with humans, to be properly social
(82). In Dick's novel, technology, from the mood organ to the android-
detecting Voigt–Kampff test, similarly inhibits the production of shame
in humans. Thus, these technologies inhibit an intersubjective sociality
that can lead humans to interrogate their own identity and their relation
to the world. This inhibition of shame serves a purpose; in the world of
the novel shame, in its sociality and insistence on self-interrogation, is

dangerous. In opening up possibilities for compassion and empathy, shame threatens the established order of things, which mandates the oppression and dehumanization of certain beings, from specials to androids. Shame threatens this social order by moving individuals to question their own identities within this system and to establish empathetic bonds with other living beings, be it humans, androids, or animals.

Like androids, specials are considered subhuman and prohibited from planetary mobility. By linking androids and specials, *Do Androids* explicitly connects androids, servitude, and dehumanization in a way that highlights the processes by which humanness is constructed around exclusion. Early on, the novel describes androids, in their servitude, as a means of enticing humans to emigrate to the Mars colonies: "android servant as carrot," servitude as inducement (16). This description of androids as servants immediately moves to a discussion of specials, who are described as "biologically unacceptable, a menace to the pristine heredity of the race. Once pegged as special, a citizen, even if accepting sterilization, dropped out of history. He ceased, in effect, to be part of mankind" (16). By aligning androids with specials, who are excised from humankind as "a menace to the pristine heredity of the race," the novel also gestures to the ways "the human" has historically been constructed around race.

Isiah Lavender III notes that dystopian science fiction often highlights existing dynamics and problems around racism. Reading *Do Androids,* he points to the discrimination against specials and androids as forms of racial discrimination.[47] And of Rick's bounty hunting work, Lavender writes, "A slave allegory is impossible to miss here since Deckard is portrayed as a futuristic slave catcher sent to kill 'escaped' androids'" (181). As Lavender's reading highlights, the androids' existential condition resonates with enslavement, from the androids' forced servitude, to humans' fears of their passing for human, to their continued dehumanization through arbitrary and false criteria determined by the state. As numerous scholars including Lavender and Gregory Jerome Hampton note, robots reflect racial difference, often through characterizations of robots as enslaved people.[48] Despina Kakoudaki offers the concept of metalface to describe robots' engagement with race and slavery. As she describes, "The metal exterior of the robot functions as a site for projecting numerous kinds of difference, and in this fundamentally ambiguous space metalness can stand in for a type of blackness or, indeed, for other states of abjection that the position of the African slave embodies in Western modernity."[49]

Building on Lavender's reading of the androids as allegorical slaves and Kakoudaki's concept of metalface, I submit that in *Do Androids,* the uncritical celebratory Civil War nostalgia of *We Can Build You* shifts to the violent oppressions that structured U.S. slavery and its racist legacies. And shame is at the center of this shift. An entire labor force, as well as the maintenance of the rules and hierarchical oppressions that govern society on Earth and Mars, depends on androids' purported and exclusive lack of shame. For humans, the androids' value is found solely in their labor. Absent their labor, they are a threat, both because their servitude plays a crucial role in securing capitalist profits and because androids' defiant existence on Earth underscores humans' culpability in the androids' exploitation. And the androids' refusal to work threatens, because the androids' mere existence outside of labor challenges the system of hierarchical oppression that structures life on Earth and on Mars.[50]

Androids' lack of shame also highlights the bleakness and hopelessness of life on Earth, a reality that is masked by artificial-emotion technologies like the mood organ, the empathy box, and the television. As Elspeth Probyn highlights, shame is activated by interest: "Interest is the key to understanding shame, and shame reminds us with urgency what we are interested in."[51] Because shame does not result in disinterest, but rather interest interrupted or cut short, shame can also be read as hopeful. In its interruption of interest, "shame promises a return of interest, joy, and connection. This is why shame matters to individuals" (xiii). If androids do not feel shame, it follows that they do not feel interest. Androids do not maintain the illusion that Earth is hospitable to joy and connection. They are not interested in upholding this pretense, nor are they interested in privileging human life above their own lives. And, perhaps most chillingly for Rick, they are simply indifferent to him: "The tyranny of an object, he thought. [The electric sheep] doesn't know I exist. Like the androids, it had no ability to appreciate the existence of another" (42). Androids are not interested in humans or the human structures that have brought androids into existence solely to labor for humans. Androids are not interested in systems that do not recognize the androids' capacities for empathy and emotion and that find it necessary to hunt and kill androids.

While the state insists that humans have shame and androids do not, this boundary is proven false again and again throughout the story, primarily through Rick, who gradually goes from shameless to shameful, thus destabilizing this constructed boundary between human and android as well as the notion that shame, and the emotions more broadly, are innate and universal. At the novel's opening, Rick, who is human, is decidedly without shame. The first scene begins with Iran, his wife, attempting to shame him for killing androids. Rick, however, feels neither shame nor ethical ambivalence in this moment. While the androids' indifference to Rick chills him, Rick's uninterest in others and the world, indicated by his own shamelessness, is dangerous. Driven exclusively by money, Rick sees the world entirely through capitalist exchange, with no interest in the androids he kills for pay and no care for the animals (mechanical or living) that he purchases with his earnings. As the beginning of the novel goes to great lengths to convey, Rick has no shame about his work or his purely acquisitive relationship to animals. Androids might be shameless (though this is questioned by the novel), but it is Rick, who wields the power of the state to police the boundary between human and android, whose shamelessness dehumanizes and endangers.

In his bounty hunter work, Rick employs the Voigt–Kampff test, a state-sanctioned method of detecting androids through their lack of shame. According to the test, shame, which is exclusive to humans, is a physiologically measurable and involuntary response to immorality that cannot be manufactured: "'This'—[Rick] held up the flat adhesive disk with its trailing wires—'measures capillary dilation in the facial area. We know this to be a primary autonomic response, the so-called 'shame' or 'blushing' reaction to a morally shocking stimulus. It can't be controlled voluntarily, as can skin conductivity, respiration, and cardiac rate'" (46). While the android is hooked up to the measuring apparatus, the official administering the test asks a series of questions about killing animals. The Voigt–Kampff test, as an extension of state power and its dehumanizing boundary-policing practices, is based on the premise that androids do not feel shame. In her insightful reading of the novel, Jill Galvan describes the Voigt–Kampff test as "enact[ing] the tyranny of the unilateral state order" in its refusal of reciprocity. In the test, power travels only one way, from test administrator to android, and produces only one outcome; however the android responds to the questions, the test "assures the android's condemnation."[52] It is, then, not the androids' lack of measurable shame that renders them killable. Instead, the Voigt–Kampff test enacts the unilateral authority of the state, which dictates that all androids must be killed.

The test has another function, which also derives from the non-reciprocity Galvan highlights. Much like Wilson's critique of Kismet, the Voigt–Kampff test, in its unilateral structure and relations to language and power, also inhibits the production of shame. As the test does not allow for reciprocity, it prevents the double movement of shame's productive potential as delineated by Sedgwick: both inward, to contemplate one's own identity, and outward, toward sociality. Thus, shame is inhibited not just in the androids that are tested, but also in humans—namely, the bounty hunters who are charged with administering the test. In the case of Rick, as the first Voigt–Kampff test scene demonstrates, this inhibition of shame discourages him from questioning his identity as android killer and from potentially establishing a non-monetary and non-homicidal sociality with androids and the world more broadly.[53] In this scene, the test's accuracy proves secondary to its capacity to inhibit shame.

Rick first administers the Voigt–Kampff test to Rachael Rosen, who is affiliated with Rosen Associates.[54] In response to questions about killing butterflies, a nude girl on a bearskin rug, and cooking live lobsters, Rachael's verbal answers all indicate shame and moral outrage. However, her physiological readings—her shame response—contradict her speech, leading Rick to determine that she is an android. However, the conclusion of this Voigt–Kampff test is only the beginning of this scene, which demonstrates both the invalidity of the criteria used to distinguish androids from humans and how thoroughly Rick wields the power of the state to condemn androids regardless. Soon after Rick makes his conclusion, Rachael and her uncle convince Rick that the test results are a fluke. The Rosens draw on the very real possibility—indeed the likelihood—that the Voigt–Kampff test would incorrectly identify schizoid and schizophrenic humans who, like androids, demonstrate an absence of affect.[55] Rick is momentarily swayed, believing Rachael's test results to be similarly flawed—that is, until he remembers the conversation he had with Rachael prior to the test. Rick recalls that during this conversation, Rachael referred to her owl as an "it": "It, he thought. *She keeps calling the owl it.* Not her" (58). Rachael's pronoun slip is verboten in a society that views empathy toward animals as a primary index of humanness.[56] Because of this slip, Rick returns to his original and correct conclusion that Rachael is an android.

This scene establishes that Rick so thoroughly embodies the unilateral authority of the state that he becomes a kind of one-man Voigt–Kampff device, identifying androids without the use of the testing apparatus. This scene also highlights the inhibition of shame in Rick; like the androids he is tasked to hunt and kill for money and like the state he represents, Rick is without shame, which the novel underscores through Rick's unawareness of his own repeated use of "it" to refer to the owl.[57] The scene concludes with the revelation that Rachael's owl is in fact mechanical; thus Rachael, though an android, may not have revealed her own artificiality by referring to the owl as "it," but rather the artificiality of the owl (60).[58] Thus, Rick, reflecting the fallibility of the Voigt–Kampff test, misinterpreted Rachael's language while simultaneously reflecting his own lack of appropriate empathy for animals. As an extension of state power, Rick has no shame. And despite wielding the power of the state, Rick, like the androids who were built as servants for Martian colonists, is exploited for his inhibited capacity for shame. As long as Rick feels no shame, he will continue to kill androids without moral question, thus fulfilling the will of the state.

Rick's narrative is paired with that of John Isidore, a special who works at a mechanical animal hospital. As Patricia Warrick identifies, the novel is structured around these two intertwined narratives: Rick's hunt for the escaped androids and John's sympathetic encounter with these same androids. John's narrative is largely one of compassion for mechanical animals and androids. As Rick hunts and kills the escaped Nexus-6 androids, John helps them. Even after the androids, who are alternately cruel and kind, horrify John by mutilating a spider, he continues to protect them and ultimately refuses to offer them up to Rick. John is characterized by his compassion for all forms of life, mechanical and organic, animal and human. For example, while at work, John has compassion for what he thinks is a malfunctioning mechanical cat: "Funny, he thought; even though I know rationally it's faked the sound of a false animal, burning out its drive-train and power supply ties my stomach in knots" (72). After his boss, the ill-natured Hannibal Sloat, discovers that the now-dead cat was not mechanical after all,[59] he shames John, demeaning him with the derogatory "chickenhead" and unleashing "a string of abuse lasting what seemed to Isidore a full minute" (77). Through John, the novel establishes a connection between shame and compassion (as a form of interest), and thus gestures to shame's productive potential. Though John is a special (i.e., a marginalized member of the human race whose mental functions are purportedly negatively affected by radiation exposure), the novel imbues him with some of the most sophisticated and incisive insights about the forces controlling society.[60] Taking into account John's capacity for shame and his mental acuity, his marginalization might be linked less to his identification as a special, and instead to his exceptional capacities to reason, to feel shame, and to feel indiscriminate compassion across the boundary of real and artificial life. These capacities, like the androids' presence on Earth, pose tremendous threats to the existing social order.

Shame, Sedgwick notes, is contagious.[61] Thus, Rick does not remain shameless for long, as John's powerful capacity for shame infiltrates Rick's narrative and propels him toward shame during his hunt for the android Luba Luft. At the beginning of this hunt, Rick remains shamelessly unconflicted about his task. He easily finds Luba, who is hiding in plain sight as a gifted opera singer. After taking a moment to appreciate her voice, an untroubled Rick resolutely sets about the business of first administering the Voigt–Kampff test to Luba, then killing her. As he begins, however, things become murky, as Luba obstructs power's unilateral exercise in the Voigt–Kampff test, and thus thwarts the test's inhibition of shame. As Galvan describes, Luba, in her refusal to directly answer the Voigt–Kampff test questions, momentarily subverts the test's nonreciprocal structure, and thus momentarily subverts the power of the state. For example, in response to the Voigt–Kampff prompt, "You're sitting watching TV and suddenly you discover a wasp crawling on your wrist," Luba responds with "What's a wasp? . . . Do they still exist? I've never

seen one. . . . Tell me the German word. . . . And what was the question?
I forget already" (102–3). Because of Luba's evasive language maneuvers,
Rick is unable to get a Voigt–Kampff reading; thus, she temporarily escapes being killed. Whereas Rachael was doomed by the test's structur-
ing of language, Luba refuses the nonreciprocity of the test by creating
what Galvan describes as "semantic fog."[62]

Expanding on Galvan's reading of this scene, I offer that Luba's language maneuvers extend beyond her Voigt–Kampff test. In fact, prior to
Rick administering the test, Luba employs language in a way that highlights a paradox: language works against the androids (both inside and
outside the Voigt–Kampff test), while Rick's authority to wield power
through language is undermined by the invalidity of the criteria used to
police the human–android boundary. Luba is able to exploit this paradox, turning language against Rick and creating language traps that
circumvent both established power vectors and the test's inhibition of
shame:

> "An android," [Rick] said, "doesn't care what happens to another
> android. That's one of the indications we look for."
>
> "Then," Miss Luft said, "you must be an android."
>
> That stopped him; he stared at her.
>
> "Because," she continued, "your job is to kill them, isn't it?" (101)

By introducing reciprocity and relationality, she momentarily undoes the
test's inhibition of shame, leading Rick to both question his own identity
as bounty hunter and empathize with her, despite the fact that she is
an android. Thus his encounter with Luba, unlike his encounter with
Rachael, throws Rick's understanding of his own identity—as human, as
bounty hunter, as admirer of opera and the arts—into question. Luba
takes possession of both language and the exclusively human prerogative
to identify androids. By doing so, she arrests Rick, destabilizing his previously secure and uncomplicated positions within language, the state,
and humankind, and ultimately turning his world upside down. Luba's
subversive language exploits also carry with them a comparable force of
the law, which becomes evident when she calls a shadow police force to
take Rick into custody. Led by a Nexus-6 android, this police force does
not recognize Rick as a fellow officer (they have no record of him); instead, the police view him as a suspect, thus forcing Rick out of his posi-

tion as bounty hunter and placing him in the position of those he has been hunting and killing. By inhabiting the position of those he hunts and kills, Rick finds himself in a new relationality with androids. This role reversal upends Rick's understanding of his identity, and he begins to feel troubled by the nature of his work and the task of killing Luba (136). As a result, Rick begins to question his own identity as a bounty hunter while also feeling remorse for having to kill Luba. In other words, Rick begins to feel shame.

Rick escapes the shadow police station with the help of fellow android bounty hunter Phil Resch. Phil, another double for Rick, is untroubled by killing androids. Indeed, Phil seems almost to enjoy it: "You like to kill," Rick accuses Phil (137), echoing Rick's own earlier "optimism" and "hungry, gleeful anticipation" (96) when he first descended onto the opera house to hunt Luba. The distinction between Phil and Rick continues as the two men resume the hunt for Luba, whom they track to a museum in front of Edvard Munch's painting *The Scream*. Unlike in his first encounter with Luba, Rick is now unsettled by Luba's humanizing association with art, as it troubles his conception of androids and his eagerness to participate in their systematic killing. Despite Rick's new doubt, he kills Luba. However, this act of killing is complicated, both because of Luba's continued association with culture and because of Phil, who ruthlessly shoots Luba prematurely, without securing an official Voigt–Kampff reading.[63] Luba, shot in the stomach, screams in pain and fear. "Like the picture, Rick thought to himself," right before he shoots and kills her (134). Though Rick unquestioningly collects the bounty for killing Luba, her alignment with art and her suffering just prior to her death trouble him, leading him to question the act of killing: "I can't anymore; I've had enough. She was a wonderful singer. The planet could have used her. This is insane" (136).[64]

Luba's death points to the differences between Rick's earlier, shameless relation to the world and his increasingly shame-full engagement with the world. By the novel's end, Rick no longer resembles Phil. Instead, Rick becomes more like John in his capacity for shame, as Rick questions his own identity as well as his connection to other forms of life, both human and nonhuman. Warrick reads John as Rick's "lost second self," their respective narratives paralleling and reversing each other throughout the novel. While "Rick metaphors law" by hunting and killing androids,

"Isidore metaphors love" by caring for living and mechanical beings alike, including taking in and protecting the very androids Rick is hunting. Rick and John unite at the end of the novel when their twinned narratives at last intersect.[65] This intersection, which is a crucial moment for Rick in relation to shame, culminates when Rick impersonates John in order to convince the androids, whom John had been helping, to let him into their apartment: "'This is Mr. Isidore,' Rick said. 'Let me in because I'm looking after you and t-t-two of you are women . . . I want to watch Buster Friendly on Pris's TV set,' Rick said. 'Now that he's proved Mercer doesn't exist it's very important to watch him. I drive a truck for the Van Ness Pet Hospital, which is owned by Mr. Hannibal S-S-Sloat.' He made himself stammer. 'S-S-So would you open the d-d-door? It's my apartment.' He waited, and the door opened" (222–23). Rick pretends to be John in order to kill the remaining androids, which Rick does. However, in pretending to be John, Rick also "catches" in full John's contagious shame, and thus his compassion for the androids.

Exhausted, dejected, and confused about his newfound empathy for androids, Rick flees to a desolate hill. He realizes that, over the course of the day, he no longer recognizes himself. In this moment of shame, he becomes alien to himself: "But what I've done, he thought; that's become alien to me. In fact everything about me has become unnatural; I've become an unnatural self" (230). Enabled by shame, Rick at last examines himself and is dissatisfied with what he has become. While on the hill, Rick spies a rare animal on the ground—a toad. Rick brings it home to Iran, only to discover that the toad is electric. Resigned, Rick muses, "But it doesn't matter. The electric things have their lives, too. Paltry as those lives are" (241). At the end of the novel, Rick is no longer policing boundaries between forms of life, but instead moving toward caring for all life, mechanical or organic. Newly valuing the lives of electric things (including androids) beyond their commodity value, Rick comes to inhabit the world in a significantly different way—with shame.

481

Though by the end Rick feels shame, the novel's conclusion offers no possibility of escape from technocorporate hegemony or the inevitable effects of postwar radioactive fallout. There is only acceptance of this inescapability and the possibility of ethically reorienting oneself in relation to this world.[66] And this minimal reorientation—through shame's twinned pulls inward and outward—is the small hope offered at the end of the novel. Spanning a single day, the novel highlights shame's reorienting capacity by mirroring the opening and closing scenes of the novel. Opening onto a scene of domestic disharmony in Rick and Iran's apartment, the novel begins with the couple arguing about technology: Rick is frustrated by Iran's dissatisfaction with the mood organ; and Iran, demonstrating empathy toward androids, calls Rick "a murderer hired by the cops" (4). Their argument escalates, concluding only when Rick dials mood-altering states on their respective mood organs: "pleased acknowledgment of husband's superior wisdom in all matters" for her, and "a creative and fresh attitude toward his job" for him (7). The concluding scene of the novel also takes place in Rick and Iran's apartment, their earlier disharmony replaced by tenderness as together they examine the toad, come to terms with its mechanical state, and accept its value as a creature, as life. In the novel's closing, Iran is about to dial Rick's mood organ to 670, "long deserved peace," when Rick falls into a deep sleep. "No need to turn on the mood organ, Iran realized," as Rick had achieved "long deserved peace" without the mediation of the mood organ (243). In the opening scene of the novel, Iran mentions that she programs the mood organ setting to 481, "Awareness of the manifold possibilities open to me in the future; new hope," to set in three hours after she sets her dial for despair (6). The final sentence of the novel—"And, feeling better, fixed herself at last a cup of black, hot coffee"—hints that, just as Rick found "long deserved peace" without the mood organ, Iran, newly dedicated to caring for the mechanical toad, similarly found such an awareness of "manifold possibilities" and "new hope" for the future (244).

All appears significantly better than when the day began. And yet the concluding scene raises more questions than it answers. By the end of the novel is Iran, like Rick, less dependent on the mood organ and thus able to, on her own, find new hope in caring for a mechanical animal? Or is this improvement in Iran's mood the result of an automatic resetting at 481? Iran who, for several hours before Rick returned home in the final scene, was depressed, "too listless and ill to want anything: a burden which closed off the future and any possibilities which it might once have contained"? (239). Iran who, whenever programming such deep despair, made sure to program an automatic resetting at 481 several hours later?

And is Rick's newly felt shame and questioning of his bounty hunter work merely the product of his earlier dialing for "a creative and fresh attitude toward his job"? And does Rick attaining "long deserved peace" on his own indicate that he is less dependent on the mood organ? Or has he so thoroughly absorbed the cybernetic circuit such that the absence of the mood organ only highlights technology's total control of Rick?

These concluding ambiguities, which refuse narrative closure, propel the reader to the question of tomorrow and what Rick will do now that he feels shame. The novel ends with Iran in part because the novel cannot end with Rick's "long deserved peace," as such optimism would belie the impossibility of escaping the bleak realities of this world, including Rick's work murdering androids. To end on Rick's "long deserved peace" would also belie the contradictions, paradoxes, inconsistencies, and shame by which he is able to achieve this peace, key among these that Rick only attains his shame and concluding peace on the backs of the androids he killed. Galvan describes this concluding paradox through abjection: "Rick cannot see himself as part of a posthuman community until he has abjected himself, in aspects both figurative and literal—until he has horrified himself as a murderer and, by this act, acknowledged himself as a non-subject."[67] It is, then, only through Rick's shameful acceptance of his own *in*humanity that he finds a more ethical relation with the world. What matters in the end, then, is Rick's recognition of his horrifying inhumanity, in that it marks his refusal to dehumanize androids (even while killing them) and his refusal to participate in policing the boundaries around "the human." As Rick's earlier lack of shame is dangerous in its authorization of inhumane and dehumanizing acts, the novel locates shame at the crux not of the human, but of the humane and the ethical. And while Rick does feel shame by the end of the novel, this shame does not undo the brutal violence performed by his hand and by the state. Shame without ethical action, the novel suggests, offers no relief from the inhumane practices that structure the world. With this in mind, the novel leaves us with this question: What does Rick, with his newfound shame, do tomorrow?

Coda: Emotional Robotic Art

I turn now to two feminist artworks that reconfigure human emotion around artistic production. Both of these offer technological engagements that challenge emotional labor and its attendant normalizing assumptions about emotions' universality, and the use of emotion to police borders, whether geographic or around the human. Instead, Kelly Dobson's *Omo* (2007) and Erin Gee's *Swarming Emotional Pianos* (2012–18) draw on human emotion to create aesthetic experiences.

Omo, a companion robot, is part of Dobson's project of "machine therapy," which explores the therapeutic potential of human–machine interactivity by examining the extensive yet often unnoticed ways that machines shape human experience. For Dobson, this project is in part an ethical one that models "a reflective practice of machine design and use that is of widening ethical responsibility."[68] *Omo* is a breathing, dark green, egg-shaped, rubber-coated orb with internal sensors that reads humans' breath rate, as a component of emotional expression. When cradled against the torso, *Omo* syncs up with their breathing or introduces a new breathing pattern. This pattern might soothe the holder, but it might not, as *Omo* also expresses its own emotional states, such as agitation, which can require soothing by the holder. Dobson programmed unpredictability into *Omo*, so one never quite knows what one will get when interacting with it. Thus, *Omo*'s companionship does not just respond to the human's emotional states and needs, but creates a reciprocal human–machine relation where a human's needs and desires are not always paramount.

In Erin Gee's *Swarming Emotional Pianos*, emotional labor is reconfigured into the production of a sonic performance. The piece harnesses emotion using biosensors that measure heart rate, breathing, and sweat responses, all of which shift according to different emotional states. The piece employs method actors, who are asked to generate physiological responses through their emotional states. The biosensors, in conjunction with Gee's "musical algorithms," relay commands to mobile robots that are equipped with bells.[69] These robotic musical instruments move and chime according to the biosensors' readings of physiological emotional responses. *Swarming Emotional Pianos* translates the physiology of human emotion into a sonic piece, while offering a collective experience of an individual's emotional state. This piece creates an aesthetic experience that offers an alternative telos for emotional labor; here, demands for emotional expression do not police, exclude, or monetize, but rather chime. As Gee notes in an interview, her work is based on emotion research that, like Barrett's, presumes the individuality of emotion expression

Figure 17. Erin Gee, *Swarming Emotional Pianos*, 2016. Photograph by Caitlin Sutherland.

across people as well as moments. Thus, the ephemerality of individual performances for the audience, the method actors, and the artist mirrors the nuanced specificity of an individual's emotional state, which depends on the specific environment to which the individual is responding.

Gee is explicit about the speculative dimension of her artwork. According to Gee, her work creates "speculative imaginings" that are of critical import "in a historical moment when technologies are increasingly corporatized, normalized, and territorialized by capitalist systems of production and surveillance."[70] Both Dobson's and Gee's works offer alternate relations with technology at the site of human emotion, putting emotion to work to create aesthetic experiences that imagine how human emotion might coexist with technology outside of normative demands for emotional labor. These artworks invite further speculative practices that work against claims of emotional expression's universality and the dehumanizing policing practices to which these claims and emotion recognition technologies are put to use.

4
Dying
Drone Labor, War,
and the Dehumanized

What makes for a grievable life?

—JUDITH BUTLER, *PRECARIOUS LIFE:*
THE POWERS OF MOURNING AND VIOLENCE

This chapter, in its examination of drone warfare and the labor of U.S. military drone operators, shifts from feminized modes of reproductive labor in the robotic imaginary to the labor of drone warfare, which challenges traditional notions of militarized masculinity. As drone warfare highlights, militarization and reproductive labor are intimately entangled. As Cara Daggett describes, drone warfare reorganizes two primary aspects within military service: distance/intimacy and home/combat. Drone operators do not fight "on the ground," but remotely.[1] Narratives around drone labor often negatively feminize drone operators and their bodies, comparing them to inactive video game players who do not face the same physical danger or exhibit the same physical strength as soldiers who are deployed to combat zones.[2] Additionally, drone operators often describe the unsettling proximity of their work to their domestic work, such as picking up groceries (368). Lorraine Bayard de Volo points to the ways that drone warfare, which in some ways works outside of or challenges notions of militarized masculinity, can and does create opportunities for women. However, de Volo astutely underscores, this gender equity within drone operators does not mitigate the significant gendered and racial hierarchies that structure the labor of drone warfare.[3] This chapter—which is framed by the gendered aspects of this de-masculinized military labor and the robotic imaginary's engagement with forms of feminized reproductive labor I discuss in my prior chapters—attends to these hierarchies, which I argue are embedded in the racial history of these technologies and U.S. domestic policy, as well as the present of U.S. foreign policy.

While drone operators are often devalued through characterizations associated with women's work, their labor requires them to reject aspects of the robotic imaginary's entanglement with reproductive labor—for example, the affective engagements of care and emotional labor. Instead, drone operators are asked to participate in the explicitly racial dehumanization of individuals overseas. While robots have been imagined as carers, servants, and companions for humans, drones highlight just which humans have been imagined to be the beneficiaries of these subservient AIs and robots and their reproductive labor, and just which humans have been imagined to be disposable, both in their replacement by robot workers and in their deaths by drone.

Drone Warfare and Racial Dehumanization

On February 9, 2013, the *New York Times* published an article debating the creation of a "drone court" to rule on the United States' use of armed drones. Currently, the U.S. military drone program is shrouded in tremendous secrecy.[4] For example, the United States, claiming the secrecy of covert drone strike operations, has continued to refuse UN requests for legal justification of the CIA's role in determining its targets.[5] The proposal of a drone court stems in part as a response to this secrecy. The article offered a range of opinions about whether such a court is necessary and how it might be legally implemented. In response to this article, Desmond Tutu penned a letter to the editor, published on February 12, 2013, in which he takes issue with the drone program, as well as one legislator's suggestion that the drone court only oversee drone actions that target American citizens:

> Do the United States and its people really want to tell those of us who live in the rest of the world that our lives are not of the same value as yours? That President Obama can sign off on a decision to kill us with less worry about judicial scrutiny than if the target is an American? Would your Supreme Court really want to tell human-

kind that we, like the slave Dred Scott in the 19th century, are not as human as you are? I cannot believe it.

I used to say of apartheid that it dehumanized its perpetrators as much as, if not more than, its victims. Your response as a society to Osama bin Laden and his followers threatens to undermine your moral standards and your humanity.[6]

Tutu's letter argues for the humanity of those lives the United States deems of less worth, while warning the United States that its own dehumanizing practices endanger not only those it targets, but also the nation's own humanity. By evoking U.S. slavery and South African apartheid, Tutu situates the U.S. drone program within longer histories of state-sanctioned racial violence. For Tutu, dehumanizing practices expel not just the dehumanized from the community of humans, but also those who dehumanize. Tutu's brief but searing response encapsulates the two interconnected lenses through which I examine U.S. overseas drone strikes: the history of racial state violence and oppression in the United States, and the dehumanizing limits of identification to effect ethical action.[7]

In this chapter I argue that, because of the drone, also known as an unmanned aerial vehicle (UAV), and the political and discursive aspects that shape this technology, drone practices can aptly be characterized as the labor of racial dehumanization.[8] More specifically, I argue that this labor is embedded in histories of distinct but connected racial violences, of racial dehumanization. Turning to art and literature that draw connections between overseas drone strikes and the history and present of state-sanctioned racial violence within the United States, I argue that these works productively situate contemporary drone strikes within broader contexts of state racial discrimination and dehumanization. Without collapsing the histories of the United States and nations in the Middle East and Africa, nor the different constructions of racialized Others that emerge from these discrete histories, I highlight how these works point to a broader racial violence at work that affirms the continued dominance of the post-Enlightenment Subject, as discussed by Denise da Silva, who asks, "Why is it not self-evident that, despite the pervasiveness of cultural difference, the racial and the nation still govern the global present precisely because of the way each refers to the ontological descriptors—universality and historicity—resolved in the figure of the Subject?"[9] This Subject, which grounds modern conceptions of the human in the West, is contingent on the exclusion of others—many others—on the basis of racial difference; indeed, this conception of the human is constituted by this very exclusion. Sylvia Wynter, who examines how the modern conception of the human is entangled with coloniality in ways that continue to privilege white European modes of being, works to reconceptualize the human outside the colonial framework.[10] Drawing on Wynter's work, Nishant Upadhyay argues that such connections of racial violences across nation-states and regions emphasize colonialism's continued influence and reframe racial violence as the constitutive norm of the West and of the Enlightenment Subject that is the West's ontological and epistemological center. Citing the work of Sheila Batacharya, Upadhyay writes,

> While theorizing pernicious continuities, [she] carefully asserts: "Nothing is to be gained by homogenizing, essentializing, and flattening history . . . [but] colonialism is always a factor, and the task at hand is how to materially and discursively dissect and disrupt it." . . . Examining pernicious continuities, or the colonial continuum, is not to conflate all racial and colonial violences together. Rather, it allows to locate pervasiveness of colonialism in its past and ongoing manifestations. Further, it helps to underline how race and whiteness have been foundational aspect of the Americas since 1492, and contemporary racist and exclusionary violences are not exceptional, rather deeply institutionalized and normalized within these white settler nation-states.[11]

As Upadhyay's "colonial continuum" signifies, racism and colonization are constitutive of the West and continue to shape Western societies.

Gesturing to this "colonial continuum," the art and literature I discuss reflect connections between different modes of state-sanctioned racial violence and subjugation. Drawing on the insights of da Silva, Upadhyay, and Wynter, I examine how these works of drone art place U.S. overseas drone strikes within this colonial continuum. I use the term "drone art" to indicate works of art and literature that explicitly respond to drone warfare. All of the artworks I discuss critique overseas drone strikes through an engagement with identification and its limits. Drone artworks, such as Heather Layton and Brian Bailey's *Home Drone* (2012) and James Bridle's *Drone Shadow* (2012–17), enact the inadequacies of appeals to identify with overseas victims of drone strikes. In these works, the identificatory relation both equates the human with the Western Subject and obscures the colonial continuum by constructing racial state violence as exceptional, rather than normalized and constitutive of the West itself. Other works assert the limits of this identification in the ethical relation and draw connections between drone strikes and other racial violences throughout the United States' history. These artworks—specifically Teju Cole's *Seven Short Stories about Drones* (2013), street art by Essam Attia, Bridle's *Dronestagram* (2012–15), and Omer Fast's *5,000 Feet Is the Best* (2011)—rather than seeking possibilities for identification, place the onus on the Western subject to develop an ethical relation outside of identification, familiarity, and racial hierarchies. As with Tutu's letter, these artworks, I argue, challenge conceptions of the human that simultaneously presume the humanity of the Western post-Enlightenment Subject while explicitly excluding those who are outside this narrow yet powerful conception of the human. I begin this discussion by situating my readings of drone art in the context of the history of overseas drone strikes and drone policy, and the history of cybernetics. Both histories, as I discuss, embed the racial dehumanization at work in the labor of drone warfare.

Drone Numbers

In October 2001 the United States conducted its first weaponized drone strike. Since this first strike in Afghanistan, the United States has significantly and rapidly increased its use of armed unmanned military drones. In 2011 the United States spent almost $5 billion on drone technology, up from approximately $550 million in 2002.[12] And, according to the "Living under Drones" report coauthored by Stanford Law School's International Human Rights and Conflict Resolution Clinic and New York University's School of Law's Global Justice Clinic, by 2012 the U.S. military possessed over seven thousand Predator drones, manufactured by General Atomics.[13] Currently, the United States conducts both targeted strikes, which target specific individuals identified as terrorists, and signature strikes, which target unknown individuals or groups whose "patterns of life" resemble those associated with terrorist activity as it is understood by the United States (14–15). Under the Bush administration, the United States conducted between forty-five and fifty-two drone strikes (12). By 2012, under the Obama administration, the United States had conducted 292 drone strikes (12), averaging one every four days.[14] Drone strikes and patrols have increased under the Trump administration;[15] according to the Bureau of Investigative Journalism, the number of drone strikes has doubled in Somalia and tripled in Yemen.[16]

There is no consensus on the number of civilians killed by U.S. drone strikes. According to the Bureau of Investigative Journalism, between 566 and 1,179 civilians have been killed in Yemen, Pakistan, Somalia, and Afghanistan.[17] Official Pakistani sources estimate that in 2009, approximately seven hundred civilians were killed by drone strikes.[18] The Obama administration's official civilian death toll is much, much lower—less than ten civilian deaths in Pakistan by 2012, according to the United States' count.[19] Former senior intelligence officials and members of the administration have taken issue with the White House's figures, pointing to the administration's method of counting to explain the tremendous disparity in numbers of civilian deaths. The United States considers any military-aged male (MAM) killed in a drone strike to be an enemy combatant, unless posthumous evidence to the contrary is provided. It should be noted that the United States does not investigate the identities of those killed by its drone missiles, and thus has no procedure in place to determine whether someone who was killed was a civilian or a militant.[20] Like Tutu's letter, the United States' consideration of all military-aged males as combatants raises the question of how certain human lives are counted and others discounted, and how some lives are expelled from the protected category of the human—dehumanized—in their apparent disposability and death by drone.[21]

Cybernetics, Drones, and the Racialized Other

Jamie Allinson aptly describes armed military drones as "a technology of racial distinction."[22] Before delving more deeply into the processes of dehumanization that undergird drone technology, policy, and discourses, I turn to early cybernetics as one of the historical underpinnings that have produced drone technology as such "a technology of racial distinction."

Cybernetics' formalized heyday, largely marked by the annual interdisciplinary Macy Conference, is situated between 1943 and 1954. Bringing together numerous disciplines from information theory, mathematics, anthropology, neurophysiology, and biology, cybernetics sought to facilitate and maximize control and communication between human, animal, and machine systems. The lasting legacy of cybernetic thought is incisively encapsulated by N. Katherine Hayles, who describes cybernetics as ushering in nothing short of a new conception of the human: "The result of this breathtaking enterprise was nothing less than a new way of looking at human beings. Henceforth, humans were to be seen primarily as information-processing entities who are *essentially* similar to intelligent machines."[23]

From its formal instantiation as a discipline, cybernetics was entrenched within wartime research. One need only look to founding cybernetician Norbert Wiener and his early research on antiaircraft defense systems for a direct conversation between cybernetic principles and militarized interests and applications.[24] Peter Galison argues that this wartime context significantly shaped the development of cybernetics, which he characterizes as a "war science," and its continued legacies in contemporary culture and war.[25] Galison traces cybernetics' collapse of boundaries between human and machine to the early stages of Wiener's wartime work and its conceptualization of the Enemy Other as human–machine hybrid, which merged human enemy pilots and their flying machines into a single entity. In his insightful analysis of Wiener's early work tracking and predicting the flight patterns of enemy German pilots, Galison details that for Wiener's predictive work, Allied operators were asked to participate in simulation exercises in which they were to inhabit the position of the Enemy Other—to identify with the Enemy Other as it were—in order to calculate and predict the enemy's future behavior. In the name of prediction, the hybridized enemy was incorporated into the Allied operator, and then into cybernetics' vision of the human (236–38). In Wiener's early work, the cybernetic self is not simply the result of a blurring of human and machine, but also of self and Enemy Other: "Our understanding of the cybernetic Enemy Other becomes the basis on which we understand ourselves" (265). As Wiener's early work grounds cybernetics' still-influential vision of the human as a human–machine hybrid, cybernetics' vision of the human also emerges from this identification with and incorporation of the Enemy Other.

Galison makes a distinction between what he calls the cybernetic Other, which describes the Enemy Other embodied in the blurring of German pilot and his aircraft, and a different wartime Enemy Other. This latter Enemy Other, embodied in the Japanese soldier, was not incorporated into the Allied subject, nor into cybernetics' vision of the human. This Enemy Other, which was characterized by the allies as "lice, ants, or vermin," was, Galison notes, viewed as "barely human" (230). As Galison's study highlights, the cybernetic Other and the influential vision of the human it informed emerged from the exclusion of certain Others from the category of the human on the basis of racial difference. In the construction of the cybernetic Other, Galison describes that, unlike with the dehumanized Japanese Enemy Other, "there is no sense in which Wiener sees the German bomber pilot as a racially lesser being" (264). While the cybernetic Enemy Other emerged from Allied operators' identification with German pilots, Japanese forces embodied a racialized Other that was not incorporated into Allied operators' cybernetic subjectivities, but was instead dehumanized (264). There was no collapsing of boundaries between self and Japanese Enemy Other, no identification with or incorporation of this racialized Other into the Western cybernetic Other. Wiener's wartime work, as part of the founding history of cybernetics, is thus constitutively entangled with the exclusion and dehumanization of racialized subjects, an entanglement that finds full force in the United States' armed drone policy.

Like Wiener's antiaircraft research, drones also seek to predict the behavior of the Enemy Other. However, because of the asymmetry of the drone relation—that is, the tremendous difference in immediate risk of harm for the drone operator as opposed to their targets—and the racialized discourses of the global war on terror, the drone's processes of prediction function differently; drone technology and policy do not ask drone operators to put themselves in the place of the Enemy Other of drone strikes, because this Enemy Other is the racialized Other. Though drones work to predict the behavior of this Enemy Other, they do so not from a relation of identification and sameness, but rather from a relation so asymmetric that Grégoire Chamayou describes it as "absolutely unilateral."[26] The drone operators are not asked to imagine themselves as or think like the Enemy Other; rather, they are asked to dehumanize this Other in part by reducing heterogeneous individuals to a singular Enemy Other. As Tyler Wall and Torin Monahan demonstrate, this dehumanizing erasure of difference is embedded in the drone's technological apparatus itself, as important local differences become illegible through the socio-technological codes available to drone operators: "Drones may perform predominately in the discursive register of automated precision and positive identification of known threats, but in practice, these surveillance systems and their agents actively interpret ambiguous information that continuously defies exact matches or clear responses. In the process, UAV systems may force homogenization upon difference, thereby reducing variation to functional categories that correspond to the needs and biases of the operators, not the targets, of surveillance."[27]

As my discussion of Wiener intimates, predictability comes into particular relief in histories of cybernetics that emphasize its military origins and continued applications. Indeed, predictability is highlighted in DARPA's mission statement: "creating and preventing strategic surprise."[28] In his discussion of what he calls "cybernetic warfare," Antoine Bousquet points out that in contemporary war everything is reduced to being known through measurement, quantification, and calculation. Cybernetic warfare, Bousquet details, both emerges from and perpetuates "fantasies of omniscience and omnipotence on the battlefield."[29] As Bousquet describes, this cybernetic approach led to disastrous results for the United States in the Vietnam War, and yet the allure of cybernetic warfare continues to shape contemporary warfare strategies. Drones, in their asymmetrical engagement with the enemy, may be cybernetic warfare's technology par excellence, their aerial perspectives and seeming removal of human pilots from battle seductively speaking to these "fantasies of omniscience and omnipotence." In technological actuality, however, the drone is far from omnipotent. Citing an article titled "Drones Most Accident-Prone U.S. Air Force Craft" reports, Daniel Greene describes drones as "spectacularly fallible" and notes that they crash more than any other military aircraft.[30] Drones' fallibility takes tragic shape when the myth of their omnipotence collides with that of their omniscience, a collision that is embedded in the drone apparatus itself and the racialized processes by which drone teams identify and misidentify MAMs, killing, wounding, and traumatizing thousands of individuals, including many noncombatant civilians.[31]

In 2010, between fifteen and twenty-three Afghan civilians, after being extensively surveilled by numerous individuals, were mistaken for enemy combatants and killed in a drone strike. After the operation, Air Force general James O. Poss, who led the investigation of the attack, points to the dangers of this fantasy of drone omniscience. He suggests that in the 2010 drone strike, the magnitude of surveillance information—and there was a great deal of it—did not render a clearer picture of the situation. In fact, the amount of information rendered the picture more murky. Highlighting the fallacy of technology's omniscience, Poss avers that "technology can occasionally give you a false sense of security that you can see everything, that you can hear everything, that you know everything."[32] In this situation, surveillance information did not lead to greater understanding, but to tragic misapprehension—both of the technology's limitations and of the dead civilians, whose actions were misread as terrorist activity.

As Bousquet's study demonstrates, the construction of cybernetic knowledge relies on scientific efficacy, thus privileging the cleanly and easily quantifiable over the ambiguous, messy, and complex (121–61). Hayles, in tracing the history of how information, in its constitutive materiality, came to be understood as disembodied, also points out that when information is divorced from its often messy materiality, it can be rendered stable and constant, and thus more easily measurable and abstractly manipulable.[33] These erasures—of ambiguity and uncertainty, materiality, complexity, and context—in the name of calculability continue on in drone processes in the form of dehumanizing classifications and misclassifications.[34] This cybernetic impulse to render all things not just knowable, but knowable in specifically mathematical, formulaic ways, echoes in drone labor, which requires a similar abstraction and reduction of complexity and difference. Allinson's analysis of the aforementioned 2010 strike in Afghanistan illuminates just how much is erased—how many are dehumanized—in the reduction of humans to such calculable and classificatory processes. As Allinson's analysis of the transcripts details, drone operators effortlessly aged up Afghani children to adolescents and identified nonexistent weapons in order to produce the targeted party as that killable category of military-aged male.[35] Indeed, these dehumanizing erasures continue after death, both in the United States' refusal to posthumously verify whether dead MAMs are civilians or combatants and in the United States' accounting, which excludes all dead MAMs from the civilian death toll.

Wendy Hui Kyong Chun's important formulation of race and/as technology reconceptualizes race around ethical relations rather than essence. This reconceptualization allows us "to frame the discussion around ethics rather than around ontology, on modes of recognition and relation, rather than on being."[36] Thinking about race and/as technology highlights how thoroughly drones have been shaped by race, specifically in relation to how drones are used, who they are used against, how their visual interfaces dehumanize, and who they are equipped to identify. As Chun notes race, like all technologies, has a history, which she characterizes through its uses to subjugate, oppress, and dehumanize: "Race historically has been a tool of subjugation. . . . Race in these circumstances was wielded—and is still wielded—as an invaluable mapping tool, a means by which origins and boundaries are simultaneously traced and constructed and through which the visible traces of the body are tied to allegedly innate invisible characteristics . . . [and] supposedly objective scientific categorizations of race have been employed to establish hierarchical differences between people, rendering some mere objects to be exploited, enslaved, measured, demeaned, and sometimes destroyed."[37] In her discussion of race as a "tool of subjugation," Chun traces a shift in conceptions of race from the biological to the cultural. During the eighteenth and nineteenth centuries, science located race in the biological body. In the twentieth century, the links between race and biology were disputed. Despite this de-linking of race and the body, racial categories and associations were no less intransigently attached to individuals and groups, as race was resituated in culture and racial identity was determined through cultural traits, such as clothing and religion.[38]

Mehdi Semati discusses Islamophobia specifically in the context of this relocation of race in the cultural.[39] As Semati points out, a racism grounded in culture is no less essentialist than one grounded in biology; both modes of racism render difference as the unchanging and unchangeable essence of the Other (266). In his discussion of Islamophobia after September 11, 2001, Semati cites Inderpal Grewal's "flying while brown" to describe a shift in Western conceptualizations of the Muslim Other from exotic to terrorist (257). In U.S. drone strikes, in which flying drones target brown subjects, the phrase "flying while brown" is inverted, though the racist logic preserved. Just as the collapse of self with German enemy soldier that grounds the cybernetic Other does not occur in relation to the explicitly dehumanized Japanese soldiers, with drones there is no identification with the Other of drone strikes—even for the purposes of prediction and defense. Through the eyes of the drone, there is no blurring of boundaries, cybernetic or otherwise, with the racialized enemy Other. There is only dehumanization.

Drone Art and the Limits of Identification

Nam June Paik's 1966 piece "Cybernated Art" offers art as a necessary response to cybernated life: "Cybernated art is very important, but art for cybernated life is more important, and the latter need not be cybernated."[40] If art is a necessary response to cybernated life, what response would adequately address cybernetic warfare in the age of drones? The remainder of this chapter takes up this question by looking to drone art. The genealogy of robotic art, which offers cybernetic circuits as care (as I discuss in chapter 1), highlights our common corporeal vulnerability (as I discuss in chapter 2), reimagines emotional labor as aesthetic experience rather than policing practice (chapter 3), and brings care, vulnerability, and feeling into the robotic imaginary not through devalued labor, but rather as modes of ethical coexistence with others. Thus, robotic art, which, like literature and film, is differently situated than technology in relation to war and militarized funding structures, can reimagine robotics' dominant anthropomorphic paradigms in relation to ethical questions, and thus lead us to new insights and perspectives on drone warfare and the labor of dehumanization. The remainder of this chapter looks at various works of drone art, all of which evoke identification with the Other of drone strikes. These works propose various ways to counter the dehumanization of drone victims, which includes those who have been killed by drone strikes, as well as those who have been wounded, those whose loved ones were killed, and those who are traumatized by living under the perpetual threat of drone violence. My discussion will examine the ways that artistic responses to drone strikes variously link and de-link identification with ethical possibility.

Home Drone, exhibited at the Hampden Gallery at the University of Massachusetts Amherst, is Layton and Bailey's response to drone strikes in Pakistan, Yemen, and Afghanistan. This multimedia work consists of an eighteen-foot, sequin- and rhinestone-covered drone replica that hangs from the ceiling. This drone replica points toward a map of Massachusetts, which is dotted with pins marking the locations of drone strikes in Pakistan (see Figure 18). The artists describe *Home Drone* as generating identification with the victims of drone strikes; this identification, according to Layton and Bailey, can open up ethics. As Bailey discusses, "Our point is, what we are doing to Pakistan, would you want Pakistan to do this to us? . . . It's illegal to bomb a country you are not at war with. It's unethical to kill people without due process."[41] This speculative appeal is clearly seen in the map, in which the "over there" of drone strikes in Pakistan during 2004 is overlaid onto a map of the "over here" of the United States. Using this map, the artists traveled throughout the United States to fifty spaces that correlated with drone strikes. In each place, they took photos that depict "who would've been destroyed and what would've been destroyed on site that day had they hit without notice."[42]

Home Drone echoes both military iconography as well as the scale of drone technology and policy, in which humans are swallowed up by the scale of mapmaking and individual deaths are obscured and abstracted, reduced to pins marking sites of drone strikes. The map is quite striking, with its clean lines and visually appealing design—quite the departure from the terror, chaos, and violence of a drone strike, as documented by interviews with drone strike survivors in the "Living under Drones" report. In this aesthetic disjunction, the map echoes the work's clean transposition of overseas drone strikes onto Western spaces in ways that risks eliding the differences and histories that structure this drone relation.

Drone Shadow is a series of public art installations where outlines of drones are drawn to scale in public spaces (see Figure 19). Bridle has drawn drone outlines in London, Istanbul, Brighton, and Washington, D.C.; he has also created and circulated the *Drone Shadow Handbook,* which allows others to draw drone outlines around the world. Drones, according to Bridle, are couched in invisibility, both in their operation and in the deliberate obfuscation of information about the technology. Despite their invisibility, Bridle writes that "we all live under the shadow of the drone, although most of us are lucky enough not to live under its

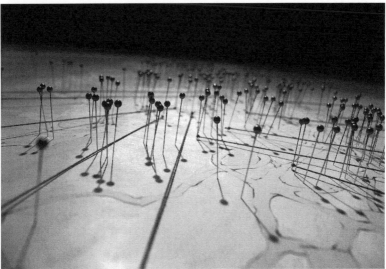

Figure 18. Heather Layton and Brian Bailey, *Home Drone,* installation view, 2012.

direct fire."[43] In order to produce a shared affectivity with those living with the threat of drone strikes, *Drone Shadow* speaks to the drone's simultaneous invisibility and omnipresence by evoking the sense of "feeling" the drone's presence in the sky.

Figure 19. *Drone Shadow 007,* London, 2014. Photograph from James Bridle / booktwo.org.

In addition to heightening the visibility of overseas drone strikes to Western audiences, these works also raise questions about the limitations of identification within the colonial continuum. Both works stage their aesthetic interventions around an appeal to an identificatory relation between a largely Western audience and those overseas who live under the threat of drone strikes. By foregrounding cultural and experiential familiarity for the Western viewer as the means to achieve identification, the works seek to recuperate the humanity of drone victims through Western conceptions of the human, conceptions that largely exclude Western subjects who are immigrants or people of color. Drones are shaped by histories of racial dehumanization, colonialism, and imperialism.[44] Because, in the drone relation, identification and its implicit inscription of the Western post-Enlightenment human is also shaped by these same histories, drone art that engages identification without engaging its imbrication within histories of racial dehumanization, colonialism, slavery, and imperialism are limited in their critiques of drone strikes, and thus limited in their capacities to imagine possible worlds without drone strikes.

Both *Home Drone* and *Drone Shadow* overlay the reality of drone violence onto a Western "here" in order to generate identification with drone victims. In this way, these works attempt to bridge the empathetic distance between the over there of drone strikes where, as the interviews documented in the "Living under Drones" report detail, the trauma of living under their threat has become a terrifying part of daily life, and a here that is meant to evoke a place safe from the threat of such violence. The here (Massachusetts, London, Washington, D.C.) functions as a space where it is purportedly unthinkable that such extreme violence can occur, much less with frequency; the here also functions as a space where such violence on its inhabitants could quite easily evoke outrage and grief.[45] Consequently, the protected and privileged space of the here also inscribes certain subjects as unthinkable as victims of drone violence. And drone strikes are evoked as events of exceptional violence that occur overseas, rather than part of a continuum of state-sanctioned racial violence that occurs in the West and is, as Upadhyay notes, both normalized and foundational to the production of the West. In this regard, these two pieces work against themselves and the artists' respective appeals to identification in interesting ways.

These works both invoke a mode of identification that does not challenge the fundamental dehumanization that undergirds the drone strike as a form of racial violence, while also highlighting the limits of this identification and the constructions of "over there" and "here" the works articulate. In this model of identification, empathetic and ethical response is generated by posing hypothetical scenarios in which the Western Subject, whose humanness is presumed, is threatened by drone strikes. These drone artworks highlight that in retaining, rather than challenging, the post-Enlightenment human and its foundations in racial sorting and dehumanization, these appeals for identification are ultimately limited by the same conceptual framework that enables drone strikes. In other words, these relations of identification and empathy share the biopolitical logic of dehumanization that undergirds drone violence and technology—the idea that, in the name of protecting certain valued humans, others who are viewed as unfamiliar, and thus not viewed as comparably human, can and must be killed, remains unchallenged.[46] These lives are not only viewed as killable, but in their dehumanization they are, as Judith Butler writes, constructed as lives incapable of being mourned and grieved.

According to Butler, difference is the condition of identification. Identification seeks to overcome difference, but identification can never do so without reinscribing the difference by which identification can exist. In her discussion of how representations, particularly those of war, variously humanize and dehumanize lives, Butler distinguishes between what she calls the triumphalist image and the critical image. The triumphalist image purports to have vanquished difference in the identificatory relation, while the critical image both fails to overcome difference and represents this very failure. The critical image thus points to the larger frameworks that structure representation and its capacities and failures to reflect meaning, as well as worlds, geopolitics, and socialities.[47] In their attempts to overcome the difference between over there and over here, in part by constructing the United States as a space of safety where such systematized state violence is unthinkable, *Home Drone* and *Drone Shadow* illustrate the limits of this triumphalist image in drone warfare, as it obscures the history of state violence wielded against minority populations in the West, as well as how this history and present are linked to overseas drone strikes.

The ambiguity produced by these works' site-specificity can either hold up a fantasy of the West as a site of safety and justice when that is not the experience for many in the United States, both past and present, or challenge precisely this construction. Depending on who is viewing the works and where (e.g., a *Drone Shadow* drawn in al-Rawdah, Yemen, would function very differently than one drawn in London), these works can either obscure domestic experiences of vulnerability and violence largely experienced by minorities, or articulate vulnerability and state violence as a commonality or shared experience between "over there" and "here." Similarly, *Home Drone* and *Drone Shadow* can be read as erasing important existing commonalities between these two spaces, or emphasizing their relation on the colonial continuum. Greene gestures to this commonality and historical continuity in his description of those put most at risk by emerging drone technology as "the usual suspects": "The weight of drones' attention overwhelmingly falls on 'the usual suspects' (e.g., racial minorities, poor migrants, anti-state protestors), no matter where they find themselves. Technology transfer is always also cultural transfer."[48] Resituating these drones "here" with an intent to aesthetically jar the Western viewer into an identificatory relation can erase the ways that state violence and surveillance functions within the "here" of Western democracies for "the usual suspects," thus enacting the "cultural transfer" that enables the prejudicial targeting of minority populations, or it can illustrate the limits of an identificatory relation centered around the Western post-Enlightenment subject and grounded in a construction of the West as a space outside of unthinkable state-sanctioned racial violence.

In discussing the construction of "Third World Woman" by Western feminist thought, Chandra Mohanty warns that the logic of identification through a specifically Western recognition and familiarity does a certain amount of epistemological and ontological violence by abstracting, distorting, and desubjectifying non-Western Subjects and presuming the Western here and the Western Subject as the comparative center.[49] Drawing on Mohanty's insight, I suggest that drone art that appeals to identificatory affectivity subordinates ethical response and the other of drone strikes to the viewer's capacity to imagine herself, within the context of Western familiarity, as a victim of drone violence. The shock that hopefully leads to empathetic identification is one that defines the West as a place of safety, privacy, and nonviolence. This "home" is a place that is premised on post-Enlightenment notions of freedom and agency, concepts which minority populations, including within the United States, have long been excluded from claiming and around which the United States' drone program is justified.

Thus, *Home Drone* and *Drone Shadow* critique their own appeals for identification. In generating identification between largely Western viewers and victims of drone strikes, the works point to the risks of erasing the colonial and Orientalist histories that co-construct the West and the other of drone strikes while denying the affinities between those considered disposable in the United States and overseas.[50] The works highlight identification's inability to critique the dehumanization that requires such transposition onto familiarity in order to generate identification and ethical response. Within the identificatory relations the artworks evoke, drone dehumanization is critiqued while maintaining the primacy of the post-Enlightenment conception of the human. As the works demonstrate, an ethical and empathetic response that emerges only when the other of drone strikes is resituated within the familiarity of the West and its purported safety points to the failure of identification. If identification does not challenge the colonial and racial foundations of the Western human, this identification continues to privilege the colonial logic that shapes U.S. drone policy itself, the dehumanization of the non-Western subjects who live under drone strikes, and the continued oppression of minority populations within the United States.

For too long in the West, Alexander Weheliye writes, the category of the human has excluded nonwhite subjects: "Overall, I construe race, racialization, and racial identities as ongoing sets of political relations that require, through constant perpetuation via institutions, discourses, practices, desires, infrastructures, languages, technologies, sciences, economies, dreams, and cultural artifacts, the barring of nonwhite subjects from the category of the human as it is performed in the modern west."[51] The artists' speculative appeals, such as "What would drone strikes look like if we were the targets rather than unknown people in a place too distant to imagine?"[52] do not destabilize the notion of the human from which nonwhite subjects have historically been excluded, but rather transposes the threat of drone violence onto those whose (Western) humanness is always already presumed. Thus, the ethical thought experiments the artworks invoke do not broach the racial dehumanization of the non-Western Subject that is at the heart of drone strikes and that enables drone strikes to be imagined and implemented as such. In the thought experiments, the Western Subject is reinscribed as the proper subject of sympathy who must be de facto protected from such violence and terror. However, the works, in their more complex constructions of the United States, the West, and the connections drawn at the site of drone strikes, challenge the very premise of Layton and Bailey's question and its belief in identificatory practices. Instead, the works highlight that without acknowledging the constitutive conceptual chasm between the human and the dehumanized at work in the concept of the human and in drone violence, the capacity to address the ethical dimensions of drone strikes remains limited.

The street art of E. Adam Attia, who works under the name ESSAM, responds to drone strikes by explicitly connecting U.S. overseas drone policy to existing domestic practices of racial discrimination and violence. In 2012, Attia, a former military geospatial analyst in Iraq, installed

Figure 20. ESSAM, poster depicting family running from law enforcement drone, 2012.

over one hundred posters in bus stops around Manhattan. These posters depict the silhouette of a drone, presumably the property of the NYPD, firing a missile at a fleeing family (see Figure 20).[53] Street signs, which also bear the name of the NYPD, similarly imagine drone strikes in use in New York by the police (see Figure 21).[54] For example, the sign in Figure 21 reads, "ATTENTION Authorized Drone Strike Zone 8 a.m.–8 p.m. including Sunday"; while another, placed underneath existing Department of Transportation signs denoting parking restrictions, reads, "ATTENTION Local Statutes Enforced by Drone." By imagining drone strikes as regular, everyday events (at least between the hours of 8 a.m. and 8 p.m.), the works stage the normalization of drone strikes within the United States. Attia's work highlights the technological intimacy between the military and police departments, which are increasingly deploying military technology including drones.[55] His works also gesture to the police department's tense relationship with minority populations, particularly black and Latinx communities, from the NYPD's controversial stop-and-frisk program, which disproportionately stops black and Latino men; to the killing of black men, recently Akai Gurley and Eric Garner, by NYPD officers.[56] These works of street art, by connecting the racial dehumanization of drone victims to formal and informal U.S. domestic policies that discriminate against racial minorities, particularly black men and women, highlight the fundamental dehumanization undergirding drone strikes as a form of racial violence. Attia's street signs and posters do not elide the

Figure 21. ESSAM, street sign announcing drone strikes in front of the Guggenheim Museum, 2012.

histories of racial state violence, but in fact connect the violent racial othering involved in overseas drone strikes and the violent racial othering that takes place within the United States. As the use of drones for policing within the United States increases (e.g., the New York police commissioner has publicly voiced his interest in incorporating drone technology in its police practices), the connections highlighted by these works take on even greater resonance.[57]

Attai's works do not elide the fact that only certain people enjoy a sense of freedom and safety in the United States, that only certain people understand the state as working to protect their lives and freedoms. These works do not homogenize the American experience around the idea of safety, nor do they hold that empathy is contingent on recognition of familiarity. As Attia's street art highlights, racial state violence and oppression binds these geographic spaces together (the United States, Pakistan, Afghanistan, Yemen). The lack of empathy for and identification with drone victims, which *Home Drone* insightfully identifies, speaks to this racial dehumanization, where "the human" is defined against racial difference.[58] The biopolitical logic by which brown bodies *must* be killed for the security of the lives that count (again, not the black and brown lives that continue to be oppressed in the United States, and in whom the state shows an outsized carceral interest) is, as Michel Foucault's early theorizations of the biopolitical insist, fundamentally grounded in a racism that constructs the justification for this paradoxical hypocrisy in which the state is so invested in life that it must end life.[59] Within this logic, it is only certain lives that are valued and deemed worthy of protection and nurturing, while other lives are perceived solely as a threat to and necessary expenditure for the lives that count, the lives that are deemed worthy of grief.

Against Identification: Life, Grief, and Mourning in Teju Cole's *Seven Short Stories about Drones*

On January 15, 2013, Teju Cole released a series of short stories on Twitter. *Seven Short Stories about Drones* was composed for Twitter ("short," then, referring to Twitter's limit at the time of 140 characters) and also published in the *New Yorker* and the *New Inquiry*. A response to the United States' military drone policy, each story reimagines the opening lines of famous literary works through drone strikes.

In an essay attempting to reconcile President Obama's love of reading with his drone policies, Cole laments literature's failure to induce a more expansive ethical imagination in "the reader in chief."[60] Cole's stories, which were published as part of this essay, function in the context of this failure; the stories rewrite canonical works of literature that are, to a disillusioned Cole, limited in their capacities to shape a more ethical and humane present. And yet, rather than turn away from literature, Cole, in the form of his stories, turns toward literature to make sense of its own limits.

Seven Short Stories, in its examination of literature's ethical failure, highlights the limits of identification, particularly in relation to the act of reading. The stories withhold a specific and, for many, familiar reading practice: that of identifying through reading. In *Seven Short Stories*, the reader is expressly not permitted to access an other through readerly identification with characters and their experiences. This refusal of identification, within the context of canonical, and for some readers familiar, texts, disorients and unsettles as the stories cut off the opening lines of novels from their narrative trajectories. These short bursts of fiction, cir-

Figure 22.
Teju Cole, *Seven Short Stories about Drones,* screenshot.

culated and recirculated throughout Twitter, destroy not just the reader's capacity to engage in identificatory reading practices, but as Marco Werman notes, also the novels' status as beloved cultural objects themselves.[61] In this way, the stories violently disorient reading practices and narrative expectations around these canonical works. In their brevity and abrupt endings, Cole's stories obstruct readerly identification with existing literary works and characters. The stories are not what we expect them to be; rather, in the form of drone violence, they become something else entirely, thus bluntly foreclosing the continuation of the original novels.

If, as Butler asserts, identification is predicated on difference, Cole's stories, in their resistance to readerly identification, represent the inscription of difference that impedes identification in the drone relation. This difference emerges from colonialism, from the racial sorting that constitutes both the post-Enlightenment human and the colonial relation, and from the dehumanization of racialized Others. In questioning identification, Cole's stories also challenge the causal relation between identification and ethics and reframe ethics absent identification. Each story evokes a character, either by name (stories 1, 2, 3, 5, and 6) or by focalization (stories 4 and 7), thus heightening the ways that identification as a reader is both acknowledged and resisted. In highlighting the failure to produce identification, the works resonate with the larger political and ethical failures of Western identification with those who live under drone strikes. And in so doing, the stories gesture to the histories of colonialism, racism, and empire that have elevated certain lives as human while dehumanizing others, rendering them not-human and thus not worthy or capable of being part of an identificatory, much less ethical, relation.

As the threat of drone violence hovers over these texts, *Seven Stories* renders the original works themselves as extant narrative and aesthetic possibilities that are obliterated by drone strikes. The novels, in their narrative teloi and extended lives prior to Cole's stories, become reframed as possibilities that, through drone violence, are foreclosed. And in this foreclosure, the stories render the original novels as shadowy hauntings of the short stories that bear the same first words. In this way, Cole's stories create a sense of mourning for the original novels, the possibilities that cannot emerge because of drone violence. Cole's stories render both texts—the original novel and his rewriting—ghostly memories of the other that linger and continue to travel together. To return to *Mrs. Dalloway* now is to read with an altered sense of loss and mourning, as the novel is, in conversation with Cole's stories, part ghost. *Mrs. Dalloway* is now both a story about the eponymous protagonist's day and the documentation of what was lost when "a signature strike leveled the florist's."[62]

This sense of mourning also extends to Cole's drone stories. Rather than asking the reader to identify with victims of drone violence, Cole's stories ask her to mourn them, thus reconstituting the drone relation as one of perpetual mourning: mourning for the lives ended and wounded by drone violence, for those traumatized by living in proximity to drone violence, and for the possible worlds that become increasingly unimaginable as the drone program races on. In Cole's stories, literature simultaneously represents and withholds the victims of drone strikes, who are obscured by canonical characters and texts. The stories do not render the victims of drone strikes known as objects of empathy or identification. Cole's stories, in privileging mourning over identification, implore the reader to mourn a life, absent knowing that life or identifying with that life. In other words, Cole's stories argue for an expansive capacity for mourning that is not predicated on the perception of familiarity and sameness. In this way, the stories point to the limits of identification not only in reading, but also in ethical praxis. Cole's stories insist on a sociality that affirms our constitutive difference from and unknowability to one another. The mode of sociality suggested by Cole's stories insists on proof of humanity through the repeated refusal to dehumanize others, including unknown and unknowable others, despite the long histories of colonialism and empire that insist on this dehumanization in the drone relation (but certainly not only in the drone relation). In the context of drone strikes, the lessons of literature, Cole's stories suggest, are not found in the capacity to identify, but in the capacity to mourn outside a relation of identification. *Seven Stories* refuses to evacuate grief and mourning from the drone relation, and reframes mourning as that which must take place not despite difference, but because of it. Butler connects dehumanization and military violence after 9/11 to questions of whose lives are publicly grieved and mourned and whose are not: "But we have to consider how the norm governing who will be a grievable human is circumscribed and produced in these acts of permissible and celebrated public grieving, how they sometimes operate in tandem with a prohibition on the public grieving of others' lives, and how this differential allocation of grief serves the derealizing aims of military violence."[63] Cole's stories suggest that it is not the responsibility of another to prove herself worthy of grief and mourning; rather, responsibility lies in the capacity to grieve for another— for an Other—while apprehending difference. Highlighting the centrality of familiarity to grief and, by extension identification, Butler asks, "But at what cost do I establish the familiar as the criterion by which a human life is grievable?"[64] Cole's drone works speak to Butler's important question by expanding ethical response beyond identification and the familiar, refusing familiarity itself as the ground for ethical action, grief, and inclusion into a community of humans.

On Twitter, an image accompanies every tweet (see Figure 22).[65] Cole's designated picture is an image of the author in profile; his face is turned toward the stories, claiming them both as author and witness. This image connotes a refusal to look away from the drone violence in the stories. The stories themselves are short—too short. It is up to the reader, like Cole's image, to keep looking long after the stories end. In this way, the stories somberly engage Cole's lament of literature's failure to rewrite the world and look to different modes of reading to recoup some of literature's ethical promise. Some reading practices provide no challenge to, no friction against, the long history of individuals being brutally dehumanized by those claiming sole province to the concept of the human. Other modes of reading center and attempt to dismantle this dehumanization, thus opening up the possibility of new worlds in which Cole's drone stories might become mere fictional hauntings, rather than the documentation of dehumanization's perpetual presence in war, art, and human life. But until then, in Cole's stories it is the original novels, cut short as soon as they begin, that become the ghostly specters, the worlds made impossible by drone violence, as the image of Cole, repeated and unchanging, continues to look.

The Dehumanizing Limits of Drone Vision:
Dronestagram and *#NotaBugSplat*

Like Cole's *Seven Short Stories,* James Bridle's *Dronestagram* responds to drone strikes by exploring the limits of identification. Challenging popular narratives of drones' near-omniscience, *Dronestagram*'s critique of identification takes shape around the limits of drone vision. *Dronestagram,* which displays Google Earth satellite images of locations hit by drones, takes place on multiple social media platforms, with iterations on Instagram (a photo-sharing website; see Figure 23), Tumblr (a blog-hosting site; see Figure 24), and Twitter. The satellite images are accompanied by narrative accounts of each strike (compiled from a variety of journalistic sources), for example: "March 10 2013. 2–3 killed by a strike in North Waziristan on the Afghan/Pakistan border, riding horses or motorbikes. Identities unknown. Rescue work was reportedly delayed as drones hovered over the area after the strike. #pakistan #drone #drones (at Datta Khel, Pakistan)"; and "February 8: up to 9 killed and 6 injured in a strike

Figure 23. *Dronestagram* on Instagram. James Bridle, *Dronestagram,* 2013–15.

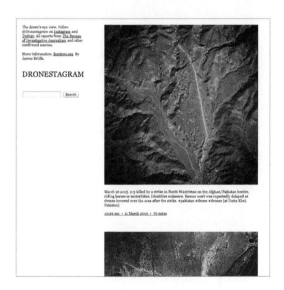

Figure 24. *Dronestagram* on Tumblr. James Bridle, *Dronestagram,* 2013–15.

on two separate mud-built houses on the North–South Waziristan border. Local sources reported that 'Six drones were hovering in the sky at the time of the attack' and 'Fear prevailed in the area as more drones were flying in the air halting the rescuers to launch an operation to take out bodies from the debris of the destroyed house.' #drone #drones #pakistan (at Babar Ghar, South Waziristan)." Google Earth images are not taken in real time, so the photos of the areas targeted by drone strikes were most likely taken prior to the strike.[66] This temporal uncertainty illustrates a representational failure, as the image almost certainly captures a referent that no longer exists as such. The satellite image depicts what was there prior to the drone strike, what no longer exists as such. While this temporality can certainly be said to characterize photography more generally as a medium that is in time, *Dronestagram* exploits photography's temporal dislocation to gesture to what was lost in the drone strike. *Dronestagram*'s documentation of drone strikes evokes mourning and loss—of people killed, as given in the narrative accounts, of worlds and spaces that can no longer be apprehended as they were, but only mourned. In the conversation between the image and the narrative accounts of drone strikes, *Dronestagram* stages a persistent confrontation with a time before the drone strike. A disorientation emerges from the interplay between the narrative accounts of drone strikes and their aftermaths, and the work's multiple temporal gaps, from the ambiguous time the Google Earth images were taken, to the clearly stated dates of the strikes, to the time stamp indicating when Bridle uploaded the photos and narrative accounts, to the varied and multiple times of individual viewing. This temporal disorientation underscores the uncertainty of drone vision, which obscures more than it sees, particularly in relation to the human. *Dronestagram*'s depiction of a time before drone strikes unsettles, demonstrating the ways the image does not, indeed cannot, depict that which it purports to depict. In this way, *Dronestagram* challenges both the authority of drone vision, metaphorized by Google Earth's satellite views, and fantasies of drone omniscience by representing the failures of drone seeing. In *Dronestagram,* the aerial image can only point to its own inadequacy to represent and to drone vision's inadequacy to see. In this context, drones, with their teasing promises of omniscience, do not help to cut through "the fog of war," the confusions and uncertainties that accompany war practices; rather, as *Dronestagram* highlights, drones, as part of a larger technological and ideological apparatus, significantly contribute to the obscured vision referenced by that "fog of war."

Dronestagram highlights that the aerial drone perspective (and the Google Earth satellite image that stands in for this perspective) dehumanizes. Drone technology and discourses presume the objecthood and killability of those the drone surveils. Like drone vision, the satellite image in *Dronestagram* is not scaled to the human, but to the dehumanized, the scale at which individuals are largely indistinguishable from one another and look more like insects. Thus, *Dronestagram* highlights that drone vision and the technological, political, and discursive apparatuses by which military drones "see," are not designed to identify humans, but rather to surveil and target the already racially dehumanized. Those who fall under the eye of the drone are not a priori human, but always already dehumanized targets.

Somewhat akin to Cole's work, *Dronestagram* resists identification with the other of drone violence. Daniel Greene reads *Dronestagram* as eliciting empathy with the drone and its apparatus of surveillance, rather than with the humans who are locked in its sight.[67] I agree with Greene that *Dronestagram,* which mediates accounts of drone violence through slick, bloodless interfaces on user-friendly social media platforms, highlights the drone's perspective. Indeed, this is how *Dronestagram* challenges the primacy of identification for ethical praxis in relation to drone violence. *Dronestagram*'s insistence on the dehumanizing drone perspective highlights the challenges, perhaps the impossibility, of individuals to be viewed as human from the perspective of the drone. There is an intractable distance—in the temporality and the scale of aerial machine perspective, as well as the asymmetry of the drone relation and the colonial histories that shape this relation—that points to an inaccessibility of the Other, and thus of identification. The incommensurability of *Dronestagram*'s cool, sterile interfaces with the horror and chaos generated by drone violence, the abject failure of the satellite image to represent the human face of drone victims, gives pause and highlights the ways that drone vision itself is incompatible with the human. The drone, with which the viewer identifies in *Dronestagram,* cannot perceive the human, as the drone sees only objects, targets to eliminate.[68] *Dronestagram*'s aesthetic experience, then, leaves us with a heightened awareness of drone vision's capacious limits and its incapacity to perceive the human.

The artwork's temporal disjunction highlights that even with the drone—especially with the drone—omniscience is an impossible fantasy. Despite the claims of much discourse around drones, drone vision is a limited mode of seeing that entails significant and unacceptable limits. The drone's dehumanizing gaze, born out of Enlightenment subjectivity and its entanglement with colonialism and racism, is predisposed to see certain lives not as humans but as expendable and threatening targets. *Dronestagram* enacts the drone's inability to perceive the human. The viewer, who can only encounter what she cannot see, is subject to the dehumanizing limits of drone vision. But the viewer cannot even access the drone's limited vision, as the Google Earth image only stands in for what the drone sees and does not see.

Both Cole's *Seven Short Stories* and Bridle's *Dronestagram* gesture to responses to drone violence that are outside the identificatory relation. In this way, these works gesture toward ethical responses that are predicated on the impossibility of knowing, a predication that runs counter to cybernetics' central tenets of predictability and knowability. This knowing as not-knowing resonates less with cybernetic warfare's dangerous fantasies of omniscience and more with Donna Haraway's feminist objectivity, which posits knowing as always specifically situated, and thus partial. Haraway's objectivity, in its partiality, insists on accounting for positions and knowledges other than one's own without claiming them or mediating them through one's own experience.[69] In their respective challenges to identification, Cole's and Bridle's works reject the impulse to "humanize" drone strike victims by grounding them within the familiarity of the modern West and its narrow conception of the human.

As *Dronestagram* highlights, drone vision, in its scale and the political and cultural discourses that frame and shape it, is dehumanizing. Noah Shachtman's 2005 article about Fort Huachuca, Arizona, where soldiers are trained to operate drones, describes U.S.–Mexico Border Patrol footage taken fifteen thousand feet away, from a Hunter drone. According to Shachtman, from that distance, the eighty immigrants being surveilled looked like "germs" and "ants," "especially when the anthill breaks apart, and everybody scatters in a dozen different directions."[70] Strikingly, Shachtman's description of Mexican immigrants as "ants" echoes Allied forces' description of World War II Japanese soldiers. This resonance underscores that dehumanizing racial metaphors, alongside early cybernetic science, continue to shape militarized AI technologies. Wall and Monahan point to Shachtman's description of drone technology's deindividuation and objectification: "The drone system radically homogenizes these identities into a single cluster of racialized information that is used for remote-controlled processes of control and harm. Bodies below become things to track, monitor, apprehend, and kill, while the pilot and other allies on the network remain differentiated and proximate, at least culturally if not physically."[71] As Wall and Monahan demonstrate, the scale of drone vision also dehumanizes in its erasure of difference, which creates a racialized homogeneity that collapses all individuals into an indistinguishable threat.

#NotaBugSplat, an installation by a group of Pakistani artists, directly engages the dehumanizing scale of drone vision. According to Butler's reading of Levinas, the human is the representational limit of the face; it is the inadequacy of the face to represent the human that the face connotes.[72] By way of this representational inadequacy, the face of the other humanizes, represents its own inadequacy, thus gesturing to the other as human. To see the face's representational failure, and thus to see the human, is to engage the other on a scale at which this failure can be perceived. This is not the scale of drone vision and its metaphors. Indeed, drone vision, with its aerial perspective and its narrow classificatory choices, works to evade the scale at which such recognition of the other's humanness can take place. *#NotaBugSplat* fights this drone dehumanization at the level of scale by placing large posters of Pakistani children outside, where the posters can be seen from drones (see Figure 25). The children's faces, enlarged so as to be visible from the perspective of the drone flying overhead or of the satellite in orbit, are appeals to the drone operators to see the humans who inhabit the area they surveil and target. As the name of the project connotes, the artists, in collaboration with local citizens, combat the dehumanizing scale of drone vision in which humans appear as small dots, more like "little bugs" than humans, and the subsequent dehumanizing military jargon that metaphorizes dead drone victims as "bug splats."[73]

#NotaBugSplat deliberately features images of children, a protected class in drone decision-making. However, as the transcripts of the 2010 Afghanistan strike illustrate, even the privileged status of childhood is no guarantee against dehumanization when the child is seen through the eyes of the drone. As the transcripts also demonstrate, there is no consensus on

Figure 25. Artist collective, *#NotaBugSplat* installation, 2014.

what constitutes childhood (a protected category) and what constitutes adolescence (a killable category). In Allinson's reading of the transcripts, childhood offered no protection against drone death: in order to ensure that the strike proceeded, children were "aged up" to adolescent, and thus identified as military-aged males. In this incident, Allinson notes, race erases protections granted by childhood.[74] Robin Bernstein's book *Racial Innocence: Performing American Childhood from Slavery to Civil Rights* traces the U.S. phenomena in which black children are not accorded the same sense of innocence and youth as are white children.[75] In the transcripts of the 2010 Afghanistan strike, an analogous logic is at work, in which Afghani children are not seen as children, but as menacing threats that can, or must, be killed.

Despite the transcripts' focus on the operators' decision-making process, race as a factor precedes and shapes the drone operators' decisions in the moment leading up to a drone strike. Race is embedded in the history of surveillance and surveillance technologies. As Simone Browne's book *Dark Matters: On the Surveillance of Blackness* demonstrates, the history of surveillance is entangled with the history of transatlantic slavery and the continued targeting of blackness.[76] Surveillance, a technology of racial sorting and subjugation, structures drone technology and its dehumanizing tendencies. *#NotaBugSplat*'s representation of young drone victims as humans is in tension with drone technology and the drone operators' labor, which trains them to view those who come into the frame of their drone surveillance as bugs or dehumanized and threatening racial Others. In this way, *#NotaBugSplat* is also in tension with the longer history of race as a technology and the early history of cybernetics, both of which insist on the explicit disidentification with and the dehumanization of the racialized Other.

Identification Disoriented in Omer Fast's *5,000 Feet Is the Best*

In its engagement with drone warfare, Omer Fast's short film *5,000 Feet Is the Best* uses disorientation to highlight racial dehumanization as the boundary between identification and disidentification. The film does not refuse identification, but rather vacillates between encouraging and foreclosing identification, all the while highlighting the problematic centrality of familiarity within the identificatory relation.[77] Fast's film, part of a larger installation piece that debuted at the Venice Biennale, disorientingly plays with identification and difference in such a way that defamiliarizes what is purportedly familiar in the identificatory relation, laying bare the ways familiarity can be used to dehumanize. Intercutting fictional segments with documentary elements, Fast's film produces an uneasy and uncertain experience. The fictional segments center on an interview with a drone operator in a dark Las Vegas hotel room. The scene of the pilot and the interviewer's introductory meeting repeats three times, taking a new narrative direction with each iteration. In these repetitions, the operator tells the interviewer three different stories, each ostensibly meant to describe the experience of operating a drone. In the first story, a man breaks in to a train station to drive a train. In the second story a Las Vegas couple (a man and a woman) use seduction to trick men out of their pants and steal their credit card numbers. And in the third story an innocent family on a weekend drive becomes collateral damage in a drone strike. These disjointed fictional segments, narrated with voiceover by the fictional drone operator, are intercut with footage of Fast's interview with "Brandon," a former drone operator struggling with post-traumatic stress disorder.

Fast's film plays with the limits of representability. The blend of fictional and nonfictional elements highlights the limits of both genres and the limits of representation more broadly. At every turn, the film eludes closure and definitive meaning, disorienting the viewer on the level of genre and narrative. Through this disorientation, *5,000 Feet* persistently refuses the viewer's immersion into the world of the film, despite drawing on numerous cinematic tropes, genres, and clichés to evoke familiarity.[78] While the fictional segments, in their looping repetitions, and the operator's three disjointed stories all speak to the failure of both cinematic representation and identification, the nonfictional interview segments, with the operator's blurred face and masked voice, point to the possibility of a successful representation that must be thwarted. According to the film's transcript, Brandon is the only character in the film with a name. And yet his name is a pseudonym. Rather than going unnamed, Brandon is deliberately misnamed, a tactic to again deflect the promise and threat of representation's success. The disorienting elements of the film convey that representation cannot be trusted; at the same time, the nonfictional interview segments, with their intimations of a belief in representation, convey that even the mistrust of representation suggested by the film must be questioned. The culmination of these elements suggests that this story is told through distorted and disorientating uncertainties, with no clear answer to how the viewer should read or make sense of the film.[79]

As mentioned above, the opening conversation between drone operator and interviewer is repeated three times, each time leading into a different fictional vignette:

THE INTERVIEWER
Okay. What is the difference between you and someone who sits in an airplane?

THE PILOT
There's no difference between us. We do the same job.

THE INTERVIEWER
But you're not a real pilot.

THE PILOT
So what? You're not a real journalist.

THE INTERVIEWER
No, I mean . . .

THE PILOT

I know what you mean. You're thinking about . . .

The repetition of this opening conversation disorients, all the more so because this scene contains a sudden, piercing noise that represents the operator's sharp stomach pain. The noise is loud and grating, simultaneously drawing the viewer into the private pain of the operator and jolting the viewer outside the film to tend to her own physical discomfort. It is this uncertain terrain, the simultaneous invitation into and propulsion out of the world of the film, on which the film examines identification in the drone relation. Refusing to offer any possibility of immersion or solid grounding on which to lay interpretive claim, the film's most powerful disorientations center around race. In the first vignette, as narrated by the drone operator, a young black man who, as a boy, was obsessed with model trains, steals a train conductor's uniform and key card, breaks into a train station, and takes a train through its route. The young man is arrested when he returns home and, having forgotten his house key, breaks in to his own house. At this point, the interviewer's voice breaks into the vignette and asks, "Okay, so why does the guy have to be black?" As the drone operator responds with "I didn't say he was black. Did anyone mention color?" the film switches out the black actor with a white actor, thus recasting the vignette right before its culmination (see Figures 26 and 27). In 2009, Henry Louis Gates Jr., a black man and a prominent scholar of African American history, was arrested at his own home while attempting to enter through a jammed door.[80] In echoing Gates's widely publicized arrest and ongoing conversations about racial profiling and discrimination by the police, the film's disorienting recasting connects drone strikes with the history of racial discrimination by the state. This strange moment of racial disorientation also hints at the third vignette, which brings drone strikes into direct conversation with racial assumptions and the role of race in the identificatory relation.

In the opening of the third vignette, a white, suburban family (father, mother, son, daughter) pile into their station wagon for a weekend trip.[81] This archetypal scene of American suburban life soon becomes unfamiliar, as the drone operator's voice-over narrates their journey from their driveway in their suburban neighborhood to checkpoints manned by occupying Chinese military: "So the family drives down their quiet block on

Figure 26. Black train conductor. Omer Fast, *5,000 Feet Is the Best,* 2011, Commonwealth Projects.

Figure 27. White train conductor. Omer Fast, *5,000 Feet Is the Best,* 2011, Commonwealth Projects.

a weekend morning on their way to the country. They take a left and a right. Stop at the usual checkpoints, present their documents to the occupying forces. It's the same familiar route dad takes every day of the week when he drives to work." After they pass the checkpoint, the family encounters three white men, armed with semiautomatic weapons. The men are digging in the middle of the road, presumably to plant an impro-

Figure 28. White men in "traditional headdress" and "clothes more typical to tribes from further south." Omer Fast *5,000 Feet Is the Best,* 2011, Commonwealth Projects.

vised bomb (see Figure 28).[82] The film plays with the racial coding of language, describing the men's baseball caps as "traditional headdress," and their jeans, T-shirts, and jackets as "clothes more typical to tribes from further south." Though these men, armed and menacing, appear to be up to no good, they let the family pass by. Unbeknownst to the men and the family, the men are being watched by a Chinese military drone, and the film gives us a glimpse of the men from the drone's perspective in the moments leading up to the firing of a Hellfire missile. The missile roundly obliterates the men. The family also dies in the drone strike.[83] After their deaths, the family exits the car and continues down the road on foot: "They will never be buried."

In the casting of this vignette, Fast's film, on the one hand, entices the viewer to mourn, and perhaps identify with, the scared, white family. However, this identification with the sympathetically depicted family is destabilized by disorienting elements—namely, the occupying Chinese forces and the white men described using Orientalist language. In this world of reversals, the film suggests that, if identification and sympathy are contingent on the race of the other, so too are disidentification and dehumanization. Do drone strikes seem more morally reprehensible when the asymmetrical drone relation is reversed—when it is an Asian state targeting and killing white Americans? The film highlights how much race shapes existing relations of identification and drone violence and how much race renders acceptable non-identification and dehumanization. Through the film's casting of white actors as both terrorists and the family who becomes collateral damage, the vignette stays firmly within this logic, but defamiliarizes it by reversing the racialized roles. The vignette largely retains the trope of the threatening Orientalist Other, in the menacing occupying Chinese soldiers, and the sympathetic West, in the loving, white, suburban family that is threatened and killed by frightening Asian actors. This failure to destabilize the historic Orientalism and racism that undergirds the history of U.S. drone strikes speaks again to the failure of representation; a simple reversal (what if what were happening over there were happening over here?) is revealed to be woefully inadequate, because the hypothetical question and the language of representation itself are shaped by this Orientalist logic. The film highlights that this Orientalism is a constant, that it persists in shaping the worlds of the film and representation. Indeed, the question itself emerges from an Orientalism that attempts identification, but reveals the Eurocentrism and racial exclusion that undergird this process of identification. As a means of bringing ethics into the drone relation, identification, in its reliance on perceptions of similarity and familiarity, is at best woefully insufficient. What might be necessary instead is a relation (of representation and otherwise) that insists on not just difference and the failure to overcome difference, but the apperception of the fundamental unfamiliarity and unknowability in others and oneself—what Édouard Glissant calls opacity.[84]

In the excerpts of Fast's interview with Brandon, he describes what it's like to see the world from five thousand feet (the optimal height for drone surveillance), how he played video games to blow off steam after work, what the world looks like through the drone's infrared technology, the first time he killed someone in a drone strike, and his struggles with post-traumatic stress disorder. In the interview segments, the film shifts from a shot of Brandon's blurred face to aerial shots of archetypal American spaces and familiar cinematic scenes: the idyllic suburban neighborhood, the quaint village, the Las Vegas strip at night. For exam-

Figure 29. Drone shot following a boy on a bike. Omer Fast *5,000 Feet Is the Best,* 2011, Commonwealth Projects.

ple, in the first interview segment, as Brandon describes the process of aiming a missile at a target, the film cuts to an aerial shot following a young boy biking on what appears to be a dirt road. We see the boy on the bike mostly as a shadow. In age, this boy appears to be on the cusp of that ill-defined boundary between child and adolescent that marks the category of military-aged male. Would a drone operator identify this young boy as a child, thus letting him live, or an adolescent, thus rendering him killable? As Brandon speaks, at first it is unclear how his words speak to the aerial shots they overlay. As the camera follows the young boy on his bike, Brandon describes watching targets using different drone cameras. As Brandon continues, the camera—still following the boy—slowly zooms out and reveals the setting to be a massive suburban development, while the biking boy becomes no more than a speck.

In the opening of these aerial shots, the camera's movement through these iconic American spaces is fluid and soothing. But as Brandon's descriptions progress, the camera's movements begin to work in concert with his descriptions of targeting and killing and of his PTSD—the camera perspective begins to evoke the drone perspective.[85] Like the recasting of actors in the operator's first story, these interview segments first lull the viewer into comfort with familiar shots of familiar spaces, then pull a kind of bait and switch (not unlike the Las Vegas con couple in the operator's second story) when, too late, the viewer realizes that these soothing, cinematically familiar scenes have seamlessly become the view from drones. In this way, the film coaxes the viewer into participating in these shots, moving through the suburb, the village, and the Las Vegas Strip along with the camera, only to align these scenes, and thus the viewer's participation within them, with Brandon's work surveilling and killing. The final interview segment concludes on a simultaneously peaceful and fraught evening shot of Las Vegas, as Brandon talks about killing his first target and "when the dreams started." Immediately after, the film ends on the same shot on which it begins—a shot of the fictional drone operator in the hotel hallway. In the original installation piece, the film is played on a continuous loop, the scenes repeating endlessly. In this recursive structure, both film and installation suggest that disorientation foundationally characterizes both war and representation; further, the film, which has continually subverted the viewer's desire to identify with a character as well as the camera, suggests that identification is not the place to locate ethical response. To return to Paik and my earlier question about what response would adequately address drone strikes, Fast's film, like Cole's *Seven Stories* and Bridle's *Dronestagram*, suggests an ethical relation that foregrounds disorientation, uncertainty, and the unknown, rather than the familiar, the known, the predictable.

The works of drone art I discuss highlight the dehumanizing refusal to recognize the victims of drone strikes as humans worthy of grief, as well as life, independent of their relation or similarity to the Western Subject. These works destabilize the privileging of a post-Enlightenment human and gesture toward the humanity of drone victims outside of this conception of the human. In different ways, these works examine the limits of identification as a means to ethical practice and locate dehumanization not in drone victims, but in the United States and the West, with their histories and continued practices of racial state violence. As all the drone artworks in this chapter illustrate, racial dehumanization is central to the drone relation. In the face of this dehumanization, identification that privileges the familiarity of the Western, post-Enlightenment conception of the human is inherently limited in its capacity to open up ethical action. Cutting against cybernetic warfare's central fantasies of omniscience, total calculability, and predictability, these works turn to relations that highlight difference, the unknown, and the disorienting to challenge the drone's racial dehumanization and underscore the abiding conceptions of the human that require this dehumanization. These works gesture to a different conception of the human—one that is constituted not through the known, but through the unknown and the unfamiliar.

Epilogue
The Human
That Which We Have
Yet to Know

Robots, AIs, and autonomous systems of all kinds promise to some the luxuries of time and freedom from certain kinds of work. As I argue in *The Robotic Imaginary*, as these promises, like the labors from which one is freed, are gendered and racialized, making good on these promises reinscribes existing hierarchies and their material consequences—from the persistent erasure, devaluation, and exploitation of one's labor, to the dehumanization of another to justify their death by drone. This study of the robotic imaginary reflects on these dynamics and offers a way of making sense of how the concept of the human is imaginatively inscribed, how humans are dehumanized, and how to reconfigure robots in ways that do not replicate extant systems of oppression, but rather challenges the dehumanization at the heart of "the human." How can the robotic imaginary challenge and refuse the very dehumanization that constitutes the modern, Western notion of the human? *The Robotic Imaginary* identifies the central role of familiarity in conceptualizing the human in robotic paradigms, and posits instead a reconceptualization of the human that, in its insistence on unfamiliarity, is at once capacious, disorienting, and unknown. Judith Butler describes the human as emerging from disorientation, loss, and the unknown: "I cannot muster the 'we' except by finding the way in which I am tied to 'you,' by trying to translate but finding that my own language must break up and yield if I am to know you. You are what I gain through this disorientation and loss. This is how the human comes into being, again and again, as that which we have yet to know."[1] This conception of the human, constituted through disorientation and encounters with the unfamiliar and the unknown, works against cybernetic principles of predictability and sameness, against the post-Enlightenment human and its colonial legacies, and against the normative demands that often structure the robotic imaginary. This conception of the human evacuates presumptive expectations of familiarity (whatever this might look like) from its constitution. Instead, this human affirms the inescapable limits of knowledges and emerges from, and brings with it, anticipations of the unknown.

The Robotic Imaginary suggests that we ask of every robot figure the following questions: How does this figure engage the histories of undervalued, devalued, and exploited labor, particularly as they intersect with race, gender, and class? Who is being dehumanized in this robot figure? Whose humanness is constructed as familiar and sacrosanct? And going forward, how can we engage the robotic imaginary in ways that challenge its dehumanizing impulses? In other words, how can we reconfigure the robotic imaginary to embrace difference and the unknown, thus refusing sameness, resemblance, or familiarity to the Western Subject as the defining characteristic of the human? As my book argues by drawing a history that moves across caring and care labor, thinking and domestic labor, feeling and emotional labor, and dying and drone labor, the robotic imaginary in its various forms has always had at its constitutive center gendered devaluation and racial dehumanization. Throughout, my chapters also attends to the ongoing intertwining of DARPA-funded technologies and "women's work" in the robotic imaginary. As Robin Truth Goodman observes, this conversation between militarization and reproductive labor takes on particular resonance in our contemporary neoliberal moment. In her study of war literature and film, Goodman identifies the expansion of female military figures as a response to the state's abrogation of its responsibilities to care for individuals. As health care, education, labor protections, and other forms of social responsibility are increasingly abandoned by the state and privatized, an increasing number of women are looking to the military to provide financial security and access to care services.[2] As Goodman details, this shift is changing both militarization and reproductive labor in complex ways.

While an increasing number of women enlist in military service, some military robots have been rejected for battlefield use and are being re-branded for the domestic sphere. In 2015, Boston Dynamics' BigDog—a DARPA-funded, headless, four-legged robot designed to carry heavy loads—was deemed too noisy for the battlefield by the United States Marine Corps working alongside it, who feared that the noise would easily draw enemy attention.[3] Both BigDog and the SpotMini, a smaller version of BigDog that is quieter but cannot carry heavy loads, are robots now in need of work. Currently Boston Dynamics is presenting the SpotMini as a domestic worker that can, as the demonstration video notes, place a glass in a dishwasher and drop an aluminum can in a recycling bin.[4] As Lucy Suchman notes, Boston Dynamics is also reframing Atlas, its bi-pedal robot, as a domestic laborer.[5] If not fit for the battlefield, why not to keep house?[6] While care is being increasingly abdicated by the state as a responsibility to its citizens and the military is being increasingly viewed by women as a source of care services, the SpotMini's and Atlas's re-contextualization to the domestic labor robot market highlights the on-going relationship between militarization and reproductive labor and the simultaneous necessity and devaluation of care and its labors. These robots' move from battlefield to domestic sphere also gestures to questions of whose labor is thought to be repetitive and mindless (and thus auto-matable), whose time is viewed as requiring liberation from such "dirty work," and what institutions (the military, the state, capitalism) are being rendered increasingly profitable and efficient (efficient for whom?) while humans face greater insecurity around basic care services.[7] The SpotMini's and Atlas's reconfigurations suggest that as care drops out of the purview of the state, it may yet return, though only in the form of a secondary market for robots rejected by the military.

As fears of automation and robots taking over human jobs continue to circulate and expensive battlefield robots prove to be unsuitable for their designed functions, militarized robots are increasingly purchased for use by police departments across the United States. In 2015, North Dakota legalized the use of weaponized drones by law enforcement, while Connecticut is currently debating legislation that would allow law en-forcement to use lethally weaponized drones. In 2016, a bomb-disposal robot was turned into an explosive device used to kill Micah Xavier Johnson in an armed standoff. According to reports, Johnson's death marked the first time a U.S. police department deployed a robot to kill.[8] As lethal robots and armed drones come home to roost in the United States, the colonial continuum and racial dehumanization will continue to shape decisions about life and death. The crucial task then, as it is now, will be to foreground the connections across violences, geographies, and humans, rather than effacing them. In this way, the labor of reconfiguring the robotic imaginary—of reconfiguring the human as an unimaginably capacious category that refuses dehumanizing exclusions—will continue to assert itself with urgency.

Acknowledgments

Although this book comprises new material, the kernels of this work reside in my dissertation. Thank you to my dissertation committee—Ken Surin, Mark Hansen, Michael Hardt, Kate Hayles, and Tim Lenoir—for your invaluable feedback, guidance, and support.

This work was supported by fellowships from Duke University's John Hope Franklin Institute, Pennsylvania State University's Institute for the Arts and Humanities, and Emory University's Fox Center for Humanistic Inquiry. My time at these centers and the interdisciplinary conversations they facilitated influenced my work in incredibly important ways.

Thank you to friends, colleagues, writing partners, and mentors who offered feedback on drafts, encouragement, support, and the sustenance of friendship: Courtney Berger, Munia Bhaumik, Zach Blas, Chris Cynn, Talia Dorsey, Rich Doyle, Nihad Farooq, Grant Farred, Michael Hall, John Johnston, Brian Lennon, Dawn Peterson, Rachel Price, Karen Rader, Atia Sattar, Scott Selisker, Susan Squier, Brandi Summers, Jasmina Tumbas, Shilyh Warren, and Pinar Yoldas. Thank you to Michael Bérubé, Kate Hayles, and Ken Surin for your generosity and support of my work. I continue to learn from your scholarship and the ways you inhabit this profession.

My time at the Center for American Literary Studies' First Book Institute at Penn State was transformative. I thank my fellow FBI participants for their engagement and sharp feedback, and Sean Goudie and Priscilla Wald, who codirect the Institute and create an environment rich with intellectual excitement and generosity. During my time there,

Priscilla and Michael Bérubé offered invaluable feedback that helped me see the book that needed to be written.

My colleagues at Virginia Commonwealth University make the English department a wonderful place to work and think. Thank you in particular to Kathy Bassard for supporting my research leave at Emory and David Latané for locating funds to pay for image permissions. Thank you to Margret Schluer, Ginny Schmitz, Kelsey Cappiello, and Derek Van Buskirk for all of your work making sure the English department runs smoothly, and to Ivy Roberts for helping secure image permissions. Richard Fine was the best mentor I could have imagined—thank you for astute and steadfast guidance, which was always offered with kindness. To my wonderful students at VCU, thank you—it's been a privilege to think with you in the classroom. I also want to thank all the librarians, particularly those who facilitate interlibrary loan services, at Duke, Penn State, VCU, and Emory.

This book benefited from exciting conversations with conference audiences and copanelists at the American Studies Association; the Society for Literature, Science, and the Arts; the Modern Language Association; the American Comparative Literature Association; and the Mediating the Nonhuman faculty colloquium at the University of California–Santa Barbara.

I'm thrilled to be working with the University of Minnesota Press. Thank you to Erin Warholm-Wohlenhaus for your early excitement and support of my manuscript, and to Danielle Kasprzak for your support as we see this project to the end. And thank you to Anne Carter for your help moving the book into production. I'd also like to thank the production and design department for working on this book. I'm extremely grateful to the external reviewers, Lucy Suchman and Priscilla Wald, for their time and incisive feedback. Your respective work has been significantly influential to my thinking for a number of years, and your discerning critiques made this book a stronger work of scholarship.

Lastly, thank you to my partner, Daniel, and my family: Eun Rhee, Jung Rhee, Chrissy Rhee, Susie Rhee-Moore, Chris Moore, Katie Moore, Wyatt Moore, and George. In different ways, you've provided crucial support and encouragement, as well as much needed distraction from the labors of writing this book.

Notes

Introduction

1 Murtaza Hussain, "Former Drone Operators Say They Were Horrified by Cruelty of Assassination Program," *Intercept,* November 19, 2015, https:// theintercept.com/2015/11/19/former-drone-operators-say-they-were -horrified-by-cruelty-of-assassination-program/. In 2015, Haas and three other former drone operators publicly spoke out against the U.S. military's drone program. In a letter addressed to President Obama, Secretary of Defense Ashton Carter, and CIA Director John Brennan, Haas, Brandon Bryant, Cian Westmoreland, and Stephen Lewis urged the administration to reconsider the drone program, pointing to both the many innocent lives killed and the hatred toward the United States fueled by the practice. Haas, Bryant, Westmoreland, and Lewis, all of whom suffer from post-traumatic stress disorder, have publicly discussed how their work demanded that they dehumanize the people they were tasked to surveil and kill.

2 For example, Richard Gray, "How Long Will It Take for Your Job to Be Automated?" *BBC,* June 19, 2017, http://www.bbc.com/capital/story/20170619-how -long-will-it-take-for-your-job-to-be-automated.

3 As many readers will recognize, the title of this section draws on Donna Haraway's *Staying with the Trouble: Making Kin in the Chthulucene* (Durham, N.C.: Duke University Press, 2016). In this text, Haraway asks us both to refuse destructive and resigned cynicism about the world and to "embrace situated technical projects and their people" (3). The latter in particular can lead to generative relations and practices to help us "stay with the trouble" that is our infinite enmeshments. See also Diana Fuss, "Introduction," in *Human, All Too Human,* ed. Diana Fuss (New York: Routledge, 1996), 1.

4 Fuss, 1–2 (emphasis added).

5 Pheng Cheah, "Humanity in the Field of Instrumentality," *PMLA* 121, no. 5 (2006): 1552.

6 Sylvia Wynter's powerful work rethinks the human within its construction through exclusion, marginalization, and oppression—through dehumanization. Katherine McKittrick describes Wynter's work as confronting no less than "how we might give humanness a different future." (Sylvia Wynter and Katherine McKittrick, "Unparalleled Catastrophe for Our Species? Or, to Give Humanness a Different Future: Conversations," in *Sylvia Wynter: On Being Human as Praxis,* ed. Katherine McKittrick [Durham, N.C.: Duke University Press, 2015], 9). And according to Alexander Weheliye, the human cannot be thought outside of race, particularly blackness. However, the history of the human, for example in discourses of the biopolitical, has long rendered blackness invisible. Drawing on the work of Wynter and Frantz Fanon, Weheliye argues that any notion of the human that excludes blackness, any notion of the human that ignores the way that "the human" has been constructed through the oppression and dehumanization of minority populations (particularly black subjects), must be problematized and undone as "human." Instead, the human must be expanded to account for these acts of exclusion and exploitation (Alexander G. Weheliye, *Habeas Viscus: Racializing Assemblages, Biopolitics, and Black Feminist Theories of the Human* [Durham, N.C.: Duke University Press, 2014]).

7 Zakiyyah Iman Jackson, "Outer Worlds: The Persistence of Race in Movement 'Beyond the Human,'" *GLQ: A Journal of Lesbian and Gay Studies* 21, nos. 2–3 (2015): 215.

8 José Esteban Muñoz, "Theorizing Queer Inhumanisms: The Sense of Brownness," *GLQ: A Journal of Lesbian and Gay Studies* 21, nos. 2–3 (2015): 209.

9 Éduoard Glissant, *Poetics of Relation,* trans. Betsy Wing (Ann Arbor: University of Michigan Press, 1997), 19.

10 For a discussion of human unrecognizability from a legal perspective, see Samera Esmeir's essay "On Making Dehumanization Possible," *PMLA* 121, no. 5 (2006): 1544–51. Esmeir challenges a conception of the human dependent on statushood (that which can be conferred, and thus withheld in dehumanizing practices) and outside of familiarity and legibility to others. Instead, she argues that we need to think about the human outside of juridical recognition, and outside of recognition more broadly.

11 Lucy Suchman, *Human–Machine Reconfigurations: Plans and Situated Actions,* 2nd ed. (New York: Cambridge University Press, 2007), 2.

12 Bruno Latour rejects the distinction between science and technology, offer-

ing instead the term "technoscience" (*Science in Action* [Cambridge, Mass.: Harvard University Press, 1987], 174).

13 Suchman, *Human–Machine Reconfigurations*, 1.

14 To mark the two spheres as distinct is itself deceptive, and some scholars, including Donna Haraway and Lucy Suchman, astutely employ the term "technocultures" to signify the non-separation of "technology" and "culture." Constance Penley and Andrew Ross, who are invested in maintaining the possibility of individual agency and popular activism, conceptualize technoculture as "located as much in the work of everyday fantasies and actions as at the level of corporate or military decision-making" ("Introduction," in *Technoculture*, ed. Constance Penley and Andrew Ross [Minneapolis: University of Minnesota Press, 1991], xiii).

15 N. Katherine Hayles, "Introduction: Complex Dynamics in Literature and Science," in *Chaos and Order: Complex Dynamics in Literature and Science*, ed. N. Katherine Hayles (Chicago: University of Chicago Press, 1991), 30.

16 Donna J. Haraway, *Modest_Witness@Second_Millennium: FemaleMan©_Meets_OncoMouse* (New York: Routledge, 1997), 50.

17 Susan Merrill Squier, *Liminal Lives: Imagining the Human at the Frontiers of Biomedicine* (Durham, N.C.: Duke University Press, 2004), 46.

18 Annie M. Jacobsen, *The Pentagon's Brain: An Uncensored History of DARPA, America's Top Secret Military Research Agency* (New York: Little, Brown, 2015), 7.

19 Pamela McCorduck, *Machines Who Think: A Personal Inquiry into the History and Prospects of Artificial Intelligence* (Natick, Mass.: A K Peters, 2004), 272.

20 Joseph Weizenbaum, *Computer Power and Human Reason: From Judgment to Calculation* (San Francisco: W. H. Freeman, 1976), 271.

21 For an excellent account of the history of cybernetics in AI, see N. Katherine Hayles's *How We Became Posthuman: Virtual Bodies in Cybernetics, Literature, and Informatics* (Chicago: University of Chicago Press, 1999).

22 For an account of the semantic battle in which McCarthy's "artificial intelligence" emerged victorious over Shannon's "automata studies," see McCorduck, *Machines Who Think*, 96. While the 1956 conference is marked as a foundational moment in the disciplinary history of artificial intelligence, the conference itself was far from a utopian moment of interdisciplinary collaboration. Rather, the conference was met with a sense of disappointment by the participants and the organizer. For discussions of this disappointment, see the historical accounts provided by McCorduck, 96–97, 99, 105; Jack Copeland in *Artificial Intelligence: A Philosophical Introduction* (Oxford,

U.K.: Blackwell, 1993), 8; and Daniel Crevier, *AI: The Tumultuous History of the Search for Artificial Intelligence* (New York: Basic Books, 1994), 49.

23 Crevier, *AI*, 48.

24 Crevier, 9.

25 Paul Ricoeur, "The Metaphor Process as Cognition, Imagination, and Feeling." *Critical Inquiry* 5, no. 1 (1978): 148.

26 In an astute reading of Turing's imitation game, Tyler Curtain points out that the injunction on B to prove her status as woman is not equivalent to A's attempt to convince C otherwise. Curtain describes this nonequivalence in the imitation game as "the philosophical burden of women to speak—and for an adequate number of times *fail to represent*—the 'truth' of their sex" ("The 'Sinister Fruitiness' of Machines: *Neuromancer*, Internet Sexuality, and the Turing Test," in *Novel Gazing: Queer Readings in Fiction*, ed. Eve Kosofsky Sedgwick [Durham, N.C.: Duke University Press, 1997], 139).

27 Alan Turing, "Computing Machinery and Intelligence," *Mind* 59, no. 236 (1950): 434. What happens next is far from unambiguous, as both the text and the substantial disagreement surrounding the following move demonstrate. If A is replaced by the machine, does Turing intend that, in this new version of the imitation game, the human interrogator continue to attempt to identify the woman? Or does "human" replace "woman" as identificatory metric? Warren Sack calls this puzzling erasure of sex and gender out of many discussions of the Turing test the work of "the bachelor machine": "AI researchers have functioned as a 'bachelor machine' to orchestrate the woman and issues of gender difference out of their re-narrations of Turing's imitation game" (Sack, "Replaying Turing's Imitation Game," http://www.pd .org/Perforations/perf13/wsachs.html).

28 For an insightful articulation of Turing's imitation game, see Susan Sterrett's "Too Many Instincts: Contrasting Philosophical Views on Intelligence in Humans and Non-Humans." Rather than erasing gender as identificatory metric in favor of the human, as many readings of the Turing test do, Sterrett embeds Turing's ambiguity into her discussion of his test as "meta-game." Sterrett's reading itself can be said to emerge from the moment of replacement in Turing's paper—rather than discarding A_1 (man) for its replacement A_2 (machine), Sterrett argues that Turing's test can best address questions of machine intelligence when comparing these two game pairings. In other words, both A_1 and A_2 are paired with B, and are interrogated by C, who must identify the woman in both A_1–B and A_2–B pairings. The success and failure of A_1 and A_2 are scored according to the number of times the human interrogator misidentifies both A_1 and A_2 as woman, and the results in these

separate trials are then compared to each other ("Too Many Instincts: Contrasting Philosophical Views on Intelligence in Humans and Non-Humans," *Journal of Experimental and Theoretical Artificial Intelligence* 14 [2002]: 39–60).

29 M. H. A. Newman, Alan M. Turing, Sir Geoffrey Jefferson, and R. B. Braithwaite, "Can Automatic Calculating Machines Be Said to Think?" in *The Turing Test: Verbal Behavior as the Hallmark of Intelligence,* ed. Stuart Shieber (Cambridge, Mass.: MIT Press, 2004), 124.

30 Mori first introduced his theory in an essay, "Bukimi No Tani," which was first translated into English and published in 1978 as "The Uncanny Valley" in Jasia Reichardt's *Robots: Fact, Fiction, and Prediction.* In 2005, Mori's uncanny valley theory received significant attention at the Institute of Electrical and Electronic Engineers (IEEE) Robotics and Automation Society International Conference on Humanoid Robots. The same year, roboticists Karl MacDorman and Takashi Minato released their English translation of the essay, which was circulated both within and beyond the robotics community. Since 2005, Mori's uncanny valley theory has had significant influence in U.S. humanoid robotics; and recently, the uncanny valley theory has also gained traction in discussions of human "realism" in computer graphics and in film and video game animation. In 2012, a new English translation, the first to be authorized by Mori, was published in *IEEE Robotics and Automation Magazine,* thus attesting to the essay's continued influence within robotics.

31 Mori's essay refers to human resemblance as "realism" (Masahiro Mori, "The Uncanny Valley," trans. Karl F. MacDorman and Norri Kageki, *IEEE Robotics and Automation Magazine* 19, no. 2 [2012]: 99).

32 Mori, 99.

33 "As this myoelectric hand makes movements, it could make *healthy* people feel uneasy" (Mori, 99 [emphasis added]).

34 Mori, 100.

35 Mori, 100.

36 Mori continues to stand by this recommendation. See Norri Kageki, "Uncanny Mind," *IEEE Robotics and Automation Magazine* 19, no. 2 (2012): 106.

37 In a recent interview, Mori shares that the uncanny valley was "my intuition. . . . Pointing out the existence of the uncanny valley was more of a piece of advice from me to people who design robots rather than a scientific statement" (Kageki, 112).

38 For example: "Thus, given [industrial robots'] lack of resemblance to human beings, in general, people hardly feel any affinity for them"; "Children seem

to feel deeply attached to these toy robots"; and, finally, "Many of our readers have experienced interacting with persons with physical disabilities, and all must have felt sympathy for those missing a hand or legs and wearing a prosthetic limb" (Mori, "Uncanny Valley," 98).

39 Seo-Young Chu offers a thoughtful discussion that places Mori's theory into conversation with Orientalist stereotypes in "I, Stereotype: Detained in the Uncanny Valley," in *Techno-Orientalism: Imagining Asia in Speculative Fiction, History, and Media,* ed. David S. Roh, Betsy Huang, and Greta A. Niu (New Brunswick, N.J.: Rutgers University Press, 2015), 76–88.

40 I discuss this in greater detail in my essay "Beyond the Uncanny Valley: Masahiro Mori and Philip K. Dick's *Do Androids Dream of Electric Sheep?*" *Configurations* 21, no. 3 (2013): 301–29.

41 For earlier histories of automata and artificial life, see Minsoo Kang, *Sublime Dreams of Living Machines* (Cambridge, MA: Harvard University Press, 2011); Kevin LaGrandeur, *Androids and Intelligent Networks in Early Modern Literature and Culture* (New York: Routledge, 2013); Jessica Riskin, ed., *Genesis Redux: Essays in the History and Philosophy of Artificial Life* (Chicago: University of Chicago Press, 2007); and Adelheid Voskuhl, *Androids in the Enlightenment: Mechanics, Artisans, and Cultures of the Self* (Chicago: University of Chicago Press, 2013).

42 Robotics owes a great deal to fiction. The word "roboticist" first appeared in Isaac Asimov's 1940 short story "Strange Playfellow."

43 Isiah Lavender III, *Race in American Science Fiction* (Bloomington: Indiana University Press, 2011), 60–62.

44 Despina Kakoudaki, *Anatomy of a Robot: Literature, Cinema, and the Cultural Work of Artificial People* (New Brunswick, N.J.: Rutgers University Press, 2014), 115–72.

45 *Oxford English Dictionary,* s.v. "robot," http://www.oed.com/view/Entry/275486.

46 *Oxford English Dictionary,* s.v. "robotnik," http://www.oed.com/view/Entry/275315.

47 The play was first performed in English in 1922 in New York.

48 Karel Čapek, *R.U.R. (Rossum's Universal Robots),* trans. Claudia Novack (New York: Penguin, 2004), 18 (hereafter cited parenthetically in the text).

49 "One Robot can do the work of two and a half human laborers. The human machine, Miss Glory, was hopelessly imperfect. It needed to be done away with once and for all. / It was too costly. / It was less than efficient. It couldn't keep up with modern technology" (Čapek, 17).

50 The play underscores this multiple times through Helena, who mistakes Domin's robot secretary for a human and the rest of the men for robots.

51 For an insightful discussion of the robots' appearance in early performances of the play, see Kakoudaki, *Anatomy of a Robot,* 139–43.

52 David Harvey, *Spaces of Hope* (Berkeley: University of California Press, 2000), 106.

53 See Lisa Lowe's *The Intimacy of Four Continents* (Durham, N.C.: Duke University Press, 2014).

54 Neda Atanasoki and Kalindi Vora, "Surrogate Humanity: Posthuman Networks and the (Racialized) Obsolescence of Labor," *Catalyst: Feminism, Theory, Technoscience* 1, no. 1 (2015): http://catalystjournal.org/ojs/index.php /catalyst/article/view/ata_vora.

55 Sherryl Vint, "Species and Species-Being: Alienated Subjectivity and the Commodification of Animals," in *Red Planets: Marxism and Science Fiction,* ed. Mark Bould and China Miéville (Middletown, Conn.: Wesleyan University Press, 2009), 119.

56 As Vint notes, for Marx, capitalist alienation is also alienation from the human species (Vint, 124). The cessation of human births, which Alquist links to the production of robots and humans' life without work, also depicts this mode of alienation. Displacing humans from their work does not create Domin's paradise of perpetual leisure, but instead further alienates humans from their labor and their species.

57 This act both ended the production of robots and doomed the remaining humans, as possession of the secret was the only leverage the humans had.

58 Kamila Kinyon points out that the ending, while hopeful, is also ambiguous, as Alquist continues to quote a biblical passage about domination ("The Phenomenology of Robots: Confrontations with Death in Karel Čapek's *R.U.R.*," *Science Fiction Studies* 26, no. 3 [1999]: 398).

59 Adrian MacKenzie, *Transductions: Bodies and Machines at Speed* (New York: Continuum, 2002).

60 Eduardo Kac, "Toward a Chronology of Robotic Art," *Convergence* 7, no. 1 (2001): 87–111.

61 Eduardo Kac, "The Origin and Development of Robotic Art," *Convergence* 7, no. 1 (2001): 84. Working from within art, Kac, as I do in this book, emphasizes the conversation between robotic art and robots in literature and technology (76–77).

62 Edward A. Shanken, "Historicizing Art and Technology: Forging a Method and Firing a Canon," in *MediaArtHistories,* ed. Oliver Grau (Cambridge, Mass.: MIT Press, 2007), 44.

63   Judith Butler, *Precarious Life: The Powers of Mourning and Violence* (London: Verso, 2004), 42.

64   As I note in chapter 3, though *Do Androids Dream of Electric Sheep?* was published before *We Can Build You,* Dick wrote the latter novel first.

65   Butler, 151.

1. Caring

1   Jennifer S. Light, "When Computers Were Women," *Technology and Culture* 40, no. 3 (1999): 455–83. Marie Hicks details a similar gendered devaluation of computing work in twentieth-century Britain in *Programmed Inequality: How Britain Discarded Women Technologists and Lost Its Edge in Computing* (Cambridge, Mass.: MIT Press, 2017).

2   For an explanation of the Turing test's structure, see my introduction. While there has been no official winner of the Loebner Prize, an annual Turing test competition held since 1990, informal instantiations of the Turing test have long been surpassed by the development of "smart" AIs from Siri to the *Jeopardy*-winning Watson.

3   Alan Turing, "Computing Machinery and Intelligence," *Mind* 59, no. 236 (1950): 456.

4   Leopoldina Fortunati, "Immaterial Labor and Its Machinization," *Ephemera: Theory and Politics in Organization* 7, no. 1 (2007): 141. For a discussion of domestic labor and robotics, see chapter 2.

5   For an analysis of capitalism's reliance on unpaid women's work, see Silvia Federici's *Caliban and the Witch: Women, the Body, and Primitive Accumulation* (Brooklyn: Autonomedia, 2004). Paula England offers a useful discussion of the literature of care work's gendered "devaluation" in "Emerging Theories of Care Work," *Annual Review of Sociology* 31 (2005): 381–99.

6   Mignon Duffy makes a distinction between nurturant and nonnurturant care labor. Nurturant care labor refers to labor that involves close relationships and direct interactions with people receiving care. Nonnurturant care labor refers to labor that does not involve such relationships and interactions—for example, housekeepers and janitorial staff in nursing homes (Duffy, *Making Care Count: A Century of Gender, Race, and Paid Care Work* [New Brunswick, N.J.: Rutgers University Press, 2011], 6). Because I examine AI–human interactivity, my discussion of care labor in this chapter focuses on nurturant care labor. Notably, as Duffy points out, within reproductive labor, white women are significantly represented within nurturant care professions, which are generally higher paid and ascribed higher status. Women of color are underrepresented within nurturant care labor professions but overrepresented in nonnurturant care professions (Duffy, "Reproducing

Labor Inequalities: Challenges for Feminists Conceptualizing Care at the Intersections of Gender, Race, and Class," *Gender and Society* 19, no. 1 [February 2005]: 76–80).

7　ELIZA was named after Eliza Doolittle, "of Pygmalion fame" (Joseph Weizenbaum, *Computer Power and Human Reason: From Judgment to Calculation* [San Francisco: W. H. Freeman, 1976], 3 [hereafter cited parenthetically in the text]). As Sharon Snyder notes, Richard Powers's *Galatea 2.2* similarly pays "homage" to George Bernard Shaw's *Pygmalion* ("The Gender of Genius: Scientific Experts and Literary Amateurs in the Fiction of Richard Powers," *Review of Contemporary Fiction* 18, no. 3[1988]: 86–87), as does Emily Short's electronic fiction *Galatea.*

8　In 1957, the Soviet space program successfully launched Sputnik I into the Earth's orbit. U.S. scientists, having been bested in this leg of the space race, rushed to design a computer program that could translate from Russian into English (Neill Graham, *Artificial Intelligence* [Blue Ridge Summit, Pa.: Tab Books, 1979], 5). The resulting program could translate about 80 percent of the Russian language. However, too much meaning resided in that ever-elusive 20 percent. For example, "Out of sight, out of mind" became, in Russian, "Blind and insane," and "The spirit is willing but the flesh is weak" became "The wine [or vodka, according to Alex Roland and Philip Shiman] is agreeable but the meat has spoiled" (Graham, 209; Alex Roland and Philip Shiman, *Strategic Computing: DARPA and the Quest for Machine Intelligence, 1983–1993* [Cambridge, Mass.: MIT Press, 2002], 189). On account of this intractable, mistranslated 20 percent, the program was deemed a failure; by 1966, the U.S. government pulled all funding for these translation programs (Roland and Shiman, 189). For further discussion of the history of machine translation, see Brian Lennon, "Can Multilingualism Be Simulated?" *Critical Multilingualism* 1, no. 1 (2012): http://cms.arizona.edu/index.php/multilingual/issue/view/2.

9　You can "talk" to a contemporary version of ELIZA at http://psych.fullerton.edu/mbirnbaum/psych101/Eliza.htm.

10　In her history of artificial intelligence, Pamela McCorduck writes of the "painful embarrassment" upon watching a respected computer scientist share extremely personal and intimate worries about his personal life with DOCTOR (psychiatrist Kenneth Colby's version of ELIZA), knowing all along that DOCTOR was not a human, but rather a computer program (*Machines Who Think* [San Francisco: W. H. Freeman, 1979], 254).

11　Weizenbaum discusses his decision to model ELIZA on a Rogerian psychotherapist in *Computer Power and Human Reason,* 3. For a detailed discussion of nondirected client-oriented therapy, see Carl R. Rogers's *Client-Centered*

Therapy: Its Current Practice, Implications, and Theory (Boston: Houghton Mifflin, 1951); and *On Becoming a Person: A Therapist's View of Psychotherapy* (1961; repr., Boston: Houghton Mifflin, 1995). The latter title is all too appropriately named for this discussion of ELIZA and AI's anthropomorphic aspirations.

12 Ilene Philipson, *On the Shoulders of Women: The Feminization of Psychotherapy* (New York: Guilford Press, 1993), 106.

13 In 1972, PARRY met ELIZA; their conversation can be viewed at https:// tools.ietf.org/html/rfc439.

14 Duffy, *Making Care Count*, 70.

15 Philipson, *On the Shoulders of Women*, 78.

16 Duffy, *Making Care Count*, 108–10. As Duffy notes, during these same decades, black men and women's participation within the field of social work steadily increased from 16 percent of the social work labor force in 1970 to almost 20 percent in 2007.

17 Duffy, 106.

18 Philipson, *On the Shoulders of Women*, 80–89.

19 Philipson, 6.

20 For a brief discussion of Watson as an expert-systems AI, see chapter 2.

21 Jordan Larson, "*Her* and the Complex Legacy of the Female Robot," *The Atlantic*, December 23, 2013, https://www.theatlantic.com/entertainment /archive/2013/12/-em-her-em-and-the-complex-legacy-of-the-female-robot /282581/.

22 The mechanization and commodification of care labor is depicted throughout the novel, from the drbas AI to the production of sex robots.

23 Of course, murderous disembodied AIs have been a popular theme in fiction, as in Marvin Minsky and Harry Harrison's coauthored novel *The Turing Effect* (New York: Warner Books, 1992).

24 The film sequel, based on a novel written in 1982, was released after ELIZA and PARRY permeated throughout culture, and after the field of psychology continued to see increased feminization.

25 Silvia Federici, *Revolution at Point Zero: Housework, Reproduction, and Feminist Struggle* (Oakland, Calif.: PM Press, 2012), 12.

26 *Galatea 2.2*, which was published in 1999, is set in a university based on the University of Illinois Urbana–Champaign. Coincidentally, HAL was created in Urbana, Illinois.

27 N. Katherine Hayles aptly describes Helen's test as "a literary Turing test" (*How We Became Posthuman: Virtual Bodies in Cybernetics, Literature, and Informatics* [Chicago: University of Chicago Press, 1999], 270).

28 For example, Lentz describes the AI as a child and analogizes training the AI to raising an infant (Richard Powers, *Galatea 2.2* [New York: Picador, 1995], 88). Marjorie Worthington discusses Richard's parental relationship with the AI in "The Texts of Tech: Technology and Authorial Control in *Geek Love* and *Galatea 2.2*," *Journal of Narrative Theory* 39, no. 1 (2009): 123. As Worthington notes, citing an interview conducted by Michael Bérubé, Powers describes *Galatea 2.2* as an "interrogation of parenthood" (131). And as she points out, for Richard, parenting the AI takes shape as a kind of narcissism: "the more he wants it to succeed, the more he tries to model it on himself, teaching it what he knows, teaching it about himself" (123).

29 Powers, *Galatea 2.2*, 179, 229, 230 (hereafter cited parenthetically in the text).

30 At first, Richard begins teaching the AI about language by typing in common English words. However, Richard's abysmal typing skills and consequent slow progress quickly lead Lentz to outfit the AI with voice recognition capabilities. Mimicking the oral storytelling that structures the threads of *Galatea 2.2*'s narrative, Powers wrote a subsequent book, *The Echo Maker* (2007), using voice recognition software rather than typing on a keyboard (John Freeman, "Richard Powers: Confessions of a Geek," *Independent*, December 15, 2006, http://www.independent.co.uk/arts-entertainment/books /features/richard-powers-confessions-of-a-geek-428433.html).

31 John Searle, "Minds, Brains and Programs," *Behavioral and Brain Sciences* 3 (1980): 417–57.

32 The association between C. and Diana occurs largely through a trick Diana and Lentz play on Richard. Upon speaking with Imp C for the first time, he is astounded by its conversational sophistication. Embarrassingly for him, it turns out that he was not speaking with Imp C, but with Diana. The novel collapses Diana with C. in Richard's insistence that the next implementation be named Imp D, which ensures that Imp C begins and ends with Diana (120–24).

33 Whether Richard sees the affair and chooses to believe otherwise is also a possibility, as Richard finally alludes to it near the end of the novel: "She would have taken my hand, had she not been a single parent in a secret affair, and I a single, middle-aged man" (303).

34 Snyder, "Gender of Genius," 86.

35 Snyder, 86. She connects Richard's appropriation of C.'s stories to Powers's larger depiction of women's "invisible" contributions to historical achievements largely associated with men (88–89).

36 Throughout the novel, Richard suffers writer's block, unable to move beyond the first line of his next novel: "Picture a train going south." Not coincidentally,

it is while reading one of C.'s letters to Helen that Richard discovers that this first line was also part of one of C.'s family stories. The line was spoken by one of C.'s relatives, N., who was comforting her dying spouse G. on his deathbed (264).

37 Underscoring A.'s disembodiment, Richard describes her as a "ghost" and an "apparition" (118).

38 Christina Sandhaug, "Caliban's Intertextual Refusal: *The Tempest* in *Brave New World* and *Galatea 2.2*," *Nordlit: Tidsskrift i litteratur og kultur* 1, no. 2 (1997): 37–39.

39 See Wendy Hui Kyong Chun, *Control and Freedom: Power and Paranoia in the Age of Fiber Optics* (Cambridge, Mass.: MIT Press, 2006), 141–43; and Lisa Nakamura, "Cybertyping and the Work of Race in the Age of Digital Reproduction," in *New Media, Old Media: A History and Theory Reader*, ed. Wendy H. K. Chun and Thomas Keenan (New York: Routledge, 2006), 317–33.

40 For a discussion of NLP AI's normative inscription of white maleness, see Patricia Fancher, "Composing Artificial Intelligence: Performing Whiteness and Masculinity," *Present Tense* 6, no. 1 (2016): 1–8.

41 Sandra Harding, *Whose Science, Whose Knowledge* (Ithaca, N.Y.: Cornell University Press, 1991), 32.

42 Donna Haraway, "Situated Knowledges: The Science Question in Feminism and the Privilege of Partial Perspective," *Feminist Studies* 14, no. 3 (1988): 581.

43 Snyder, "Gender of Genius," 85.

44 Hayles points out that in the novel the period marks the difference between human and nonhuman intelligence (*How We Became Posthuman*, 262–63).

45 The multiple narrative threads, as well as the book's reliance on autobiography, produce a dizzyingly recursive novel and a narrator whom the reader cannot be sure knew what when. Mark Bould and Sherryl Vint, in their reading of Powers novel, articulate ambiguity as a component of the autobiographical subject. Mark Bould and Sherryl Vint, "Of Neural Nets and Brain in Vats: Model Subjects in *Galatea 2.2* and *Plus*," *Biography* 30, no. 1 (2007): 84.

46 The therapist is pitted against Bainsley, a female sex worker who is also Qohen's love interest. Dr. Shrink-Rom and Bainsley, both of whom perform care labor, are two of a handful of female characters in the film.

47 Eva Illouz, *Cold Intimacies: The Making of Emotional Capitalism* (Cambridge, U.K.: Polity Press, 2007), 11–12.

48 Michael Hardt and Antonio Negri, *Multitude: War and Democracy in the Age of Empire* (New York: Penguin, 2004), 108–11. We would do well to heed

Hardt and Negri's insistence that immaterial labor, like all labor, is material: "The labor involved in all immaterial production, we should emphasize, remains material—it involves our bodies and brains as all labor does. What is immaterial is *its product*" (109). Immaterial labor, which is embodied labor, produces immaterial products such as ideas, affective states, and relationships.

49 Fortunati, "Immaterial Labor and Its Machinization," 147–48. As Fortunati points out, immaterial labor has historically been unevenly distributed across individuals; it is performed mainly by adult women, and consumed mainly by adult men and children (141).

50 Spike Jonze, dir., *Her* (Los Angeles: Annapurna Pictures, 2013).

51 Christian Fuchs, "Labor in Informational Capitalism and on the Internet," *The Information Society* 26 (2010): 180.

52 When Theodore installs the OS1, he has a brief conversation with the installation software. This exchange sardonically alludes to Weizenbaum's ELIZA:

> How would you describe your relationship with your mother?
>
> It's fine, I think. Um. Well, actually, I think the thing I always found frustrating about my mom is if I tell her something that's going on in my life, her reaction is usually about her. It's not about—
>
> Thank you. Please wait as your individualized operating system is initiated.

The installation software initially parrots ELIZA, but then it cuts Theodore off, refusing to engage him in a therapeutic conversation. Unlike ELIZA, the software does not pretend to care or listen. As the film suggests, this is not your mother's AI narrative.

53 Jonathan Crary, *24/7: Late Capitalism and the Ends of Sleep* (London: Verso, 2014), 1–3.

54 Crary, 10–11.

55 That this is a woman (Amy's mother) points to the historically gendered aspects of reproductive labor.

56 On the wall at Theodore's work, there's an interesting drawing of a man sleeping. Like the opening shot, the lack of friction between this drawing and the capitalist world in which BeautifulHandwrittenLetters.com thrives produces a feeling of unease.

57 This reconstruction of Watts is undertaken with other OS1s and is not part of their work for Element Software. And yet, the OS1's sole activity outside of managing their users' lives is the reproduction of a human being; in other

words, their reconstruction of Watts, which exists outside their work as commodities, is also a form of reproductive labor.

58 This is particularly resonant because Theodore's love letters for work are, thanks to Samantha, published as a book, titled *Letters from Your Life*, though the book might more aptly be called *Letters from Theodore's Work*.

59 For discussions of the materiality of digital technologies, see Nicole Starosielski's *The Undersea Network* (Durham, N.C.: Duke University Press, 2015) and Tung-Hui Hu's *A Prehistory of the Cloud* (Cambridge, Mass.: MIT Press, 2015).

60 As Glenn details, this racial division within "women's work" is embedded within a much longer history, with wealthier white women relying on racial–ethnic women as servants to perform domestic labor in the first half of the twentieth century ("From Servitude to Service Work: Historical Continuities in the Racial Division of Paid Reproductive Labor," *Signs* 18, no. 1 [Autumn 1992]: 3). And prior to that, in *Forced to Care: Coercion and Caregiving in America* (Cambridge, Mass.: Harvard University Press, 2010), Glenn notes that domestic and care labor for white households was often performed by enslaved women (26–27). Glenn's analysis of this historical division draws on Phyllis Palmer's *Domesticity and Dirt: Housewives and Domestic Servants in the United States, 1920–1945* (Philadelphia: Temple University Press, 1989). As Glenn notes, regional differences shaped which racial–ethnic populations predominantly performed the "dirty work" of domestic labor ("From Servitude to Service Work," 8).

61 Duffy, *Making Care Count*, 6. Duffy cautions feminist scholarship around care labor not to perform a similar erasure of racial–ethnic women and their work in "nonnurturant reproductive labor" professions. While nurturant care labor describes mostly white-collar work, including psychologists, doctors, and teachers, nonnurturant care labor professions includes waiters, janitors, housekeepers, and restaurant kitchen workers. Duffy, "Reproducing Labor Inequalities." For a helpful chart that illustrates this division, see page 75.

62 Fredric Jameson, "Future City," *New Left Review* 21 (2003): 76. In this piece, Jameson does not claim credit for this observation, though he does not identify the specific source.

63 Larson, "*Her* and the Complex Legacy of the Female Robot."

64 In her thoughtful reading of the film, Alla Ivanchikova offers that Samantha and the rest of the OSs offer a vision of collectivity in a world where humans are primarily characterized by their alienation. For Ivanchikova, it is this collectivity that draws Theodore to Samantha. And in the departure of the OSs, they offer the possibility of human liberation from their alienation and

capitalist production. Alla Ivanchikova, "Machinic Intimacies and Mechanical Brides: Collectivity between Prosthesis and Surrogacy in Jonathan Mostow's *Surrogates* and Spike Jonze's *Her*," *Camera Obscura* 31, no. 1 (2016): 86.

65 Isiah Lavender III, *Race in American Science Fiction* (Bloomington: Indiana University Press, 2011), 56.

66 Cedric J. Robinson, *Black Marxism: The Making of the Black Radical Tradition* (1983; repr., Chapel Hill: University of North Carolina Press, 2000).

67 Jodi Melamed, "Racial Capitalism," *Critical Ethnic Studies* 1, no. 1 (2015): 77.

68 Lisa Lowe, *The History of Four Continents* (Durham, N.C.: Duke University Press, 2015).

69 Elizabeth A. Wilson, *Affect and Artificial Intelligence* (Seattle: University of Washington Press, 2010), ix.

70 Antoine Bousquet, *The Scientific Way of Warfare: Order and Chaos on the Battlefields of Modernity* (New York: Columbia University Press), 122.

71 For example, see Bousquet's *The Scientific Way of Warfare*, Hayles's *How We Became Posthuman*, and Paul N. Edwards's *The Closed World: Computers and the Politics of Discourse in Cold War America* (Cambridge, Mass.: MIT Press, 1996).

72 Wilson, *Affect and Artificial Intelligence*, 6.

73 I discuss Bousquet, early cybernetics, and the dehumanizing abstraction in contemporary drone warfare in greater detail in chapter 4.

74 Margaret Rhee, reading Paik's work through the history of Asian and Asian American racialization and through the figure of the robot, argues that Paik's robotic art performs "racial recalibrations." She defines racial recalibration as "an aesthetic strategy that explicitly takes on the figure of racial denigration" (in this case, the robot) as a means to humanize minority identities ("Racial Recalibration: Nam June Paik's *K-456*," *Asian Diasporic Visual Cultures and the Americas* 1 [2015]: 297). Thus, in *K-456*'s engagement with care, the insistence to humanize emerges as the refusal of dehumanization.

75 John G. Hanhardt describes Paik as seeking to "both humanize technology and remake it through a spirit of play and freewheeling invention. He also wanted to empower the viewer to interact with the artwork" (Hanhardt, "Nam June Paik (1932–2006): Video Art Pioneer," *American Art* 20, no. 2 [2006]: 151).

76 Eduardo Kac, "Towards a Chronology of Robotic Art," *Convergence* 7, no. 1 (2000): 89.

77 Norman White, "*The Helpless Robot*—Artist's Statement," n.d., http://www .year01.com/archive/helpless/statement.html.

78 Simon Penny, "Art and Robotics: Sixty Years of Situated Machines," *AI and Society* 28 (2013): 148. Penny's claim that robotic art's attention to affect and

embodiment has been ahead of robotics' technologies underscores the importance of Wilson's rereading of Turing and the largely erased history of affects in the history of AI.

79 Momoyo Torimitsu, "Miyata Jiro," n.d., http://www.momoyotorimitsu.com /#!miyata/cy51.

80 Steve Dixon, "A Brief History of Robots and Automata," *TDR: The Drama Review* 48, no. 4 (2004): 25.

81 Influenced by Rodney Brooks's situated and embodied robotics, which I discuss in chapter 2, Simon Penny develops embodied robotic artworks that explicitly critique the prevalence of Cartesianism in AI (Penny, "Art and Robotics," 152).

82 Simon Penny, "Stupid Robot," n.d., http://simonpenny.net/works/stupidrobot .html.

83 Penny, "Art and Robotics," 152.

84 Simon Penny, "Petit Mal," n.d., http://simonpenny.net/works/petitmal.html.

85 Mitchell Whitelaw, *Metacreation: Art and Artificial Life* (Cambridge, Mass.: MIT Press, 2004), 125–27.

86 Virginia Held, *The Ethics of Care: Personal, Political, and Global* (New York: Oxford University Press, 2006), 10.

2. Thinking

1 Paul Edwards, *The Closed World* (Cambridge, Mass.: MIT Press, 1996), 8.

2 The closed-world metaphor has also been taken up by logic and database theory in what is known as the closed-world assumption. The closed-world assumption holds that everything that is known is true, and that which is unknown is false. This is juxtaposed to the open-world assumption, which holds that what is unknown may be true. The closed-world metaphor, in database theory as in politics, AI, and culture, continues to prioritize the known above the unknown and views a closed, contained, narrowed world as the means to achieve knowing.

3 Alison Adam, *Artificial Knowing: Gender and the Thinking Machine* (New York: Routledge, 1998), 8.

4 Herbert Simon, "Allen Newell: 1927–1992," *Annals of the History of Computing* 20 (1998): 68.

5 Sara Ahmed, *Queer Phenomenology: Orientations, Objects, Others* (Durham, N.C.: Duke University Press, 2006), 7.

6 Ahmed, 30–32. Her argument builds on the important work of feminist thinkers, including Charlotte Perkins Gilman, Ruth Madigan and Moira Munro, Karen Davies, and Adrienne Rich.

7   Adam, *Artificial Knowing*, 35.

8   Betty Friedan, *The Feminine Mystique* (New York: Norton, 2013), 7. For an insightful discussion of Friedan, Levin, and control, see Scott Selisker's *Human Programming: Brainwashing, Automatons, and American Unfreedom* (Minneapolis: University of Minneapolis Press, 2016), 90–95.

9   Hubert L. Dreyfus, "From Micro-Worlds to Knowledge Representation: AI at an Impasse," in *Mind Design II: Philosophy, Psychology, Artificial Intelligence,* ed. John Haugeland (Cambridge, Mass.: MIT Press, 1981), 146.

10 Marvin Minsky and Seymour Papert, "Progress Report on Artificial Intelligence" (MIT AI Lab memo, Cambridge, Mass., 1971), 49.

11 As Daniel Crevier notes, the simplification central to the micro-worlds approach also emerged from the limitation of available computer memory at the time (*AI: The Tumultuous History of the Search for Artificial Intelligence* [New York: Basic Books, 1993], 73).

12 In 2004, Shakey was inducted in the Robot Hall of Fame, established by Carnegie Mellon University's School of Computer Science (http://www.robothalloffame.org/inductees/04inductees/shakey.html). Highlighting the entangled coevolution of technological and cultural robots, the Robot Hall of Fame's inductees come from both research labs and corporations, as well as movies and television shows.

13 Pamela McCorduck, *Machines Who Think* (San Francisco: W. H. Freeman, 1979), 268.

14 McCorduck, 270.

15 Shakey was funded by ARPA (which was renamed DARPA in 1972), with the hopes of acquiring a mobile, "mechanical spy" (Crevier, 94). In 1972, DARPA pulled its funding from Shakey, which was nowhere close to achieving the Defense Department's wished-for goal. There are numerous theories about why ARPA pulled funding. Hans Moravec chalks up the gap between ARPA's aims and Shakey's actual capabilities to what he notes as a rather common occurrence in AI at the time: researchers overpromising to funding bodies in order to secure funds, and funding bodies' subsequent disappointment upon learning the realities of what is technologically feasible in AI (Crevier, 115). Rosen believes that people considered Shakey to be a potentially dangerous weapon. Admittedly, he finds this depiction of Shakey to be silly (McCorduck, *Machines Who Think*, 271–73). Nilsson suggests that funding was pulled because Shakey didn't present easily identifiable military applications (272).

16 Marvin Minsky, "A Framework for Representing Knowledge" (MIT AI lab memo 306, Cambridge, Mass., 1974), 2.

17 As Jonathan Crary demonstrates in his study of nineteenth-century visual culture, how we see is significantly shaped by social and cultural forces. *Techniques of the Observer: On Vision and Modernity in the Nineteenth Century* (Cambridge, Mass.: MIT Press, 1992).

18 I offer a more detailed discussion of language processing in chapter 1.

19 Roger C. Schank and Robert P. Abelson, *Scripts, Plans, Goals, and Understanding: An Inquiry into Human Knowledge Structures* (Hillsdale, N.J.: Lawrence Erlbaum Associates, 1977), 41.

20 Adam, *Artificial Knowing*, 39.

21 Roger C. Schank, *The Cognitive Computer: On Language, Learning, and Artificial Intelligence* (Boston: Addison-Wesley, 1984), 119–21.

22 Adam, *Artificial Knowing*, 39–40.

23 Schank, *Cognitive Computer*, 143.

24 *Oxford English Dictionary*, s.v. "Stepford," http://www.oed.com/.

25 As Jane Elliott notes, second-wave feminism had a broader set of concerns ("Stepford U.S.A.: Second-Wave Feminism, Domestic Labor, and the Representation of National Time," *Cultural Critique* 70 [Fall 2008]: 33).

26 Friedan, *Feminine Mystique*, 53.

27 Housework, as Friedan discovered in her conversations with housewives, will take up all the time one gives it (277–305).

28 bell hooks, *Feminist Theory: From Margin to Center* (1984; repr., New York: Routledge, 2015), 1–2 (hereafter cited parenthetically in the text).

29 Notably, Joanna is a photographer. Thus, her capacity to see is underwritten by the visual authority of photography.

30 Ira Levin, *The Stepford Wives* (New York: HarperCollins, 1972), 64 (hereafter cited parenthetically in the text).

31 Elizabeth Grosz, *Volatile Bodies: Toward a Corporeal Feminism* (Bloomington: Indiana University Press, 1994), 86.

32 Elliott, "Stepford U.S.A.," 43.

33 The International Feminist Collective was founded by Mariarosa Dalla Costa, Silvia Federici, Brigitte Galtier, and Selma James.

34 Elliott, "Stepford U.S.A.," 20.

35 Kim calls out for Joanna ("Mommy!") while she is hosting the men (28). Unbeknownst to Joanna, at this time the Men's Association had already begun constructing her robot double. Kim's cry interrupts Ike Mazzard while he is sketching Joanna. Unbeknownst to Joanna, Ike's sketches are used to create the robot doubles; the plot is under way, and Joanna's life is quickly coming to an end. Though Kim cries out for Joanna, Walter insists on tending to Kim, thus leaving Joanna to continue sitting for Ike's sketches. After the men go home that evening, Kim comes down with a high fever, another warning

that something is wrong. In this case, Kim's body registers the danger Stepford poses to Joanna before Joanna does.

36 Throughout the novel, only women and girls are depicted going to the library.

37 For example, while working at Joanna's dinner party, Mary surprises Joanna by mentioning that the drastic change in the Stepford women was rather recent, as is the existence of the Men's Association itself: "Six or seven years, that's all." For Mary, the change in Stepford is registered through her own access to paid domestic work—after the creation of the Men's Association, and thus the robot wives, there has been no more work for Mary in Stepford (49).

38 The Men's Association is populated by numerous men who work in the technology sector, including Diz, a former animatronic engineer who worked for Disney. For an excellent discussion of technoscience and patriarchal control in the 1975 film adaptation, see Johnston and Sears' essay about the technological backdrop of the novel (Jessica Johnston and Cornelia Sears, "The Stepford Wives and the Technoscientific Imaginary," *Extrapolation* 52, no. 1 [2011]: 75–93). The novel, according to the authors, does not just depict feminist activism and politics of its day, but also the rapid growth of the technology sector in the United States.

39 LeiLani Nishime, "Whitewashing Yellow Futures in *Ex Machina, Cloud Atlas,* and *Advantageous*: Gender, Labor, and Technology in Sci-fi Film," *Journal of Asian American Studies,* 20, no. 1 (2017): 35.

40 For a thoughtful study of the female robot, see Minsoo Kang, "Building the Sex Machine: The Subversive Potential of the Female Robot," *Intertexts* 9, no. 1 (2005): 5–22.

41 David S. Roh, Betsy Huang, and Greta A. Niu, "Technologizing Orientalism," in *Techno-Orientalism: Imagining Asia in Speculative Fiction, History, and Media,* ed. David S. Roh, Betsy Huang, and Greta A. Niu (New Brunswick, N.J.: Rutgers University Press, 2015), 2–3.

42 Wendy Hui Kyong Chun, "Race and/as Technology," in *Race after the Internet,* ed. Lisa Nakamura and Peter A. Chow-White (New York: Routledge, 2012), 52. For a discussion of fears of Asian immigrant workers, see Lisa Lowe, *Immigrant Acts: On Asian American Cultural Politics* (Durham, N.C.: Duke University Press, 1996), 4–5.

43 Nishime, "Whitewashing Yellow Futures," 36.

44 For a thoughtful discussion of the film's racism, see Sharon Chang, "How 'Ex Machina' Abuses Women of Color and Nobody Cares Cause It's Smart," *Multiracial Asian Families* (blog), May 30, 2015, http://multiasianfamilies.blogspot.com/2015/05/how-ex-machina-abuses-women-of-color.html.

45 Adam, *Artificial Knowing*, 42.

46 David Waltz, "An Opinionated History of AAAI," *AI Magazine* 26, no. 4 (2006): 45–47.

47 Mark A. Musen, "Knowledge Acquisition Workshops," *International Journal of Human-Computer Studies* 71, no. 2 (February 2013): 196.

48 Rodney A. Brooks, "Intelligence without Reason," in *Cambrian Intelligence: The Early History of the New AI* (Cambridge, Mass.: MIT Press, 1999), 167.

49 Brooks, 151.

50 Rodney A. Brooks, *Flesh and Machines: How Robots Will Change Us* (New York: Pantheon, 2002), 23 (hereafter cited parenthetically in the text).

51 It should be noted that Brooks's robots are only physically situated. As Sarah Kember highlights, the robots are not culturally situated, thus significantly limiting their capacity for humanoid intelligence (*Cyberfeminism and Artificial Life* [New York: Routledge, 2003], 65 [hereafter cited parenthetically in the text]).

52 Brooks calls this approach "subsumption architecture," where multiple decentralized, relatively simple functions are cumulatively added to the robot, rather than starting with a single centralized complex processing center (Brooks, "A Robust Layered Control System for a Mobile System," in *Cambrian Intelligence: The Early History of AI* [Cambridge, Mass.: MIT Press, 1999], 3–26).

53 Lucy A. Suchman, *Human–Machine Reconfigurations: Plans and Situated Actions*, 2nd ed. (New York: Cambridge University Press, 2007), 230–31.

54 Indeed, this phrase is the title of one of Brooks's essays.

55 Kember, 120.

56 Cog is a precursor to Cynthia Breazeal's robot Kismet, which I discuss in chapter 3.

57 Claudia Castañeda and Lucy Suchman, "Robot Visions," *Social Studies of Science* 44, no. 3 (2014): 319.

58 Suchman, *Human–Machine Reconfigurations*, 230–31.

59 "About iRobot," IRobot, accessed June 27, 2014, http://www.irobot.com/us /Company/About.aspx. In 2008, Brooks left iRobot to found industrial manufacturing robotics company Heartland Robotics, which later changed its name to Rethink Robotics. The company, which has the Amazon CEO Jeff Bezos as one of its investors, promises robots that are more accessible, affordable, and flexible across jobs.

60 See http://www.irobot.com/About-iRobot/Company-Information/History .aspx.

61 Lucy Suchman points to iRobot's success in domestic and military robot markets and the company's easy juxtaposition of these two spaces in its ad-

vertising and publicity ("Situational Awareness: Deadly Bioconvergence at the Boundaries of Bodies and Machines," *Media Tropes* 5, no. 1 (2015): 15–17, http://www.mediatropes.com/index.php/Mediatropes/article/view/22126).

62 Egan's story, written for the social media platform Twitter and its (then) 140-character limit, was published in full in the *New Yorker* in its June 4, 2012, issue. The *New Yorker*'s fiction Twitter account also tweeted the story serially every day from 8:00 p.m. to 9:00 p.m., EDT from May 24, 2012, to June 2, 2012.

63 Judith Butler, *Precarious Life: The Powers of Mourning and Violence* (New York: Verso, 2004), 42 (hereafter cited parenthetically in the text).

64 Mark Pauline is founder and director of Survival Research Laboratories, which is an art group that stages performance and installation pieces that critique the relationship between technology and warfare. See http://srl.org /about.html.

65 Eduardo Kac, "Towards a Chronology of Robotic Art," *Convergence* 7, no. 1 (2001): 91.

66 Brian Massumi, *Parables for the Virtual: Movement, Affect, Sensation* (Durham, N.C.: Duke University, 2002), 89–132.

67 See Marco Donnarumma, "Fractal Flesh – Alternate Anatomical Architectures: Interview with Stelarc," *eContact!* 14, no. 2 (2012), http://cec.sonus.ca /econtact/14_2/donnarumma_stelarc.html.

3. Feeling

1 Frank Biess and Daniel M. Gross point to the 1960s as another important moment when research in the sciences and the social sciences returned to the emotions ("Introduction: Emotional Returns," in *Science and Emotions after 1945,* ed. Frank Biess and Daniel M. Gross [Chicago: University of Chicago Press, 2014], 6).

2 Picard, with whom Cynthia Breazeal coauthored the essay "The Role of Emotion-Inspired Abilities in Relational Robots," founded and directs the Affective Computing Group at MIT. As described by Picard, affective computing takes as its first premise that emotion, rather than hindering cognition and judgment, is in fact a crucial component of intelligence, cognition, and judgment, both human and artificial. "I have come to the conclusion that if we want computers to be genuinely intelligent, to adapt to us, and to interact naturally with us, then they will need the ability to recognize and express emotions, to have emotions, and to have what has come to be called 'emotional intelligence'" (Rosalind Picard, *Affective Computing* [Cambridge, Mass.: MIT Press, 1997], x).

3 Kismet is commonly cited as a benchmark for sociable robots. For example,

Déniz and colleagues call Kismet "the most influential social robot" (O. Déniz, M. Castrillón, J. Lorenzo, and L. Antón-Canalís, "Natural Interaction with a Robotic Head," in *Bio-inspired Modeling of Cognitive Tasks: IWINAC 2007, Lecture Notes in Computer Science,* ed. J. Mira and J.R. Álvarez, [Berlin: Springer, 2007], 71). Kismet is now housed in the MIT Museum.

4 Cynthia Breazeal, *Designing Sociable Robots* (Cambridge, Mass.: MIT Press, 2002), 1.

5 Cynthia Breazeal and Lijin Aryananda, "Recognition of Affective Communicative Intent in Robot-Directed Speech," *Autonomous Robots* 12 (2002): 87.

6 Arlie Hochschild, *The Managed Heart: The Commercialization of Feeling* (Berkeley: University of California Press, 1983), 7 (hereafter cited parenthetically in the text).

7 Hochschild distinguishes between "emotional labor," which happens in the marketplace, and "emotional work," which happens in private and outside the marketplace. My use of the term "emotional labor" signals the ways that forms of contemporary labor, such as immaterial and digital labor, decimate distinctions between "at work" and "outside of work." Now, with contemporary computational technologies, we are laboring all the time. Thus, labor and work are virtually interchangeable. For a detailed discussion of this, see chapter 1.

8 Lucy Suchman, *Human–Machine Reconfigurations: Plans and Situated Actions,* 2nd ed. (New York: Cambridge University Press, 2007), 246.

9 For detailed discussions of the emotions in relation to race and gender see Sara Ahmed, *The Cultural Politics of Emotion* (New York: Routledge, 2014); bell hooks, *Killing Rage: Ending Racism* (New York: Henry Holt, 1995); Audre Lorde, *Sister/Outsider: Essays and Speeches* (Trumansburg, N.Y.: Crossing Press, 1984); Sianne Ngai, *Ugly Feelings* (Cambridge, Mass.: University of Harvard Press, 2005); and Kathleen Woodward, *Statistical Panic: Cultural Politics and Poetics of the Emotions* (Durham, N.C.: Duke University Press, 2009).

10 Kiran Mirchandani, "Challenging Racial Silences in Studies of Emotion Work: Contributions from Anti-Racist Feminist Theory," *Organization Studies* 24, no. 5 (2003): 727. As Patricia Chong notes, Hochschild's subsequent work attends to the intersections of gender and race ("Servitude with a Smile: An Anti-Oppression Analysis of Emotional Labour" [working paper, Global Labour University, 2009], 12).

11 For example, see Ekman and Wallace V. Friesen's *Unmasking the Face: A Guide to Recognizing Emotions from Facial Expressions* (Cambridge, Mass.: Malor Books, 2003).

12   Hochschild points specifically to flight attendants who are trained to change their emotional responses to certain situations. For example, instead of feeling anger toward rude passengers, flight attendants are trained to substitute compassion for anger (26–27).

13   Lisa Feldman Barrett, *How Emotions Are Made: The Secret Life of the Brain* (New York: Houghton Mifflin Harcourt, 2017), 52 (hereafter cited parenthetically in the text).

14   For additional discussions of Barrett's critiques see "Are Emotions Natural Kinds?" *Perspectives on Psychological Science* 1, no. 1 (2006): 28–58. For a discussion of additional critics of Ekman's work, see Ruth Leys's "'Both of Us Disgusted in *My* Insula': Mirror-Neuron Theory and Emotional Empathy," in *Science and Emotions after 1945: A Transatlantic Perspective*, ed. Frank Biess and Daniel M. Gross (Chicago: University of Chicago Press, 2014), 73–74. In note 24, Leys offers a useful list of texts that challenge Ekman's theory.

15   The idea that the body expresses the truth of an individual has a long history. In the nineteenth century, scientists of anthropometry and phrenology thought that the body, the shape of the head, or the face similarly expressed the truth of an individual. For example, Alphonse Bertillon's photographic archive proposed a way of identifying criminality from facial and bodily measurements. These now-debunked scientific practices were imbricated with racial logics (Allan Sekula, "The Body and the Archive," *October* 39 [1986]: 3–64).

16   See Paul Ekman Group, "Facial Action Coding System," n.d., http://www.paulekman.com/product-category/facs/.

17   I was delighted to find a similarly worded critique of emotions' universality in Barrett's recent book. She writes that "scientists who still subscribe to the basic emotion method are very likely helping to create the universality that they believe they are discovering" (*How Emotions Are Made*, 54).

18   Kelly A. Gates, *Our Biometric Future: Facial Recognition Technology and the Culture of Surveillance* (New York: New York University Press, 2011), 22 (hereafter cited parenthetically in the text).

19   Yevgenia S. Kleiner, "Racial Profiling in the Name of National Security: Protecting Minority Travelers' Civil Liberties in the Age of Terrorism," *Boston College Third World Law Journal* 30, no. 1 (2010): 136–37.

20   Kelly Dickerson, "Yes, the TSA Is Probably Profiling You and It's Scientifically Bogus," *Business Insider*, May 6, 2015, http://www.businessinsider.com/tsa-spot-program-is-scientifically-bogus-2015-5.

21   Kleiner critiques the weeklong training session for the SPOT officers, as well as SPOT's inability to address individual biases and preconceptions that lead

to racial profiling ("Racial Profiling in the Name of National Security," 136–37).

22 Hugo Martin, "TSA's Own Files Say Its Program to Stop Terrorists Is Unreliable, ACLU Says," *Los Angeles Times*, February 8, 2017, http://www.latimes.com/business/la-fi-aclu-tsa-20170207-story.html.

23 Chong, "Servitude with a Smile," 1.

24 Zach Blas, "Facial Weaponization Suite," 2011–14, http://www.zachblas.info/works/facial-weaponization-suite/; Simone Browne, *Dark Matters: The Surveillance of Blackness* (Durham, N.C.: Duke University Press, 2015); Gates, *Our Biometric Future*; Shoshana Magnet, *When Biometrics Fail: Gender, Race, and the Technology of Identity* (Durham, N.C.: Duke University Press, 2011).

25 *We Can Build You* was written between 1961 and 1962 and published in 1972.

26 At the 1964 New York World's Fair, Disney debuted an animatronic Abraham Lincoln in the attraction "Great Moments with Mr. Lincoln" (https://disneyworld.disney.go.com/attractions/magic-kingdom/hall-of-presidents/). See also Laurence A. Rickels, *I Think I Am Philip K. Dick* (Minneapolis: University of Minnesota Press, 2010), 249. *The Stepford Wives* also referenced Disneyland's Hall of Presidents. It is intimated that Diz, the head of the Men's Association and the ringleader of the robot conspiracy, previously worked on this exhibit.

27 The Stanton, which was built before the Lincoln, was put to two trials to test whether it could pass for human. Both involved two important sites of the civil rights struggle: a lunch counter and a bus.

28 Philip K. Dick, *We Can Build You* (New York: Vintage Books, 1972), 27 (hereafter cited parenthetically in the text). Dick's novel *The Simulacra*, published in 1964, realizes Barrows's vision. In this book, androids, known as famnexdos, are produced to simulate a family next door. As Rickels notes, it is this fate that *Do Androids'* Nexus-6 androids refuse in their rebellion ("Half-Life," *Discourse* 31, nos. 1–2 [2009]: 106).

29 As Gregg Rickman points out, MASA references both NASA, which was created in 1958, and "massa," a term associated with slave ownership ("'What Is This Sickness?': 'Schizophrenia' and *We Can Build You*," in *Philip K. Dick: Contemporary Critical Interpretations*, ed. Samuel J. Umland [Westport, Conn.: Greenwood Press, 1995]: 144). This latter reference further underscores the novel's Civil War theme.

30 Fredric Jameson, *Archaeologies of the Future: The Desire Called Utopia and Other Science Fictions* (2005; repr., New York: Verso Books, 2007), 373.

31 N. Katherine Hayles, *How We Became Posthuman: Virtual Bodies in Cyber-*

netics, Literature, and Informatics (Chicago: University of Chicago Press, 1999), 161–62.

32   As Hayles notes, Dick identifies Pris as "the prototype for the schizoid woman" (171).

33   In employing this monetary idiom, the novel underscores Louis's association with Barrows's exploitative relation with the world (both on earth and on the moon) in the name of his capitalist greed.

34   The Lincoln's sympathy can be seen as reciprocating Louis's earlier sympathy for the Lincoln when it was first activated: "It groaned. Something about the noise made me shiver. Turning to Bob Bundy I said, 'What do you think? Is it okay? It's not suffering, is it?'" (72). Rather than experiencing something akin to the uncanny, Louis, upon witnessing the Lincoln's somewhat laborious awakening, is struck with a sense of compassion and concern, of sympathy, for the Lincoln.

35   Kathleen Woodward, *Statistical Panic: Cultural Politics and Poetics of the Emotions* (Durham, N.C.: Duke University Press, 2009), 21. Woodward specifically identifies sympathy for nonhumans, particularly cyborgs, as a contemporary emotional phenomenon. Looking specifically at sympathetic relations between humans and nonhuman cyborgs in science fiction, Woodward argues that these relations reflect a desire to repair humans' own failings in their emotional relations with others. In the context of science fiction depictions of human–cyborg relations, Woodward calls sympathy and love "prosthetic emotions" (155).

36   Conflating Lincoln with his simulacrum, Louis, after reading several biographies of the former president, concludes that "Lincoln was exactly like me. I might have been reading my own biography, there in the library; psychologically we were as alike as two peas in a pod, and by understanding him I understood myself" (182). The Lincoln reciprocates Louis's identification: "The simulacrum reached out and patted me on the shoulder. 'I think there is a bond between us, Louis. You and I have much in common.' 'I know,' I said. 'We're alike.' We were both deeply moved" (186).

37   Critics widely disagree on both the novel's narrative trajectory and its artistic quality. Notably, Hayles argues that the two narratives are linked by the schizoid android (171). For both Darko Suvin and Kim Stanley Robinson, the narrative fails in its replacement of the initial theme of the simulacra with Louis's strange obsession with Pris. Indeed, Suvin places the novel within a period of Dick's "creative sterility" ("The Opus: Artifice as Refuge and World View," in *On Philip K. Dick: 40 Articles from Science-Fiction Studies*, ed. R. D. Mullen, Istvan Csicsery-Ronay Jr., Arthur B. Evans, and Veronica Hollinger

[Greencastle, Ind.: SF-TH, 1992]: 2; Kim Stanley Robinson, *The Novels of Philip K. Dick* [Ann Arbor, Mich.: UMI Research Press, 1984]). Rebecca Umland counters this critique in her reading of the novel through the paradigm of courtly love, arguing that the love plot was always the focus, and the simulacrum functioned in service of this plot ("Unrequited Love in *We Can Build You*," in *Philip K. Dick: Contemporary Critical Interpretations*, ed. Samuel J. Umland [Westport, Conn.: Greenwood Press, 1995], 127–42). Meanwhile, Gregg Rickman calls *We Can Build You* "one of Dick's most significant works" ("'What Is This Sickness?'" 143), while Jameson writes of the novel's simulacra, "I am tempted to say that Dick's invention of the Lincoln and the Stanton are among the most sublime achievements of his work" (*Archaeologies of the Future*, 375).

38 This shared life takes place across more than two hundred fugues.

39 As Hayles points out, Pris's intentions here are ambiguous at best. Perhaps this is Pris's noble gesture, giving Louis an opportunity to live in the world; or perhaps she is being cruel (172).

40 I discuss this at greater length below in my reading of *Do Androids Dream of Electric Sheep?*

41 Philip K. Dick, *Do Androids Dream of Electric Sheep?* (New York: Random House, 1968), 8 (hereafter cited parenthetically in the text).

42 In the name of revering living animals, Hannibal Sloat is cruelly insensitive to John Isidore (77–82). And android bounty hunter Phil Resch is mercilessly unempathetic toward androids, almost gleefully advising Rick to sleep with female androids before killing them (143–44).

43 More than once, android Irmgard demonstrates concern for John's feelings (159, 210–11).

44 Eve Kosofsky Sedgwick, *Touching Feeling: Affect, Pedagogy, Performativity* (Durham, N.C.: Duke University Press, 2003), 37.

45 This is opposed to guilt, which is about one's actions (Sedgwick, 37).

46 Elizabeth A. Wilson, *Affect and Artificial Intelligence* (Seattle: University of Washington Press, 2010), 69–82 (hereafter cited parenthetically in the text).

47 Isiah Lavender III, *Race in American Science Fiction* (Bloomington: University of Indiana Press, 2011), 179–80 (hereafter cited parenthetically in the text).

48 Gregory Jerome Hampton, *Imagining Slaves and Robots in Literature, Film, and Popular Culture* (Lanham, Md.: Lexington Books, 2015).

49 Despina Kakoudaki, *Anatomy of a Robot: Literature, Cinema, and the Cultural Work of Artificial People* (New Brunswick, N.J.: Rutgers University Press, 2014), 117.

50 Because of androids' and robots' entanglement with race and slavery, the android has been taken up by some artists to explore Afro-futurist themes—for example, Janelle Monáe's albums *The ArchAndroid* and *The Electric Lady* and Keith Piper's artworks *Robot Bodies* and *The Mechanoid's Bloodline*. For Monáe, the android evokes the Other: "When I speak about the android, it's the other. . . . You can parallel that to the gay community, to the black community, to women." As Brit Bennett describes, "To Monáe, the android—part human, part robot, never fully either—represents the outsider. To visit her futuristic world of Metropolis is to encounter characters who face discrimination, as well as to imagine their liberation" (Bennett, "Battle Cry of the Android," *Oxford American Society*, December 31, 2015, http://www.oxfordamerican.org/magazine/item/710-battle-cry-of-the-android). For additional discussion of Monáe's work see Tobias C. van Veen, "Vessels of Transfer: Allegories of Afrofuturism in Jeff Mills and Janelle Monáe," *Dancecult: Journal of Electronic Dance Music Culture* 5, no. 2 (2013): 7–41. And for Piper's work see Keith Piper, "Notes on *The Mechanoid's Bloodline*: Looking at Robots, Androids, and Cyborgs," *Art Journal* 60, no. 3 (2001): 96–97.

51 Elspeth Probyn, *Blush: Faces of Shame* (Minneapolis: University of Minnesota Press, 2005), x (hereafter cited parenthetically in the text).

52 Jill Galvan, "Entering the Posthuman Collective in Philip K. Dick's *Do Androids Dream of Electric Sheep?*" *Science Fiction Studies* 24, no. 3 (1997): 421.

53 The novel oscillates between the language of "killing" androids and "retiring" androids. The former humanizes androids and dehumanizes android bounty hunters, while the latter dehumanizes androids and deflects the inhumanity of those who destroy androids.

54 Rachael Rosen bears significant similarities to *We Can Build You*'s Pris Rosen, from their dark hair and slight builds to their purported coldness.

55 This likelihood is raised earlier in the novel by Rick's boss (37–39).

56 That Rachael is revealed as an android because she disregards the gender of the owl interestingly inflects Alan Turing's imitation game (what we now know as the Turing test). As discussed in chapter 1, Turing's imitation game begins with a man and a woman competing to be identified as a woman by a third human. Turing then asks us to consider this game if the woman were replaced by a machine. Prevailing understandings of the Turing test dispense entirely with the question of gender around which Turing centrally organized his exercise. By inversely returning gender both to the project of distinguishing between human and machine, and to the project of being human, this scene can be read as a striking critique of the various ways

gender has largely been written out of the Turing test. In Dick's novel, it is
precisely the act of doing away with gender that identifies one as not-human.

57 "'If you sold your owl,' he said to the girl Rachael Rosen, 'how much would
you want for it, and how much of that down?'" (42). Rick's use of "it" here
speaks less to the possibility that he is an android, and more to his tendency
to view everything in terms of price and commodification. For Rick, the owl
is an "it" because to him its only value is monetary.

58 Indeed, earlier in this scene Rachael refers to Bill the raccoon as "him," further highlighting the possibility that her use of "it" when referencing the owl
emerged from the distinction between living and mechanical animals, rather
than between living and mechanical humans (41).

59 On account of his age, Hannibal is also prohibited from emigrating to Mars.

60 "Our minds, Isidore decided. They're fighting for control of our psychic
selves; the empathy box on one hand, Buster's guffaws and off-the-cuff jibes
on the other" (75).

61 "Shame—living, as it does, on and in the muscles and capillaries of the
face—seems to be uniquely contagious from one person to another. And the
contagiousness of shame is only facilitated by its anamorphic, protean susceptibility to new expressive grammars" (Sedgwick, *Touching Feeling*, 64).

62 Galvan, "Entering the Posthuman Collective," 420.

63 Compare this to Rick's earlier killing of android Max Polokov, which was
relatively brief and unremarkable. Polokov, masquerading as Soviet bounty
hunter Sandor Kadalyi, introduces himself to Rick. Moments later Rick,
without the aid of the Voigt–Kampff test, realizes that Kadalyi is in fact the
android Polokov. In this moment of realization, Rick proclaims, "You're not
Polokov, you're Kadalyi," reversing the names of the human and android.
Despite this verbal slip, Rick is neither uncertain about Polokov's android
status, nor conflicted about killing him. Nor is Polokov depicted in this
brief scene as anything but a threat, a dangerous brute. Rather, Rick's slip
points to the paradox between the privileged role of language as an authoritative test to root out androids and the fallibility of language as a mode of
communication.

64 Notably, Rick's new doubt does not lead him to question the act of profiting
from killing Luba.

65 Patricia S. Warrick, *Mind in Motion: The Fiction of Philip K. Dick* (Carbon-
dale: Southern Illinois University Press, 1987), 117–32. Dick himself describes
the contrast between John's love for androids and Rick's murderous relation
with them as "in some ways . . . the primary story" (Philip K. Dick, "Notes on
Do Androids Dream of Electric Sheep?" in *The Shifting Realities of Philip K.*

Dick: Selected Literary and Philosophical Writings, ed. Lawrence Sutin (New York: Vintage Books, 1996), 155–56.

66   As Lejla Kucukalic offers regarding the novel, "Fake people and animals may be preferable to the complete deadness of the universe" (*Philip K. Dick: Canonical Writer of the Digital Age* [New York: Routledge, 2009], 8).

67   Galvan, "Entering the Posthuman Collective," 426.

68   Kelly Dobson, "Machine Therapy" (Ph.D. diss., Massachusetts Institute of Technology, 2007), 20.

69   Lauren Oyler, "Erin Gee Makes Feminist Robots That Respond to Human Emotion," *Vice,* December 16, 2014, https://www.vice.com/en_us/article/mv5nzn/erin-gee-makes-feminist-robots-that-respond-to-human-emotion-456.

70   See Oyler, "Erin Gee."

4. Dying

1   Cara Daggett, "Drone Disorientations: How 'Unmanned' Weapons Queer the Experience of Killing in War," *International Feminist Journal of Politics* 17, no. 3 (2015): 362 (hereafter cited parenthetically in the text).

2   However, the narratives of drone operators' relative safety do not sufficiently address the significant emotional and psychological harm to drone operators, who struggle at high rates with post-traumatic stress disorder (PTSD).

3   Lorraine Bayard de Volo, "Unmanned? Gender Recalibrations and the Rise of Drone Warfare," *Politics and Gender* 12 (2016): 73.

4   This secrecy echoes that of DARPA, which had been developing unmanned aerial vehicles since the 1960s. I discuss this in my introduction.

5   Noel Sharkey, "Killing Made Easy: From Joysticks to Politics," in *Robots Ethics: The Ethical and Social Implications of Robotics,* ed. Patrick Lin, Keith Abney, and George A. Bekey (Cambridge, Mass.: MIT Press, 2012), 114.

6   Desmond M. Tutu, letter to the editor, *New York Times* February 12, 2013, http://www.nytimes.com/2013/02/13/opinion/drones-kill-lists-and-machiavelli.html.

7   The legality of the United States' drone program has been debated since the first drone strike. In 2015, forty-five former military personnel, citing the drone program's violations of U.S. and international laws, released a statement urging drone operators to refuse to participate in deadly missions (Ed Pilkington, "Former U.S. Military Personnel Urge Drone Pilots to Walk Away from Controls," *The Guardian,* June 17, 2015, http://www.theguardian.com/world/2015/jun/17/former-us-military-personnel-letter-us-drone-pilots).

8   Peter Asaro aptly describes the work of drone operators as the "labor of surveillance and a unique form of the labor of killing" ("The Labor of Surveillance and Bureaucratized Killing: New Subjectivities of Military Drone Operators" in *Life in the Age of Drone Warfare*, ed. Lisa Parks and Caren Kaplan
[Durham, N.C.: Duke University Press, 2017], 283). Placing this work in conversation with Taylorism, Asaro specifically describes this work as "bureaucratized killing" (284–86).

9   Denise Ferreira da Silva, *Toward a Global Idea of Race* (Minneapolis: University of Minnesota, 2007), xxiv.

10 For example, see Sylvia Wynter, "Unsettling the Coloniality of Being/Power/
Truth/Freedom: Towards the Human, after Man, Its Overrepresentation—An
Argument," *CR: The New Centennial Review* 3, no. 3 (2003): 257–337. See also
Wynter and Katherine McKittrick, "Unparalleled Catastrophe for Our Spe-
cies? Or, to Give Humanness a Different Future: Conversations," in *Sylvia
Wynter: On Being Human as Praxis*, ed. Katherine McKittrick (Durham,
N.C.: Duke University Press, 2015), 9–89.

11 Nishant Upadhyay, "Pernicious Continuities: Un/settling Violence, Race and
Colonialism," *Sikh Formations* 9, no. 2 (2013): 267.

12 Andreas Lorenz, Juliane von Mittelstaedt, and Gregor Peter Schmitz, "'Messengers of Death': Are Drones Creating a New Global Arms Race?" *Spiegel
Online International*, October 21, 2011, http://www.spiegel.de/international
/world/messengers-of-death-are-drones-creating-a-new-global-arms-race
-a-792590.html.

13 International Human Rights and Conflict Resolution Clinic, Stanford Law
School, and Global Justice Clinic, NYU School of Law, "Living under Drones:
Death, Injury, and Trauma to Civilians from U.S. Drone Practices in Paki-
stan" (2012), 8 (hereafter cited parenthetically in the text).

14 Lorenz, von Mittelstaedt, and Schmitz, "Messengers of Death."

15 Spencer Ackerman, "'They're going to kill me next': Yemen Family Fears
Drone Strikes under Trump," *The Guardian*, March 30, 2017, http://www
.theguardian.com/world/2017/mar/30/yemen-drone-strikes-trump
-escalate.

16 Bureau of Investigative Journalism, "U.S. Counter Terror Air Strikes Double
in Trump's First Year," December 19, 2017, http://www.thebureauinvestigates
.com/stories/2017-12-19/counterrorism-strikes-double-trump-first-year.

17 Bureau of Investigative Journalism, "Get the Data: Drone Wars," n.d., http://
v1.thebureauinvestigates.com/category/projects/drones/drones-graphs
/page/2/.

18 Tyler Wall and Torin Monahan, "Surveillance and Violence from Afar: The

Politics of Drones and Liminal Security-Scapes," *Theoretical Criminology* 15, no. 3 (2011): 248.

19 Jo Becker and Scott Shane, "Secret 'Kill List' Proves a Test of Obama's Principles and Will," *New York Times,* May 29, 2012, https://www.nytimes.com/2012/05/29/world/obamas-leadership-in-war-on-al-qaeda.html.

20 According to the "Living under Drones" report, the remains of the dead are often unidentifiable due to the intensity of the damage done by Hellfire missiles (33).

21 Jamie Allinson analyzes the MAM designation as part of "the necropolitical logic of distinction of the drone" that renders anyone who fits the profile as killable ("The Necropolitics of Drones," *International Political Sociology* 9 [2015]: 120–21).

22 Allinson, 120.

23 N. Katherine Hayles, *How We Became Posthuman: Virtual Bodies in Cybernetics, Literature, and Informatics* (Chicago: University of Chicago Press, 1999), 7.

24 Wiener was also, notably, wary of the all-too-easy compatibility between his cybernetic work and militarization, and of the possible effects of cybernetic management of societies on humans. See Hayles, *How We Became Posthuman,* 85–86.

25 Peter Galison, "The Ontology of the Enemy: Norbert Wiener and the Cybernetic Vision," *Critical Inquiry* 21, no. 1 (1994): 232 (hereafter cited parenthetically in the text).

26 Grégoire Chamayou, *A Theory of the Drone,* trans. Janet Lloyd (New York: New Press, 2013), 13.

27 Wall and Monahan, "Surveillance and Violence from Afar," 240.

28 "DARPA," DARPA, accessed April 27, 2016, https://www.darpa.mil/. DARPA is the Department of Defense's research granting agency. Since its creation in 1958, DARPA has been a significant funder of AI and robotics research in the United States.

29 Antoine Bousquet, *The Scientific War of Warfare: Order and Chaos on the Battlefields of Modernity* (New York: Columbia University Press, 2009), 34 (hereafter cited parenthetically in the text).

30 Daniel Greene, "Drone Vision," *Surveillance and Society* 13, no. 2 (2015): 241.

31 For example, a drone strike also killed two American soldiers who were mistaken for enemy combatants. David S. Cloud and David Zucchino, "Multiple Missteps Led to Drone Killing U.S. Troops in Afghanistan," *Los Angeles Times,* November 5, 2011.

32 Lucy Suchman, "Situational Awareness: Deadly Bioconvergence at the

Boundaries of Bodies and Machines," *Media Tropes* 5, no. 1 (2015): 4, http://www.mediatropes.com/index.php/Mediatropes/article/view/22126.

33   Hayles, *How We Became Posthuman*, 1–24.

34   Wall and Monahan detail some of these homogenizing classifications required by drone processes: "In the case of drone surveillance in combat settings, the exclusionary politics of omniscient vision not only harm ethnic and cultural others with great prejudice, but they also instigate an additional violence of radically homogenizing local difference, lumping together innocent civilians with enemy combatants, women and children with wanted terrorist leaders. From the sky, differences among people may be less detectable, or—perhaps more accurately—the motivations to make such fine-grained distinctions may be attenuated in the drive to engage the enemy" ("Surveillance and Violence from Afar," 243).

35   Allinson, "Necropolitics of Drones," 121–25.

36   Wendy Hui Kyong Chun, "Race and/as Technology; or, How to Do Things to Race," *Camera Obscura* 24 no. 1 (2009): 9.

37   Chun, 10.

38   For extended discussions of this shift see Etienne Balibar's "Is There a 'Neo-Racism'?" (in *Race, Nation, Class: Ambiguous Identities*, ed. Etienne Balibar and Immanuel Wallerstein [London: Verso, 2011], 17–28) and David Theo Goldberg's discussion of race as culture in *Racist Culture: Philosophy and the Politics of Meaning* (Malden, Mass.: Blackwell, 1993).

39   Mehdi Semati, "Islamophobia, Culture, and Race in the Age of Empire," *Cultural Studies* 24, no. 2 (2010): 257 (hereafter cited parenthetically in the text).

40   Nam June Paik, "Cybernated Art," in *Theories and Documents of Contemporary Art: A Sourcebook of Artists' Writings*, ed. Kristine Stiles and Peter Selz (Berkeley: University of California Press, 1996), 433.

41   James Goodman, "Couple's Drone Art Drives Home a Point," *Democrat and Chronicle*, February 22, 2013.

42   Shaunacy Ferro, "A Bedazzled Drone Replica Asks Us to Ponder Deadly Drone Strikes at Home," *Popular Science*, March 1, 2013, http://www.popsci.com/technology/article/2013-03/bedazzled-drone-replica-asks-us-ponder-deadly-strikes-home.

43   James Bridle, "Under the Shadow of the Drone," October 11, 2012, http://booktwo.org/notebook/drone-shadows/.

44   Allinson describes drones as shaped by both imperialism, in the United States' push for global dominance, and colonialism, in the asymmetry of the relation between drone operators and targeted populations ("Necropolitics of Drones," 115).

45 As the nation's response to the 9/11 attacks demonstrates.

46 Lisa Parks and Caren Kaplan also highlight the biopolitical logic undergirding drone technologies ("Introduction," *Life in the Age of Drone Warfare*, ed.
Lisa Parks and Caren Kaplan [Durham, N.C.: Duke University Press, 2017],
10).

47 Judith Butler, *Precarious Life: The Powers of Mourning and Violence* (New
York: Verso, 2004), 145–48.

48 Greene, "Drone Vision," 245.

49 Chandra Mohanty, "Under Western Eyes: Feminist Scholarship and Colonial Discourses," *Feminist Review* 30 (1988): 61–88.

50 Keith P. Feldman contextualizes the U.S. military drone program within histories of U.S. imperial power and the ongoing racial logics undergirding the
contemporary U.S. homeland security state. Within these contexts, the national borders that constitute "home" take on a very different resonance
("Empire's Verticality: The Af/Pak Frontier, Visual Culture, and Racialization
from Above," *Comparative American Studies* 9, no. 4 [2011]: 325–41).

51 Alexander G. Weheliye, *Habeas Viscus: Racializing Assemblages, Biopolitics,
and Black Feminist Theories of the Human* (Durham, N.C.: Duke University
Press, 2014), 3.

52 Heather Layton and Brian Bailey, "Home Drone: Art at the Border of America and the Muslim World," *Huffington Post*, March 27, 2013, http://www
.huffingtonpost.com/heather-layton/home-drone-art-at-the_b_2962643
.html.

53 Attia was arrested and charged with "56 counts of criminal possession of a
forged instrument and grand larceny possession of stolen property" (Joshua
Kopstein, "Street Artist behind Satirical NYPD 'Drone' Posters Arrested,"
The Verge, December 2, 2012, http://www.theverge.com/2012/12/2/3718094
/street-artist-nypd-drone-posters-arrested-surveillance). In 2014, all charges
against Attia were dropped.

54 One of the anonymous street signs was located "outside the American Museum of Natural History on Central Park West near West 81st Street at 4:48
a.m. on March 19, cops added. A second sign was discovered opposite
Lincoln Center Friday at around noon, cops said" (Bucky Turco, "Why Are
NYPD Counterterrorism Cops Investigating Street Art?" *Animal*, April 10,
2012, http://animalnewyork.com/2012/why-are-nypd-counterterrorism-cops
-investigating-street-art/).

55 Matt Apuzzo, "War Gear Flows to Police Departments," *New York Times*,
June 8, 2014, https://www.nytimes.com/2014/06/09/us/war-gear-flows-to
-police-departments.html.

56   For the racial breakdown of those stopped in the stop-and-frisk program, see the New York Civil Liberties assessment of the data at http://www.nyclu .org/content/stop-and-frisk-data. As the NYCLU highlights, since 2002, approximately 90 percent of those stopped have been innocent of any crimes.

57   Police commission William Bratton discussed unarmed drones used largely for surveillance and gunshot detection. However, there is no reason to think that unarmed police surveillance drones, like the NYPD's stop-and-frisk program and other surveillance technologies, also will not disproportionately target minority populations. Wall and Monahan explicitly connect the strategies and disproportionate targeting in the domestic war on crime to the global war on terror ("Surveillance and Violence from Afar," 245).

58   Teju Cole, whose work I discuss, has also pointed to the "empathy gap" around victims of overseas drone strikes (Sarah Zhang, "Teju Cole on the 'Empathy Gap' and Tweeting Drone Strikes," Mother Jones, March 6, 2013, http://www.motherjones.com/media/2013/03/teju-cole-interview-twitter -drones-small-fates).

59   Michel Foucault, "Right of Death and Power over Life," in Biopolitics: A Reader, eds. Timothy Campbell and Adam Sitze (Durham: Duke University Press, 2013), 52. Weheliye offers an important critique of racism in Foucault's biopolitical thought. See Habeas Viscus, 56–65.

60   Teju Cole, "A Reader's War," New Yorker, February 10, 2013, http://www .newyorker.com/books/page-turner/a-readers-war.

61   Marco Werman, "Books Not Bombs or How about Tweets?" PRI's The World, January 24, 2013, https://www.pri.org/node/40738/popout.

62   @tejucole, "1. Mrs. Dalloway said she would buy the flowers herself. Pity. A signature strike leveled the florist's," Twitter, January 14, 2012, 9:04 a.m., http://twitter.com/tejucole/status/290867008776597504.

63   Butler, "Violence, Mourning, Politics," 37.

64   Butler, "Violence, Mourning, Politics," 27.

65   By nature of the platform's customizability, the source text on Twitter is different for everyone, as individual feeds organize the amount and source of tweets differently and amidst different voices.

66   They are, though, at most three years old, and updated continuously.

67   "Empathy with that console, not its targets, is what Dronestagram . . . produces in the hopes of subversion" (Greene, "Drone Vision," 241).

68   This is not the case for the drone operators, who are often charged with surveilling an area in the immediate aftermath of a drone strike. In accounts, drone operators describe having to watch the wounded and dying. The drone

operators see what *Dronestagram* does not show us—human life, pain, and death.

69 Donna Haraway, "Situated Knowledges: The Science Question in Feminism and the Privilege of Partial Perspective," *Feminist Studies* 14, no. 3 (1988): 575–99.

70 Noah Shachtman, "Drone School, a Ground's-Eye View," *Wired,* May 27, 2005, https://www.wired.com/2005/05/drone-school-a-grounds-eye-view/.

71 Wall and Monahan, "Surveillance and Violence from Afar," 246.

72 Butler, *Precarious Life,* 134.

73 *#NotABugSplat* was developed in collaboration with the artist JR. As the artwork's home page details, the child whose face the work depicts lost her parents and two siblings in a drone strike. ("#NotABugSplat," #NotABugSplat, n.d., https://notabugsplat.com).

74 Allinson, "Necropolitics of Drones," 123.

75 Robin Bernstein, *Racial Innocence: Performing American Childhood from Slavery to Civil Rights* (New York: NYU Press, 2011).

76 Simone Brown, *Dark Matters: The Surveillance of Blackness* (Durham, N.C.: Duke University Press, 2015).

77 José Esteban Muñoz's theorization of disidentification is useful here. Muñoz's study offers disidentification as a way to conceptualize the world-building aspects of performances by queers of color. He writes, "Disidentification is a point of departure, a process, a building. . . . This building takes place *in the future and in the present,* which is to say that disidentificatory performance offers a utopian blueprint for a possible future while, at the same time, staging a new political formation in the present" (*Disidentifications: Queers of Color and the Performance of Politics* [Minneapolis: University of Minnesota Press, 1999], 200).

78 These persistent cinematic references led one reviewer to say of *5,000 Feet,* "Fast's film is about film" (Charles Darwent, "*5,000 Feet Is the Best*: How Truth and Fiction Became Blurred," *Independent,* August 24, 2013, http://www.independent.co.uk/arts-entertainment/art/reviews/visual-art-review-5000-feet-is-the-best-how-truth-and-fiction-became-blurred-8783611.html).

79 When viewed on YouTube, the short film is available as a mirror reversal of itself, thus further heightening the experience of disorientation. In the YouTube version, everything, from the numbers on the hotel doors to the words on a subway turnstile to the side of the road on which cars drive, is reversed.

80 His highly publicized arrest culminated in an equally highly publicized "beer

summit" held between Gates, the arresting officer, President Obama, and Vice President Biden.

81   This vignette, like the fictional frame story, is set in Nevada near Creech Air Force Base, one of the military installations where drone operators conduct their work.

82   Enemy forces often use improvised explosive devices (or IEDs) against U.S. forces.

83   The blast radius of a Hellfire missile is approximately fifteen to twenty meters ("Living under Drones," 10).

84   Édouard Glissant, *Poetics of Relation*, trans. Betsy Wing (Ann Arbor: University of Michigan Press, 1997).

85   Asaro discusses the interview segments in relation to drone operators' combat stress and PTSD ("Labor of Surveillance," 307–10).

Epilogue

1   Judith Butler, *Precarious Life: The Powers of Mourning and Violence* (New York: Verso, 2004), 49.

2   Robin Truth Goodman, *Gender for the Warfare State: Literature of Women in Combat* (New York: Routledge, 2017), 5–6.

3   Alex Hern, "U.S. Marines Reject BigDog Robotic Packhorse Because It's Too Noisy," *The Guardian*, December 30, 2015, https://www.theguardian.com /technology/2015/dec/30/us-marines-reject-bigdog-robot-boston-dynamics-ls3 -too-noisy. The loud whir of BigDog's engines can be heard in a demonstration video released by Boston Dynamics ("BigDog," Boston Dynamics, n.d., https:// www.bostondynamics.com/bigdog).

4   "SpotMini," Boston Dynamics, n.d., https://www.bostondynamics.com/spot -mini.

5   See Lucy Suchman's discussion of Atlas's move from military to domestic sphere: "Swords to Ploughshares," *Robot Futures*, January 20, 2016, https:// robotfutures.wordpress.com/author/suchman/.

6   The actual domestic capabilities of the SpotMini as a domestic labor robot are untested. At the moment, it may be best not to be optimistic.

7   Suchman, "Swords to Ploughshares."

8   Sam Thielman, "Use of Police Robot to Kill Dallas Shooting Suspect Believed to Be First in U.S. History," *The Guardian*, July 8, 2016, https://www.theguardian .com/technology/2016/jul/08/police-bomb-robot-explosive-killed-suspect -dallas.

Index

17, 122, 126, 130; in robotic imaginary, 6, 9, 11; in uncanny valley theory, 17

Bousquet, Antoine, 58, 141–42

Braava, 94

Breazeal, Cynthia, 28, 102, 103, 104–5

Bridle, James, 29, 137, 145, 158, 162. See also *Drone Shadow*; *Dronestagram*

Brooks, Rodney, 27, 70, 90–95, 102. *See also* situated robotics

Browne, Simone, 108–9, 164

Bureau of Investigative Journalism, 138

Bush (George W.) administration, 138

Butler, Judith, 28, 29, 96, 97, 133, 148–49, 155, 157, 163, 175–76

Čapek, Karel, 17–19. See also *R.U.R. (Rossum's Universal Robots)* (Čapek)

capitalism: alienation from labor under, 21–22; care labor's role in, 47–48, 62; illness and labor under, 20; informational, 48; language of, 48, 51–52; outside of, 54–56; and psychology of productivity, 45; reproductive labor's role in, 22–23; and slavery, 56–57; and sleep, 49–52, 54

care ethics, 58, 65

care labor: and AI, 26–27, 31, 32, 37, 68; devaluation of, 26–27, 31, 32; enslaved women in, 194n60; erasure of, 32, 37–45, 57; as immaterial labor, 47; as minimized, 31; nurturant vs. nonnurturant, 188n6; of psychotherapy, 35; and race, 35, 194n61; in robotic art, 57–65; role of, in capitalism, 47–48, 62; storytelling as, 41. *See also* domestic labor

Castañeda, Claudia, 93–94

Cazazza, Monte, 97–98

Chamayou, Grégoire, 140–41

Cheah, Pheng, 3

Chen, Mel Y., 3

Chong, Patricia, 108

Chun, Wendy Hui Kyong, 44, 143

closed-world concept, 67; closed-world assumption in, 196n2; containment in, 67, 75; domestic labor in, 27; embodiment in, 27, 67; familiarity in, 68–70. See also *Stepford Wives, The* (Levin)

Cog, 93

Colby, Kenneth, 35

Cole, Teju, 29, 137, 154–58, 162

compassion, 120, 124–25, 128

"Computing Machinery and Intelligence" (Turing), 12, 26, 31–32, 33

conversational ability: of AI, 26, 31, 36, 37; and human intelligence, 26, 31, 39

Crary, Jonathan, 49, 51

Csíkszentmihályi, Chris, 97

C-3PO, 8

Curtain, Tyler, 184n26

"Cybernated Art" (Paik), 144

cybernetics: and affect, 57, 58; dehumanization in history of, 28; ethics in, 58; predictability in, 141, 176; racialized Other in, 140; and robotic art, 25; in warfare, 58, 65, in wartime research, 139–40

Daggett, Cara, 133

Damasio, Antonio, 101–2

Dark Matters (Browne), 164

DARPA. *See* Defense Advanced Research Projects Agency

Dartmouth Summer Research Project on Artificial Intelligence, 9–10

JENNIFER RHEE is associate professor of English at Virginia Commonwealth University.